Sew-It-Yourself

Sew-It-Yourself

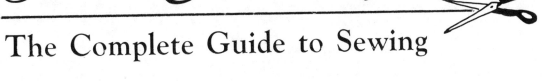

The Complete Guide to Sewing

by Dian Davis

Drawings by Rhoda Davis

Chronicle Books/San Francisco

To Maggie Baylis

whose inspiration gave my
life its new color

Acknowledgement

A special thanks to my mother, Rhoda Davis, whose outstanding illustrations and
forty years of sewing experience made this book possible.

Published by Chronicle Books
870 Market Street
San Francisco, California 94102

Library of Congress Cataloging in Publication Data
Davis, Dian.
  Sew-it-yourself.

  Includes index.
  1. Dressmaking.   2. Sewing.   I. Title.
TT515.D24   646.2   75-45426
ISBN 0-87701-074-9

Contents

Part Two: Using Your Sewing Skills

Part Three: Guides to Sewing

Part One

Sewing Step-By-Step

Chapter One

Deciding to Sew

This is a joy of sewing book. In a simple, straightforward manner it teaches you how to sew, how to enjoy it, and how to save money at it.

Sewing and Economics

With the steady rise in the cost of living, sewing has become practically an economic necessity. You can't do much about the high cost of most things short of cutting down or going without. But you **can** do something about cutting the cost of clothes without having to deprive yourself or settle for less. If you take up sewing today, you will soon be better dressed than ever before and at prices you can really afford.

Do you need to be convinced? Look at the current state of ready-to-wear clothing: It's enough to drive anyone to sew. Not only are ready-made clothes expensive, but the quality of workmanship is declining as prices rise. Check out ready-mades on the rack: Collars and necklines don't meet evenly at the center; plaids don't match. And look over the ones you've worn two or three times: Seams don't stay stitched for even that long; and crooked hems unravel for no reason. As if the situation weren't bad enough, we are paying more money than ever before for poorly made clothes that don't even fit. Few of us have the standard bodies to fit standard sizes. When was the last time you stepped into a ready-made dress that fit?

In computing the value of doing your own sewing, don't overlook the hours you invest in shopping for clothes. More often than not, you have nothing to show for your efforts at the end of a long day's search. It's not surprising that you often can't find exactly what you want. Industry executives decide what styles will be shown in the stores each year, and they base their decisions on economics and statistics. This approach may sell a lot of clothes, but it doesn't take into account your personal tastes. If you don't care for the current style you're out of luck.

For argument's sake, let's say you *do* find a dress you'd like to buy. The cost of the fabric that goes into a fifty-dollar dress is probably no more than five dollars. Most of the money you pay for the dress goes for manufacturing, shipping, and overhead expenses. The retail outlet alone marks the price of garments up one to two hundred percent.

If you make that dress—and once you read this book you'll know how—it will cost you the price of the pattern, the fabric, the zipper or buttons, and the thread.

But, you say, what about the time involved? Time is as valuable as money these days. If it takes hours of sewing to have that new dress, wouldn't it be better to buy the dress? Think again; the answer is an unqualified no! That fifty-dollar dress cost six dollars to make. Let's say it takes you five hours to assemble a comparable dress. At this rate you save nine dollars for each hour you sew. Or, to put it another way, you can pay yourself nine dollars for each hour you spend sewing and still match the price of the ready-made dress.

The amount you can save on home-made clothes varies from one garment to the next, but it's pretty safe to say that you can save at least fifty percent per garment. As your proficiency improves, you will cut down on sewing time, and the savings will increase proportionally.

You can make anything that strikes your fashion fancy. Recent innovations in pattern design have made it possible for you to buy inexpensive blueprints for virtually any garment imaginable, from bikinis to wedding dresses. Some garments take a little longer to make than others; but once you have mastered the basics of sewing, it is really no more difficult to make a coat than a blouse.

I used to make only those garments that required little fitting and a minimal investment of time, so I stayed away from blouses and jackets. Jeans, T-shirts, and lingerie were cheap, so I always bought those. But a few years ago the prices on blouses, jackets, and T-shirts soared, and it became worth the time involved to make these items myself.

I still never thought I'd see the day when I'd be making my own jeans, but when I saw jeans selling for thirty-five dollars, I knew I had to give it a try. I invested in a jean pattern, bought some denim, and whipped out a new pair of pants in no time. The cost: three dollars and four hours work! And these pants are custom made; they fit perfectly and look great. Now that I have a pattern that's altered to fit, I can afford new jeans whenever I want.

Some might consider home-sewing lingerie a bit extreme, but those little bikini panties that cost three to five dollars a pair are a snap to make. And how's this for savings? You can make seven pairs of bikinis from one yard of nylon tricot that sells for two dollars a yard. Translated into dollars and cents, this comes to twenty-eight cents a pair!

Once you learn to sew you can leaf through fashion magazines and window shop to your heart's content without suffering from a feeling of clothing deprivation. The pinch of recession needn't hit your closet. In fact, there's no time like the present to start building the wardrobe of your dreams.

It's Really "Sew Easy"

Making your own clothes sounds like a great idea. As a matter of fact, you've been idly considering taking it up for years but are wondering if you can do it. Let me put your mind at rest. Sewing is not only sensible; it's simple. There are *no* special skills involved. With a few simple lessons and a little practice, anyone can learn how to operate a sewing machine well enough to make beautiful clothes. Then it's just a matter of following instructions step-by-step. No kidding; *anyone* who can read can learn to sew.

I wasn't always convinced of how simple it is myself. My first sewing project was a disaster. I bought a beautiful wool tweed fabric to make myself a skirt for school. While putting in the zipper, I accidently stitched the back of the skirt to the front. Disgusted with myself, I threw the skirt in the corner and never touched it again. A few minutes with the seam ripper would have corrected my mistake. A little more work and I would have had a great new skirt to show for my efforts. Instead, I allowed myself to be defeated by this minor mishap. Convinced I couldn't sew, I didn't touch the sewing machine again for years.

Now I make virtually everything I wear. The only difference is that now, instead of rushing, I sew carefully and "according to the book." Patience and thoroughness are the keys to success—no gimmicks, no fancy new techniques. Just follow the directions one step at a time, and those new clothes are yours. . . . As long as you have prepared carefully, that is.

The most common complaint heard from frustrated sewers is that they've never been able to make a garment that fits right and looks well on them. Most of the sew-your-own failures I've run across were perfectly well made, but they were atrocious looking garments the makers wouldn't be caught dead in. Either the style, fabric, or color was wrong or the fit was all off.

Successful sewing is a matter of careful preparation. Select the right pattern, choose the correct fabric, alter the pattern for a perfect fit, and *then* simply follow the pattern instructions. These preparations are not difficult to learn; they are mostly matters of common sense. Once you know the inside story, you'll be well on your way to sewing success.

Sewing is not only sensible, economical, and simple—it's fun! And it's fun for everyone! Unfortunately, sewing has been classified as women's work—an arbitrary pigeonhole that has nothing to do with ability or aptitude. Traditionally, tailors, tent-makers, and net-makers have all been men. Saying that men can't sew is like saying that men can't cook—just plain silly, if not downright discriminatory.

Everyone needs a solitary activity that gives a sense of satisfaction at a job well done; a hobby that allows the expression of pent-up creative energies; a craft to explore, develop, and perfect throughout a lifetime. Keep sewing projects going and you'll have something creative, fulfilling, and fun to enrich your daily life.

Sewing By Hand

NOTE: This book is oriented toward sewing primarily with the aid of a sewing machine, but the purists who prefer to sew entirely by hand should not be discouraged. Most of us are too short on time to give hand-sewing a serious thought. Still, there is a certain sense of peace and relaxation to be found in perfectly noiseless sewing. And the feeling of pride and accomplishment that comes from making something completely unaided is not to be discounted.

If you do choose the hand-sewing route, do not start looking for another instruction book. The techniques are basically the same no matter which stitching method is used. Just substitute hand-stitching where the text reads machine-stitching.

How to Use this Book

The next eight chapters will take you through a single sewing project (any project—the basic procedures are always the same) step by step. The best way to learn is, of course, by doing. Since this is essentially an instruction manual, my advice is to actually start a project with Chapter 2 and finish it as you finish Chapter 9. The remaining chapters in the text are designed to inspire your creative imagination after you know how to sew—to broaden your horizons and give you courage to take on literally any sewing project you can think of.

The "Guides to Sewing" section of this book is very much designed for use; you should find yourself referring to it from the first chapter on, since they catalogue, alphabetically and graphically, all the in-

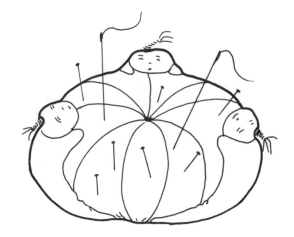

formation you will need. The first three guides are devoted to fabrics: Guide A, A Glossary of Fabrics and Related Terms; B, Fabric Qualities (what to expect of and how to care for them); and C, Sewing on Special Fabrics (look up the fabric *before* you buy it so you can prepare to meet any special problems). The next two guides are devoted to the sewing machine: D is a diagram of a standard machine, and E is a Trouble-Shooting Guide for minor problems so you don't have to drop everything and run to the dealer every time the thread breaks. Guide F is a set of Pattern-Size charts; this will be essential to you every time you buy a pattern. It will tell you how to translate body size into pattern size. Guides G and H catalogue all the information you will need for actual-ly sewing and finishing. Guide G is a glossary of sewing terms; never let an unfamiliar term slip by you, either in this book or at the fabric store, without looking it up and understanding it thoroughly. Guide H, the Sew-Easy Guide to Basic Procedures, gives you step-by-step instructions for everything you need to follow pattern instructions: how to finish seams, how to make buttonholes, how to install sleeves, etc. Everything a pattern-maker might expect you to know but wouldn't dream of explaining is in the Sew-Easy Guide in alphabetical order. Very often procedures in the text are not explained thoroughly because some other point is at issue or because space does not allow. Instructions for those procedures will be found in the Sew-Easy Guide.

Chapter Two

Getting It All Together

The Sewing Machine

Your central concern and major expense is, of course, the sewing machine. And look at what has happened to that speedy stitcher over the years. Not only do today's machines sew a straight seam, they embroider, monogram, overcast, blind-hem, appliqué, buttonhole, roll-a-hem, darn, quilt, gather, tuck, patch, tack, edge, and scallop. These innovations do make the sewing machine a versatile tool, but when in the market for a machine don't let the frills overwhelm you. The quality of a machine must be judged first and foremost by how well it executes its basic function: fastening one piece of fabric to another. This simple operation requires a dependable, even, unobtrusive but strong, straight stitch. If a machine fails in this basic function it will soon outlive its usefulness no matter how many extras it offers.

The sewing-machine market is varied indeed. The wise shopper will buy according to his needs. Once you find a machine that has a good, reliable straight stitch, look for the following features:

An even zigzag stitch that's adjustable to several widths;

A mechanism for creating buttonholes;

At least one dependable stretch stitch for sewing on knit fabrics and other stretchables.

The best choice for the beginner is a simple zigzag machine that offers the basics listed above. It is possible to buy a machine with this combination for under one hundred dollars. Stay away from complicated dials, switches, push buttons, and levers for the first years. Be sensible; keep it simple.

Let's say you've looked around a bit and are ready to buy. There's no need to rush. Take days or even weeks to make the final choice. Ask yourself these questions: Does the dealer have an established reputation for service, dependability, and helpfulness? What are his trade-in policies? Sometimes machines go on sale and often there's a gimmick to get you to buy immediately—a free sewing machine table or a brand-new vacuum. Take advantage of bargains, but don't sacrifice servicing and a good guarantee.

I travelled a few extra miles to buy my machine just so I could take advantage of a dealer's good name. The trip was well worth it. I received excellent instructions in the use of the machine; prompt and reliable service when I needed it; and a great guarantee.

Speaking of the guarantee, make sure you know what it really covers. Motor parts, servicing, labor? And who is responsible—the dealer, the manufactur-

15

er, or both? Do you have to return the machine to the manufacturer in order to take advantage of the guarantee? What happens if you move? Does the guarantee cover servicing for the machine in another town?

There is only one way to really be sure of a best buy: Put the machine to the test. A dealer who trusts his product will welcome the challenge. If he objects, do business elsewhere.

Bring some scraps of different kinds of fabrics with you to the store. Sit down at the machine and try everything in the instruction book at least once. An experienced salesperson can make any sewing machine look good; find out how well it performs for you. Most machines sew perfectly on a firm, fine-quality cotton, but many bog down on the new synthetics. Be sure the machine you buy can handle the full range of fabrics available today.

The machine's instruction manual is the home-sewer's bible. If it can't guide you effortlessly through the most trying tasks, find a machine with a manual that can.

Once you have narrowed the selection down to a few machines, consult the recent *Consumer Guide to Sewing Machine Test Reports,* available in most libraries. Look up the models you are considering and find out what the experts think.

You may be able to rent the machine you've decided on for a week or so. Make a dress with it. Put the machine through its paces and make your final decision in the comfort of your own home.

The machine you choose must come with a full set of everything it needs—attachments, foot control and cord, operator's manual, and instructions in its use. Be sure that you are getting everything you need and are not paying extra for an expensive cabinet or attachments you don't need.

If you wind up with a machine that sews a straight stitch well and does everything the manufacturer claims it will do, you've made a good deal. There are lots of machines available today; hold out for the best your money can buy.

Other Options

Rather than splurge on a new machine, make use of the one in the closet that's been gathering dust for years. Take it to the local sewing machine shop for cleaning and servicing.

My first machine was a reconditioned used one. Someone had traded in this machine to a dealer on a newer model. The used machine was then sent back to the factory to be reconditioned and stamped with a new guarantee. I got plenty of machine for my money; it worked wonders for me until I could afford a more expensive new model.

Another possibility, if you're really short on cash, is to buy a machine on time or rent one for a few months and buy when the time is right. Rentals run about ten to fifteen dollars a month, and this can often be applied to the purchase if you decide to buy the machine.

Ask a friend who is moving up to a newer model machine to sell you hers for the dealer's trade-in price. She'll be no worse off and you will most definitely come out ahead.

The Instruction Manual

The instruction manual is an essential piece of equipment; you won't make it without one. If your machine is a hand-me-down and the manual has disappeared, send immediately to the manufacturer for a duplicate or check with a dealer who sells this machine and ask if he has an extra manual.

Sometimes the wording in the manual is confusing. A good instructional picture is worth a thousand words. Rely on the diagrams when the text is unclear. (See Guide D for a basic diagram.)

With the help of the manual there is no reason why you can't do your own trouble-shooting. Every machine malfunctions once in a while. Most breakdowns are minor and no cause for alarm. See Guide E, the trouble-shooting guide. If, after exhausting that list the trouble is still a mystery, consult the instruction manual and study the diagrams closely. If you still can't solve the problem, call the dealer.

Don't Be Afraid of Your New Machine—It Won't Bite

Touch it, feel it, caress it, and love it. It's time you two became better acquainted.

Sit down in front of the machine with the instruction manual and a few scraps of fabric.

Study the machine diagram in the instruction book. Wind a bobbin, thread the machine, and you're ready to sew.

Don't run a threaded machine without placing material under the foot and always practice on double thicknesses of fabric.

Sew straight seams for a while until you get the feel of the machine. It's surprising what a little practice will do for a shaky sense of confidence.

Attachments

Modern machines come equipped with all sorts of built-in conveniences and time-saving attachments. Don't be afraid of the hem-roller or buttonholer. Once you get used to the extras they'll cut hours off sewing time. Even simple straight-stitching machines can work wonders when outfitted with a new set of attachments. Look into what's available for your machine and upgrade it to meet your needs.

Buy attachments at the local machine shop. The salesperson should be happy to give a free demonstration. Practice on scrap material a few times and then put that new addition to work for you.

Every seamstress *must* have a magnetic seam guide, unless the throat plate of the machine has a clearly marked guide line to sew by. This attachment makes perfectly uniform seams possible with almost no effort at all on your part. If your machine doesn't have one, buy one or place contact tape ⅝ inch from

FIGURE 2.1. *The sewing machine seam guide.*

the needle on the throat plate to help you guide the material (Figure 2.1).

Treat yourself to a plastic (see-through) special-purpose foot for doing decorative stitching and appliqué work (Figure 2.2). And be sure the work-kit includes a zipper foot and buttonhole foot. The cost of these extras is minor, but the time they will save you is incalculable.

Adjusting the Tension

Always use a timid touch when tampering with tension controls. The top and bottom tension should be balanced so that both threads are pulled into the

FIGURE 2.2. *The special-purpose foot.*

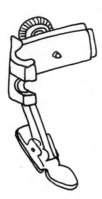

FIGURE 2.3. *The zipper foot.*

fabric evenly. If the bobbin thread pulls through to the top side of a row of stitching, the top tension is too tight—loosen it. If the needle thread pulls through to the bottom side of the fabric, the top tension is too loose—tighten it (Figure 2.4).

Don't adjust the bobbin tension! If you can't achieve a balanced tension by adjusting the top tension, get help from your dealer.

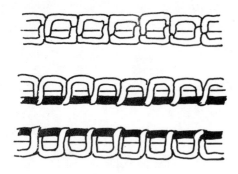

FIGURE 2.4. *Adjusting the tension.*

Preventative Medicine

There's a good way to ward off mechanical failure —keep the machine in good running order. Check the instruction manual for the straight scoop on machine

maintenance. Regular cleaning and oiling is usually all the care most machines need. Use nothing but high-quality, water-clear mineral oil on the machine and avoid the tendency to over-oil.

FIGURE 2.5. *Oiling the sewing machine.*

Preliminaries

The first step to successful sewing is the setting up of an ordered and well-equipped work space. Imagine trying to do household repairs without a hammer. You can always make do with a substitute—a heavy book-end or a large brick—but at what cost? Invariably you'll wind up with a smashed finger or two, and a few fresh dents in the newly painted wall. The same goes for sewing. Making do with inadequate equipment is more trouble than it's worth. The monetary cost of being well-equipped is minimal; the savings to the psyche is phenomenal.

Once you have assembled the necessary equipment, the next step is organization. The search-and-sew syndrome is the source of all frustration, but it's really nothing more than a bad habit. Stay sane: Organize your tools so you know where everything is before you sew a stitch.

Take time out *now* to create a sewing niche for yourself and stock it with the best gear your budget can bear. Remember, sewing is not a one-shot deal; it is a craft to be developed and enjoyed over a lifetime.

The Power Source

Your sewing center can vary all the way from a modest corner table holding the machine and a few notions to an entire room elaborately equipped to anticipate the sewer's every need. No matter which extreme you lean toward, keep a few important considerations in mind when planning the workshop of your dreams.

The chosen spot should have good connections with the electrical world. A corner fed by several outlets is ideal, but you can make do with one outlet and a three-way plug or an extension cord or two. Whatever the scheme, be sure you can plug in the sewing machine, the iron, and a lamp at the same time without causing a commotion or a major blackout.

Throw a Little Light on the Subject

The more light you have the better. Don't cheat yourself here. The eyes you save will be your own.

First choice is a place in the sun—next to a window is ideal. But an ample supply of artificial light is mandatory. Don't rely on sewing by the machine light alone. A good overhead light is essential and a high intensity lamp is recommended for close-up work.

Stay Out of the Line of Fire

If you set up in the living room, the family room, or at the dining room table, you'll live to regret the day you decided to sew. It might sound like such a good idea to cut out a new dress on the living room floor so you can keep an eye on your child or watch a favorite program while you work. It looks great on paper, but if anyone else lives in the house there's bound to be interference. The dog and cat will invariably end up doing battle right in the middle of that divine piece of cloth; and I'd rather not think of what's in store when Johnny decides he's going to help.

Locate the sewing center as far away from the mainstream of household activity as possible and sneak off to your retreat when you can.

The Work Surface and Storage Space

A work surface on both sides of the sewing machine is a must: One side is for sewing, the other for assembling. If one table is too small, set up another close by to expand the work space. Improvise with whatever extras happen to be around. A discarded typewriter stand with the leaves extended makes a great sewing machine table. An old kitchen table or card table serves well, too, and a table retired from library duty is definitely tops.

A very large table can double as a cutting surface. Penny-pinchers will be happy to know that the card table can work double-time too. Place a collapsible cutting board atop this convertible contraption for a bonus cutting surface at bargain prices.

You can build yourself a sewing table for a few extra dollars and a few hours' work. Buy an unfinished flush door from the local lumber yard or home improvement center. Finish it, paint it, stain it, or seal it, and support it with fiberboard cabinets at each end. Better yet, mount it on a wall with hinges, and you will have a table that does a fold-up, disappearing act. Support it at the end with a chest on casters that can double as a portable storage compartment.

Speaking of storage, here are a few ideas on how to make do on very little. Discount stores and import shops offer a great assortment of inexpensive baskets. The larger ones are perfect for storing fabric; the smaller ones keep pins, buttons, needles, and notions in order but out of sight.

Empty a few drawers for a simple and immediate solution to the storage space problem. Or put an idle clothes hamper to good use. Cleaned and lined with contact paper it can act as a great fabric storehouse.

Use shelves to store as a last resort. Be sure they're clean, and always fold fabric with wrong sides out to guard against dust.

FIGURE 2.6.   *Using baskets for storing fabrics and notions.*

overs. Sort buttons, pins, pencils, and chalk sticks into the individual compartments.

The Closet Caper

There are obvious advantages to leaving the sewing machine up at all times, or at least until a project has been completed. If you have managed to sequester a corner for the machine but can't stand the sight of unfinished business, screen out the mess with a decorative room divider. Get double your money's worth out of this fancy cover-up by equipping the inside with a set of hooks.

Here's another way to keep the sewing handicraft

Store all related equipment together. Think how easy the pressing will be if the sleeve board and press cloths are within reach of the iron.

Spare no effort when it comes to labeling. Put ID tags on everything. Mark the outside of boxes, drawers, and cabinets so you can find what you need at a glance. And don't forget to label fabrics. That bargain buy may not get used for a year or two. A reminder as to fabric composition, cleaning instructions, and a yardage count will be handy when it comes time to sew.

Notions are a nuisance, but there are ways of keeping them out of the way and organized for easy retrieval. For instance, a peg board or bulletin board mounted on the wall over the machine makes a tidy array of the bobbin and button jumble (Figure 2.7). Peg the board with straight hooks to hold thread spools and bobbins. Scissors and shears hang from curved cup-hooks, and snaps and zippers in original containers tack into place. Leave space on the board to pin up pattern instructions so you don't have to continually search for them as you sew.

Let a plastic silverware tray take care of the left-

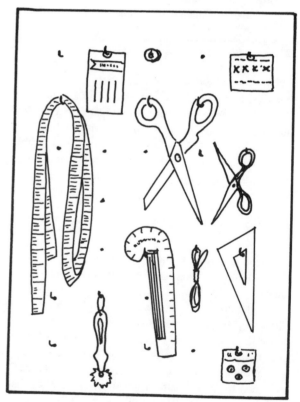

FIGURE 2.7.   *Using a peg board to organize tools.*

out of sight: Set up in a closet. I recently moved into one of those great old apartment buildings with huge walk-in closets. The old murphy bed is gone so there is plenty of space in the closet for my sewing machine, a table, and a small corner bookcase. A good overhead light makes even nighttime sewing comfortable, and storage is no problem since there are shelves to the ceiling. There's a full-length mirror on the back of the closet door and plenty of space to hang works in progress. Check out all nooks and crannies in your home for like possibilities.

An Equipment Checklist

As soon as your sewing center takes shape, stock it carefully with the tools of the trade. Don't even consider starting without *all* the proper equipment at hand. The initial investment for proper sewing equipment may seem high, but when averaged over your home-sewing career the cost per garment is minimal. Working with proper gear guarantees smooth and efficient sewing and a minimum of frustration. With the correct tools you'll be able to add professional polish to your home-made creations. No matter how you look at it, the well-equipped seamstress comes out ahead.

Don't suffer through a garment or two *before* deciding to purchase adequate tools. Do yourself a favor and equip in advance. Here is a list of the sewing essentials that every wise seamstress will have on hand. Skipping an item is like courting disaster. All the following items should be found in the notions department of your local fabric store.

Cutting Tools

Dressmaker's shears: Use bent-handled shears that are hinged with a screw and have seven- or eight-inch blades for cutting out garments. (A special model exists for left-handed seamstresses.) Buy shears

at a reputable cutlery shop since it's impossible to tell a good pair from an inferior pair without twenty years of experience. Price is a good indication of quality, so go for a more expensive pair if you can—a good pair of shears is essential. Have your shears professionally sharpened twice a year, lubricate them when they feel stiff, and *never* use them on anything but textiles. A few paper cuts will dull the sharpest edge.

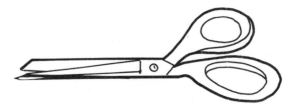

FIGURE 2.8. *Dressmaker's shears*

Scissors: For trimming and small jobs use four- or five-inch scissors with small round handles.

FIGURE 2.9. *Scissors.*

Seam ripper: Makes repairing and rearranging simple. Never use a razor blade for correcting mistakes.

FIGURE 2.10. *The seam ripper.*

GETTING IT ALL TOGETHER **21**

Cutting board: Collapsible, heavy cardboard cutting boards are available at all fabric stores for a few dollars. Even the cheap ones work well. By all means, go for economy here.

Measuring Tools

Tape measure: Indispensible! I always have two on hand. Use the sixty-inch plastic variety that won't stretch.

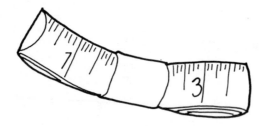

FIGURE 2.11.   *The tape measure.*

Rulers: A twelve-inch ruler and a yardstick are essential. In addition, a right-triangle ruler is a necessity for altering patterns. There's also an occasional use for a protractor.

Dressmaker's curve: A curved ruler that comes in handy during alterations.

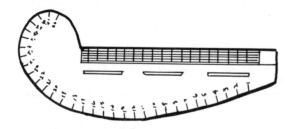

FIGURE 2.12.   *The dressmaker's curve.*

Sewing gauge: A six-inch ruler with a sliding indicator. It's great for marking hems quickly.

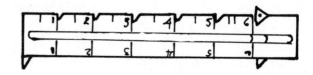

FIGURE 2.13.   *The sewing gauge.*

Scotch tape and tissue paper: These items make pattern alterations simple.

Marking Tools

Tracing wheel: A wheel with a dull serrated edge used to transfer pattern markings to the fabric.

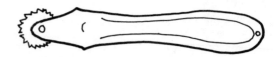

FIGURE 2.14.   *The tracing wheel.*

Dressmaker's carbon paper: The carbon paper is used with the tracing wheel to transfer construction markings. Use a color that's close to that of the fabric with just enough contrast to make the marks discernible. Dark carbons won't come out of some fabrics, so be sure to test on a fabric scrap first.

Tailor's chalk: Comes in many colors. Beware of wax chalk; it's hard to remove from some fabrics.

Sewing Aids

Thread: Have a wide assortment on hand of mercerized cotton, polyester, and silk thread. Have a spool of black and one of white available at all times.

Needles: Sharps are the most commonly used of the all-purpose needles. It's a good idea to keep a few sizes around. Keep extra sewing machine needles on hand, too. Those new self-threading needles unthread just as easily as they thread—constant rethreading becomes drudgery in no time. Think twice before buying these modern-day wonders.

Pins: Use good quality, rustproof dressmaker's silk pins. The ones with plastic coated colored heads are easy to work with and no trouble to see.

Pin cushion: Keep a good supply of pins in the cushion. Don't keep open boxes of pins around to be swept off the table every time you move your arm.

Extra bobbins: A few extra bobbins make changing from one color thread to another a simple operation.

Beeswax: A little-known aid that's a big help. Coated on hand-sewing threads, it keeps them from tangling, knotting, and breaking.

Thimble: A must for painless hand-sewing. Look for one that fits snuggly on your middle finger and wear it faithfully when doing hand-work.

Magnet: Makes cleaning up much easier. If you've ever been stabbed between the toes with a pin, you know how necessary this item is.

Full-length mirror: Necessary for fitting and great for admiring your latest creation.

Extension cord: It'll help make up for a short supply of electrical outlets.

Waste basket: Sewing's a messy business—need I say more?

Pressing Tools

Iron: One with a choice of steam or dry is best. A wide temperature range is essential and a spray mechanism can be put to good use.

Ironing board: A sturdy but adjustable board covered with a foam pad and a silicone-coated or asbestos covering is ideal.

Press cloth: A cloth to use between the iron and the garment fabric to protect the fabric during pressing. You'll probably want to have a couple of these around—a cheese cloth or muslin one for cottons and linens, and a wool one for use with woolens.

Brown paper (or a cut-up brown paper bag): To be used in a pinch instead of a press cloth. Be sure it's clean, and be doubly sure it's not waxed.

Tailor's ham: A stuffed, ham-shaped cushion used for pressing and shaping the curved areas of a garment (darts and sleeve caps). It's easy enough to make one if you can't afford to buy one. Cut two 13 by 9 inch ovals of fabric. For a professional model, cut one oval from cotton fabric and the other from wool. Sew the ovals together around the outer edge, with the right sides of the fabric facing in. Don't sew completely around the oval; leave a space for stuffing. Turn the oval right side out and stuff with *wet* kapok. Pack *tightly* for best results. Sew up the space by hand, using very small stitches.

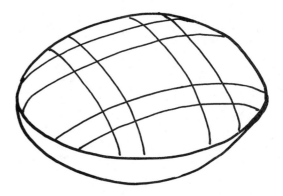

FIGURE 2.15. *The tailor's ham.*

Sleeve board: A must for pressing small slim areas that are impossible to do on a big board.

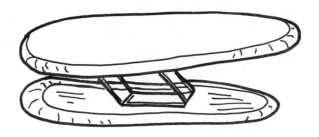

FIGURE 2.16. *The sleeve board.*

Distilled water: For the steam iron, if it needs it. Most do, although some run on tap water. If you don't go for the bottled-water routine, buy an attachment for the iron that converts tap water to distilled —all of a sudden you're self-sufficient!

Browse through the notions department from time to time. Keep up on the innovations in sewing aids and update the equipment list when you find new devices designed to cut work and time from the home-sewer's routine.

Chapter Three

Choosing the Right Pattern

Does this scene sound familiar? You decide to save a little money and get some use out of your sewing machine by making yourself a dress. You have a few minutes between errands, so you race into a local fabric store, flip through all four pattern catalogues at once, and dash out five minutes later with a few more gray hairs and no pattern. You are convinced that you haven't got what it takes to put up with the endless variety of patterns, fabrics, and colors in the yardage store. So ends your enthusiasm and your project.

The chaos is really all in your head. Yardage stores are actually well-ordered places, and sewing is based on pure logic. If you know what you want, a trip to the fabric store can be rewarding and enjoyable.

All too often the novice seamstress enters the fabric store with a half-baked idea of what she wants to make. She's overwhelmed by the choices. Frustration sets in. She makes a poor choice of pattern or can make no decision at all. Take time *before* shopping for a pattern to decide what kind of a garment to make—a skirt, blouse, jacket, dress, coat, T-shirt, or tank-top. If you can't decide what you want, go to your closet and determine what you really *need*.

Once you have decided what to make, your inclination is to jet to the store, buy a pattern, and get to

work. You know what you want and you want it now! The enthusiasm is refreshing, but you'll waste a lot of time in the fabric store if you don't know what *size* pattern you need *before* going shopping. Since pattern sizes are based on actual body measurements, to find the right pattern size you need to take measurements.

Don't shriek! It takes all of five or ten minutes to (1) measure yourself (2) determine your figure type and (3) find the right pattern size. Follow the simple procedures below, step-by-step. The wrong pattern size means time and fabric wasted in making a garment that won't fit. Davis Law Number One: If it doesn't fit you'll never wear it.

Taking Measurements

Here's how to take accurate measurements on yourself:

1. Use a good plastic tape measure and, if possible, have someone help you.

2. Always take measurements over the undergarments that you usually wear.

3. Stand in a normal posture.

4. Measure with the tape measure held snugly against the body, but don't pull it tight. (If the flesh is

25

bulging over the tape edge, you're pulling a little too tightly.)

5. Be sure to measure *carefully* and *honestly*. Those of us who are continually trying to gain or lose a few pounds are inclined to want to cheat a little when we measure ourselves. This folly will result in clothes that don't fit well. A slightly thin person will look skinny in clothes that fit too loosely. Clothes that fit too tightly accentuate the extra pounds an overweight person would love to conceal.

If you are a woman sewing for yourself take the following measurements. (If you are a man sewing for himself or a woman sewing for a man or a child, follow this procedure *and* refer to Chapter 12.)

1. *Bust:* Ideally, a friend should take this measurement for you. Measure around the fullest part of the bust; keep the tape high under the arms and straight across the back, just under the bottom of the shoulder blades.

2. *Waist:* Tie a string around your waist at the narrowest part. Measure the distance around your waist at the string. (Don't faint; no one's expected to stay a trim 24-inches forever.) Leave the string around your waist for now—it will be useful in taking other measurements.

3. *Hips:* The hip measurement is taken at the fullest part of your hips. Try the tape measure at several distances between the string at your waist and your thighs to find out where to take this measurement. Record for future reference the distance along one side of your body between your waist and the point where you take the hip measurement. For most women this distance is between seven and nine inches (See Figure 3.1).

4. *Back-waist Length:* Measure along your spine from the base of the neck to the string at your waistline.

5. *Height:* Without shoes, stand erect flat against a wall. Place a twelve-inch ruler on the top of your head, parallel to the floor, with one end of the ruler touching the wall. Lightly make a pencil mark where the ruler touches the wall and measure from this mark to the floor with a yardstick or tape measure.

Be sure to make a record of these measurements. You'll want to keep a permanent copy of these and other measurements (to be discussed) necessary in selecting and altering patterns. *Start a sewing notebook,* folder, or file instead of using your purse as a filing cabinet. Keep your measurement record in that notebook for future reference. (Recheck measurements from time to time to make sure you haven't changed pattern sizes. Those extra pounds that add inches do tend to sneak up on us.)

Before selecting a pattern size, you must determine your figure type. Manufactured patterns are made for various figure types, and for each type there is a

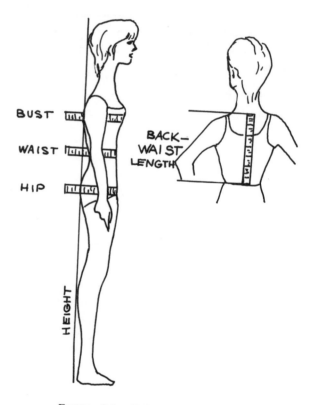

FIGURE 3.1. *Taking measurements.*

selection of sizes from which to choose. Fortunately for the home sewer, the major pattern companies in this country (Butterick, Vogue, McCalls, and Simplicity) all use the same figure type and size classification.

Finding Your Figure Type

Figure type is determined by *back-waist length, height* (without shoes), and *general body shape.* Using the brief description following each figure type listed below, decide which type pattern will be best for you. *Do not guess, be truthful,* and say goodbye to make-shift alterations in ready-made clothes (the skirt rolled several times at the waist, held precariously in place by the inconspicuous and almighty safety pin).

Misses: For the woman with a developed and well-proportioned figure; about 5'5" to 5'6" tall; back-waist length between 15½'' and 17¼''.

Miss Petite: For the shorter woman with a *Miss* figure; about 5'2" to 5'4" tall; back-waist length between 14½" and 15¾".

Junior: Designed for the well-proportioned, shorter waisted figure; about 5'4" to 5'5" tall; back-waist length between 15" and 16¼".

Junior Petite: For the woman with a well-proportioned petite figure; about 5' to 5'1" tall; back-waist length between 14" and 15¼".

Young Junior/Teen: For the developing (pre-teen and teen-aged) young lady; 5'1" to 5'3" tall; back-waist length between 13½" and 15¾".

Women's: For the woman with a larger, more mature figure; about 5'5" to 5'6" tall; back-waist length between 17½" and 18".

Half-size: For the woman with a fully developed figure and a short back-waist length; hips and waist are larger in proportion to bust than in the other figure types; about 5'1" to 5'3" tall; back-waist length 15" to 16½".

If you are a woman over 5'6" or under 5' tall, select the pattern type closest to your measurements and lengthen or shorten to fit. Altering patterns is discussed in Chapter 7.

In the pattern catalogues there is a photograph or illustration of the finished garment for each pattern. Underneath the photograph or illustration is a *pattern number.* This is usually a four-digit number. Next to or below the pattern number is a brief description of the garment. The description tells if the pattern is available in *your figure type.* Pattern catalogues are usually divided into sections by figure type for convenience.

Finding Your Pattern Size

With measurements and figure type in hand, you are ready to select your pattern size. Follow the simple rules below and you will make the correct selection each time. Remember, sewing is fun *if* you don't make costly mistakes.

1. *DO NOT buy a pattern according to the size you wear in ready-made clothes. In fact, ignore this size!*

2. Turn to Guide F, Pattern-Size Charts. You will find several sizes for each figure type. For each size there are measurements for bust, waist, and hips. Compare these measurements with your own and select the size with the measurements that match your own.

3. If you can't find a set of measurements that exactly corresponds with yours, as is often the case, select the pattern size by the *bust* measurement only for all garments except pants, skirts, and shorts. It's easier to adjust the waist and hips of a pattern than it is to alter the bust correctly. *Be sure the pattern size you select will fit well across the bust.*

4. Choose the correct size skirt, pants, and shorts by the *waist* measurement. If your hip measurement is larger than the hip measurement shown for this size, select skirt and pants patterns according to *your hip measurement*, and not waist size, and adjust the waist to fit.

5. Choose a maternity size by your bust measurement *before* pregnancy.

This may have been your first attempt at taking measurements and your first exposure to pattern-size charts. The second time through will take half as long. With a little practice rechecking a pattern size will be a snap. Be patient. Everyone feels a bit awkward trying something new for the first time.

Choosing the Right Style

A tremendous variety exists in the styles of patterns for each kind of garment. For example, turn to the *dress* section of any pattern catalogue. You'll find an A-line dress, a shift, a princess-style dress, a sheath, an empire-style dress, a dress with an asymmetrical closing, a shirt-waist, a tent, a blouson, a tunic, a dress with a yoke, a dress with a raised waist, and a dress with a low waist.

Becoming familiar with the styles that are good for you is a necessary part of sewing if the aim is to save money by consistently producing garments that look great and fit well. Avoid a costly mistake. Be sure you'll feel comfortable in a dress before you make it.

It doesn't take an experienced fashion designer to determine the best style for you. And you don't have to depend on the figure-type hints in the standard sewing manual either. You know the ones I mean. They contain such pearls of wisdom as, "Horizontal lines add width," or "Vertical lines are slenderizing"; and they suggest styles that are good for various figure types. These hints just don't hold up all the time. Trust yourself on this matter of style selections. Presumably you have been dressing yourself for sometime now. The clothes in your closet contain a

FIGURE 3.2. *The A-line dress.*

FIGURE 3.3. *The shift.*

wealth of information about which styles are best for you.

Think about your wardrobe for a moment. Some of the clothes give you a well-dressed feeling; they are comfortable and you feel special wearing them. Take these favorites out of the closet, hang them up somewhere, and take a good look at them. What is it about these garments that make them just right for you? Are they slim-fitting or loose? What kinds of neckline do they have? Do they have straight, bell-shaped, flared, or A-line skirts? What are the predominant lines of these garments; that is, do most of them have strong vertical lines—buttons or panels running down the front—or are horizontal lines more predominant? Find the common denominator in the clothes you enjoy wearing.

Now do the same analysis of those clothes in which you feel less than your best. Hang them up alongside the favorites. And don't forget to take a good look at the clutter in the closet that seldom or never gets worn. Find out what it is about these garments that you don't like. Avoid making the same mistake twice. Remember: Nothing costs money like clothes that aren't worn.

By now you're thinking I'm giving a lot of homework. If analyzing your taste in clothes seems time consuming, think about how much time you've spent shopping for a new dress with *nothing* to show for it in the end. Spend a few minutes carefully considering the style of the garment you will make and say goodbye to those frustrated shopping days forever.

A word of caution: You may find that the A-line dress is your most comfortable and complimentary style. If you play it safe and make nothing but A-line dresses you will soon have a very comfortable but very monotonous wardrobe. Variety spices up a

FIGURE 3.4. *The princess-style dress.*

FIGURE 3.5. *The empire-style dress.*

CHOOSING THE RIGHT PATTERN **29**

wardrobe as well as a life. Part of the fun of home dressmaking is that it allows us to experiment without breaking the family piggybank. Take a chance—try new things. Find a happy medium between old stand-by styles and bold new possibilities.

Trying a new style need not be a shot in the dark. Browse through a favorite dress store and try on a dress that looks great. Take a good look in the mirror. Ask the same questions of this dress as you did of the clothes from your closet. Are you delighted or disappointed? Try on those beautiful dresses you couldn't afford before—they're within your price range now. Don't be timid. Try on *all* the different styles. There's no one style for you; there are many. Don't sell yourself short.

It's a good idea to write down a brief description of a new style-find (for example, "long-sleeved dress with fitted bodice and waistline"; "A-line skirt with buttons down the front"), or make a quick sketch if you can draw. Don't trust memory here; you might not have time to look through a pattern catalogue for days after you see something you like. I speak from experience. Many times I've found *the* dress for me, only to forget what it looked like ten minutes away from the store.

Magazines are a terrific source of new ideas. Become familiar with the supply of fashion magazines at your newstand. Soon you'll be impatiently awaiting the new arrivals. And, don't limit your style search to fashion magazines. While reading through a news magazine recently I found the inspiration for my latest creation. A young woman in a cigaret advertisement was sporting the very tennis dress I'd been looking for. Keep your mind and eye open. You never know when or where a new style idea will pop up. Clip out pictures of the styles you're wild about.

FIGURE 3.6. *The tent.*

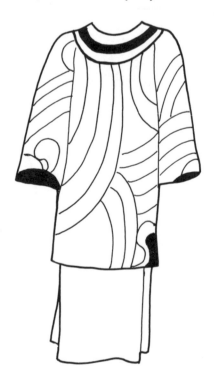

FIGURE 3.7. *The tunic.*

Keep clippings in your sewing notebook or folder along with your measurements for future use. Don't be caught with time to sew, but no idea of what to make.

Selecting the Pattern

Most stores that sell fabric also sell patterns and have copies of the current pattern catalogues from the major pattern manufacturers (Vogue, Butterick, Mc-Calls, and Simplicity). Look up local fabric stores in the yellow pages of the phone book under "Fabric." Modern department stores usually sell patterns in their home-sewing department, as do the larger what we used to laughingly call five-and-ten cent stores.

Take your measurement record, pattern size, and a small notebook to the fabric store. The notebook will come in handy in making notations. I can't count the times I have scribbled numbers on envelopes and on the back of checks, only to have them disappear.

Mothers, your small children are adorable, but they are bound to raise havoc in the fabric store where there are lots of goodies for them to get into. It is nearly impossible to keep an eye on the small folk and make a good pattern choice at the same time. Give yourself a break. Get a sitter for an hour and make the best use of your time at the store. I guarantee the sitter fee will be well worth it.

Starting Out Gradually

Don't choose overly complex patterns for your first few projects. Sewing isn't difficult, but it's a good idea to get used to working with a sewing machine before taking on a complicated design. If you pick a

FIGURE 3.8. *A dress with a yoke.*

FIGURE 3.9. *The high-waisted style.*

CHOOSING THE RIGHT PATTERN **31**

style that is too difficult for the first project you may be discouraged from sewing altogether—possibly forever. A successful first attempt will lead to more successes.

Beginning dressmakers should stick to styles that require very little fitting. The fewer the number of separate pattern pieces the better. Avoid styles with collars, buttonholes, and set-in sleeves. If you must have sleeves, choose a garment style in which the sleeve and bodice are cut all in one piece (Figure 3.11).

Some garments are easier to construct than others. Easy garments include:

shell tops
dirndl skirts
wraparound skirts
simple A-line skirts
all-in-one princess-style dresses (sleeveless)
shifts and tent dresses with no collars or sleeves
ponchos
capes
long skirts—gathered, wrap, or A-line
shawls
jumpers
vests
pants, shorts and skirts with elasticized waistbands
halter dresses
halter tops

Each major pattern manufacturer devotes a section of its pattern catalogue to "easy-to-sew fashions." Vogue makes "Very Easy Vogue" patterns; Simpli-

FIGURE 3.10. *Fashion magazines.*

FIGURE 3.11. *Sleeves and bodice all one piece.*

city has "Jiffy" patterns; McCalls has "Easy" and "Easy To Sew" patterns; and Butterick offers "Sew-and-Go", "Wrap-and-Go", and "Fast and Easy" patterns.

Beware! Those "Very Easy Vogue" and "Fast and Easy" Butterick patterns really aren't very easy at all. These patterns are more appropriate for the *ad-*

vanced beginner, someone who has successfully completed several of the garments listed above and is ready to take on set-in sleeves, buttonholes, and collars. True beginners should start with Simplicity's "Jiffy" patterns, Butterick's "Sew-and-Go" and "Wrap-and-Go," and McCall's "Easy" and "Easy to Sew."

After a few easy-sew successes, move on to the

FIGURE 3.12. *The wraparound skirt.*

FIGURE 3.13. *Using the shawl for style.*

more complicated easy-sew patterns. Collars, cuffs, and buttonholes take a little more time to construct, but the time spent pays off in more interesting and exciting clothes.

Allow enough time to construct the garment. Don't buy a pattern on Thursday and try to make an outfit to wear on Friday night. If you stay up all night to finish a last-minute project exhaustion will set in. Not only will the gala event turn into a nightmare, but the glorious new creation will take on the look of a high-school sewing project. Let's face it—all of us are proud of our creations, but heaven forbid that they look home-made. And looking home-made-in-a-hurry is the worst of all. So budget your time sensibly. Even the easy-sew styles require care and patience in the making.

If you are nervous about trying a style with a set-in sleeve, choose a pattern with a set-in sleeve that is especially designed for knit fabrics. Knits have that marvelous quality of elasticity which makes setting a sleeve into a knit bodice a relatively simple operation. (More on fabrics in Chapter 4.)

Perhaps you want to make a blouse with a front opening, but aren't quite ready to tackle buttonholes. Use mother-of-pearl cowboy snaps (they add a nice touch even if you aren't an equestrian) or decorative snap fasteners instead of buttons and buttonholes. The snaps are available in any notions department and can be installed easily in minutes. Or, take the blouse to a professional seamstress or tailor for the buttonholes.

After making a few Fast and Easy Butterick or Very Easy Vogue patterns you'll be high on confidence and ready to take on more difficult styles. But remember, the more pattern pieces there are to a style, the more time is needed for altering, cutting, fitting, and constructing the garment. No matter how good you are with the needle, when you are short on time stick to the easy-sew patterns. Avoid being rushed.

You Get What You Pay For

The cost of a paper pattern printed by one of the major pattern manufacturers varies from eighty-five cents all the way up to four dollars. Most patterns fall within the one to two dollar range. In an effort to save money you will probably be inclined to buy less expensive patterns. Pattern cost is a definite consideration, but don't lose sight of the fact that an expen-

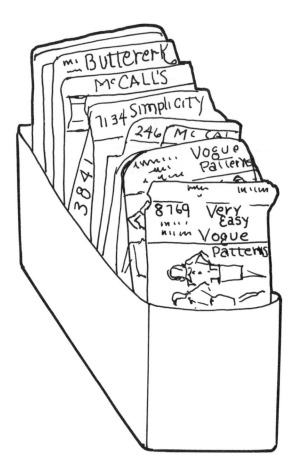

FIGURE 3.14. *Storing patterns in their original envelopes.*

sive pattern invariably has a top designer's name on it—Yves Saint Laurent, Christian Dior, Nina Ricci —and because of this the styling and fit of the finished garment will be of the highest quality. A ready-to-wear garment with a name designer's label in it costs a small fortune. If you make a Christian Dior dress at home for twenty dollars that would normally sell for over a hundred dollars in a store, the four-dollar investment in the pattern would be truly worth it.

A designer pattern greatly increases the value of a home-made garment. Think twice before you select an inexpensive pattern just to save a dollar or two.

Hold Everything!

The type of fabric to be used is an important consideration in selecting a pattern. *Do not buy a pattern until you have read Chapter 4.*

Hang on to Your Patterns

Plan on keeping all of your patterns. You can save a lot of time and money by reusing an altered pattern on a new and exciting fabric. The more experienced seamstress will want to restyle old patterns and combine pieces from different patterns to create new designs (See Chapters 10 and 11). The larger your pattern collection the more freely you can experiment.

Keep old patterns and instructions in their original envelopes and store them together in a shoe- or hatbox.

Chapter Four

Choosing the Right Fabric

Allow me to introduce the medium of the craft: Welcome to the world of textiles. Just as the painter creates illusions with oils and the potter brings life to clay, the seamstress molds and shapes fabric into an endless variety of three-dimensional designs. The medium is diverse. Each fabric carries its own special message. Velvets are plush; the message is soft and rich. Cottons speak a casual line, and knits tell the tale of comfort and action. The intricacies of lace communicate a story very different from that of the lustre of satin. And the seductive sheers, the sensuous jerseys, and the slinky crepes speak for themselves.

Each fabric has a will of its own too. Some are soft and ask to be draped; others are stiff and love to be shaped. Let each fabric speak its mind. Work *with*, rather than against, the qualities that make each textile unique. Develop a healthy respect for the cloth. In return, you can expect to see your ideas take shape just as you imagined them.

Fabric is made from fibers, natural or man-made. The fibers are spun into yarns and the yarns are woven or knitted together to give us a wealth of beautiful cloth. Cotton, linen, silk, and wool are our old favorites, the naturals. The man-made fibers are the original test-tube babies; they are created in chemistry laboratories. Recently we have been blessed with the blends. Leave it to modern technology to give us the best of both worlds in fabrics that combine the strength, durability, and comfort of the naturals with the low cost and easy care of the synthetics.

Within the broad categories the subtleties increase. For example, denim, seersucker, pique, corduroy, terry, velveteen, madras, and eyelet are all made from cotton fibers, and yet each has a special quality all its own. Seersucker has a puckered look; corduroy is covered with ridges; terry presents a field of little thread loops; and eyelet is full of holes.

Don't worry; there is no need to know all the fabrics by heart. You don't have to be a walking encyclopedia in order to sew. The fabric glossary, Guide A, lists the most commonly used fabrics, their fiber content, and the kinds of garments they are usually used for. Consult Guide B for the special qualities of each fiber and Guide C to determine if the fabric you choose requires special treatment.

The more you sew the more familiar you will

become with the types of fabric available and their properties. Don't fret about how little you think you know—just sew! When in doubt, consult the glossary.

Matching the Fabric and Pattern

Get ready to be completely immersed in a sea of fabrics. It's time to choose the gorgeous cloth that will metamorphize a flat paper pattern into a three-dimensional design.

The key to success is the match—matching your chosen pattern with the perfect fabric. Remember, fabric has a will of its own. Soft, clingy fabrics refuse to stand up by themselves; they prefer to hang on to what's round and slide from curves in folds that flow. Use these fabrics (jerseys, crepes, nylons, and knits) for the free and easy, soft and sensual look.

Forget about trying to tailor that luscious crepe. It's pure folly to think that you can break the cloth's will. After hours of aggravation, the crepe will be laid to rest in the scrap pile and you'll be tempted to join it. There is equal frustration in trying to drape a sailcloth. Team up a fabric with a pattern that is designed to enhance its unique character. Be sure you and the

FIGURE 4.1. *A basket of fabrics.*

FIGURE 4.2. *Using soft, clingy fabrics.*

CHOOSING THE RIGHT FABRIC **37**

fabric are playing the same game. Don't fight a losing battle.

Pattern manufacturers provide the information you need. They suggest fabrics best suited for each pattern, and tell you exactly how much fabric to buy. Pattern designers have experience on their side; they know what they're talking about. Follow their suggestions.

Fabric suggestions are listed underneath the diagram of pattern pieces on the back of the pattern envelope. Ask the pattern salesperson to let you see the pattern you've selected and jot down the suggested fabrics on that note pad. Patterns are not returnable, so if you are new at this game, match up a pattern with a fabric before buying either. Avoid making a costly mistake.

The pattern manufacturer will suggest a wide range of fabrics that are suitable for each design: Winter-weights, summer-weights, expensive and inexpensive fabrics. To choose among them take this book along to the store and look up each suggested fabric in the glossary at the back of the book. Ask yourself: Is it washable? Will it wrinkle? Is it best used for summer or winter-time garb? If you're braving it alone, without the book, you'll find most of the information you need at the store but it will take longer to track it all down.

Fabrics are grouped together by type and are usually marked with a sign. Let's say the pattern suggests a *crepe de Chine*. Go to the section where the *crepe de Chine* is on display. Pick up any bolt of fabric and take a look at the bolt end. The fabric qualities are usually stamped here (fiber content and laundering instructions). If you don't find any information on the bolt end, there will be an ID tag from the textile manufacturer attached to the bolt. Note the official information and then find out how easily a fabric wrinkles by giving it the crush-test.

A Fabric to Suit Your Needs

Carefully consider when and where you plan to wear this new creation. You'll be able to narrow the list down to a fabric or two. Are you planning to wear this new frock to work? Are you in too much of a

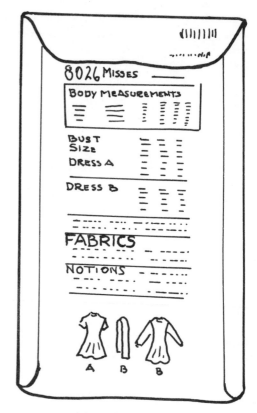

FIGURE 4.3. *Read everything on the pattern envelope.*

hurry to bother with anything but a wash-and-wear? Do you need the warmth of wool and are you ready to deal with the dry-cleaning bills? Or are you finally taking that vacation to the tropical paradise of your dreams? If that's the case, only cool and fresh, wash-and-wear drip-dry fabrics will do.

Occasionally a pattern is designed in such a way that it can be made in either a crisp or a clingy fabric. The desired effect will determine the choice. The soft fabrics drape, flow, and cling to your form. They can be seductive and revealing or graceful and flowing. Be careful with these sensual threads; nothing is left to the imagination with them. If you wear a sexy jersey when you're tipping the far side of the scales you'll feel more like Totie Fields than Sophia Loren. But the crisp fabrics take on a tailored look. They hold a shape all their own and have no trouble at all disguising the lumps and bumps. If you are in serious doubt as to how a fabric will look made up in a style, let ready-to-wear clothes be your guide.

The more advanced seamstress needn't stick to the fabric suggestions on the pattern. Be brave. Have fun. Try something new! Combine your practical knowledge of fabric with the guidelines suggested by the pattern manufacturer. Substitute at will, but remember: The new fabric should have properties similar to those of the fabrics listed on the pattern envelope.

A word of caution: If you've selected a pattern designed for knits, substitutions could lead to disaster. The for-knits-only patterns are especially designed to make the best use of the stretch qualities of knit fabrics. For instance, the darts that are essential in giving wovens their shape are often eliminated entirely in patterns for knits. You'll have a hard time getting a dartless garment to fit if it's made up in a woven fabric that won't give. The for-knits-only patterns are clearly marked in the catalogues.

What the Piggybank Can Bear

Put your note pad to good use—do a little cost accounting before you choose your fabric. But relax! You don't have to be a financial wizard to balance the fabric budget. Simply multiply the price per yard of a fabric (round it off to the nearest dollar) by the number of yards required to make the garment. The yardage requirement is listed underneath the pattern size on the pattern fabric chart, usually in the catalogue and always on the back of the pattern envelope. The fabric chart will look like this:

Bust	32½	34	36	38	40
Sizes	10	12	14	16	18
Top and Pants A					
44/45″ w/wo nap	3½	3½	3½	4	4½
54″ w/wo nap	3	3	3¼	3½	3½
60″ w/wo nap	2½	2½	3	3	3

There are usually several views to select from. "Top and pants A" means "as shown in view A." The numbers 44/45″, 54″, and 60″ refer to the width of the fabric. "W/wo nap" means "with or without nap." Read the pattern this way: If my bust measurement is 34, my size is 12. If my size is 12, I need 3½ yards of fabric that is 44 to 45 inches wide. If the fabric I choose is 54 inches wide, I need 3 yards; if it's 60 inches wide, I need 2½ yards.

Once you have determined how much fabric you'll need, multiply the yardage by the price. The rule on price when buying fabric is, *Always buy the best you can afford.* Strange advice from a sewing economy expert? Not at all. Using good quality fabrics can actually save you time as well as money. Better fabrics are easier to handle and more enjoyable to work with than cheap, sleazy ones. Pressing goes faster, the end-product looks better, and the garment holds up longer. A cheap fabric will never do for a garment that must stand up under hard wear and washing. This is especially true with children's clothes. Nothing is more frustrating than working hours on a new frock only to have it fall apart after a few washings. You only cheat yourself when you skimp on fabric quality.

The fabric quality of garments that are destined for a short life, such as the one-wear-only party dress, is not as critical as that for every-day wear. Feel free to pinch pennies here. But if you plan to put a lot of time into making a garment, you owe it to yourself to spend a few extra dollars on fabric that will hold up well.

Still, there are ways to be economy-minded *and* quality-conscious. If you want a luxurious look, but can't afford silk for fifteen dollars a yard, there's a fabric for you. Qiana is man-made fabric at its finest. It sells for between six and nine dollars a yard; it's easy to care for (just wash and wear); and it can't be beat for comfort. Men will appreciate Qiana. Qiana shirts can't be beat for prestige and comfort. And there's a bonus—you never have to iron these beauties.

Want something a little less clingy but every bit as luxurious as Qiana? Try Luftsong. It's as heavy as satin without the sheen, and it tailors beautifully with no sacrifice on elegance.

Here's a gem for bargain-hunters. No-wale corduroy (corduroy without the ridges) is relatively inexpensive but takes on the rich look of suede when made up. And like a fine wine, it improves with age. The fabric looks richer and feels softer as it gets older.

Making the Job Easier

Just as some garments are easier to make than others, some fabrics are easier to work with than others. For example, chiffon slips and slides during cutting and is difficult to sew. Ripped-out mistakes leave tell-tale signs on velvets and silks, so you'd better be right the first time. Synthetics require a bit better sewing than the naturals. Most of them won't shrink so you can't count on covering for a pucker with a fancy ironing job. Stripes, plaids, and large prints call for matching—novices should stay away from these for awhile.

Don't be discouraged, beginners; there are fabrics tailor-made for you. Small prints and textured fabrics such as tweeds and homespuns tend to hide sewing errors and are great for beginners. Linen, cotton percale, and wool flannel are easy to work with. They won't distort and if the sewing is not perfect you can correct most of the errors with an iron. Puckers disappear with a little steam-pressing.

Color It Fantastic

Wander through the fabric section of the local yardage store. What's the first thing that distinguishes one bolt from another? Color! What's the first thing you notice about a friend's new dress? The color.

By following pattern suggestions and considering price and practicality, you have eliminated all but one or two fabrics from the endless array. Now pick a color and you'll be ready to sew. Don't be a slave to the color scheme pictured on the front of the pattern envelope. Break loose! Anything goes these days when it comes to color.

Choose the color according to how it looks on you. Drape the fabric in front of your body and take a look

FIGURE 4.4. *Soft, dark, long styles for a slender look.*

in a full-length mirror. (All fabric stores provide them for customers). How does the color look next to your face? Does it enhance your natural looks, or do you look washed-out? If the fabric is a print, is it in proportion to your size, or does it overpower you. Big prints do nothing for little people and tiny prints look silly on tall, statuesque ladies.

Colors often take on strange hues under artificial store lights, so take the bolt of fabric over to a window to make sure of its true color. Find out before you get home that what you thought was American beauty velvet is really fire-engine red.

Be sure to look at the right side of the fabric. With satins and polished cottons, the lustrous side is the right side. The pile is on the right side of pile and napped fabrics. Cottons and linens are usually folded right side out. When in doubt, look at the selvage (the finished edge of the fabric)—it's smoother on the right side. Lots of fabrics can be used on either side. If it's impossible to tell one side from another, it probably doesn't matter.

Dieters! Optical illusion is a marvelous ally for those of us with skinny bodies hiding under all that fat. Avoid warm colors (reds and yellows) and light colors until the diet days are over. The same goes for rough and thick textures and shiny fabrics; they make round shapes look rounder. Dull textures, dark colors, and the cool shades (blues and greens) create an illusion of smallness. Combine one of these with a long, sleek style and inches will disappear magically.

By the way, we've all been told that vertical stripes are slimming. This is *sometimes* the case, but wide stripes add width and if the stripes have to travel over large curves they accentuate the areas they're meant to hide.

Final Considerations

Grain

Fabric falls with the grain. If you misuse the grain, you may end up with one of those disaster creations fit only for the darkest corner of the closet.

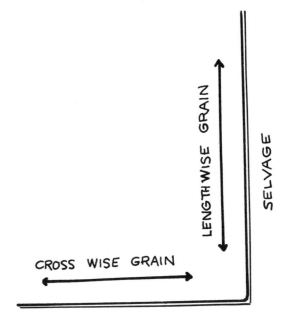

FIGURE 4.5. *Fabric grain.*

Most fabric hangs best on the vertical grain (in the direction running parallel to the selvage). The horizontal grain is best used for trim and small areas of contrast that don't need fitting.

Pay attention to the grain lines when selecting a fabric. This consideration is not too important with plain fabrics and all-over prints but it is critical with one-way designs, stripes, and some plaids. You'll be very sorry if you wait until later to figure out that the slimming vertical design must be cut with the pattern running round and round instead of up and down.

Plaids, Stripes, and One-Way Designs

Be sure that the design is printed on the grain. Otherwise you'll end up with a lopsided-looking affair. Check the design along the raw edges of the fabric (see Figure 4.60).

Plaids, stripes, and one-way designs require extra yardage for perfect matching. Use the "with nap" fabric requirements for these fabrics or buy an extra ⅝ yard.

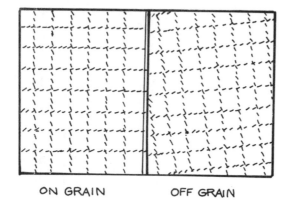

ON GRAIN   OFF GRAIN

FIGURE 4.6. *Design on fabric grain.*

Finishes

After a fabric is woven, it is often treated with a fabric finish to increase body, prevent shrinkage or wrinkling, and to make the fabric wash-and-wear, water-repellant, stain-resistant, moth-proof, drip-dry, or crease-resistant. These finishing touches are great boons to the modern homemaker, as long as the fabric is finished on the straight of the grain. Check to see that the lengthwise threads are at right angles to the crosswise threads. Once finished, a fabric can't be straightened if it's off grain, so if it's not perfect choose another fabric.

Stretch

Many of the modern woven fabrics are made to "give" with the body and spring back into shape. These fabrics are not knits, but are woven to stretch lengthwise or widthwise and sometimes in both directions. Put the stretch to good use for maximum comfort in action and neatness in fit. The stretch should run from side to side in skirts and shorts; from waist to ankle in pants; and across the shoulders in tops, dresses, and jackets.

The Big Purchase

It's finally time to buy the cloth. Take the fabric bolt to a counter and have the salesperson cut the required amount. Double-check to be sure that you don't under- or over-buy. Buy exactly the amount called for on the pattern. It's up to you to get what you pay for. Carefully check *every* piece of fabric for flaws. Just because a textile is expensive and made from the finest of threads is no guarantee that it's free from mistakes. If the fabric is flawed, negotiate with the salesperson to give you enough extra free yardage to compensate for the error. Stand firm. Refuse to buy anything that is less than perfect. (Circle the flaw with a pencil as a reminder for later. Be sure that it doesn't end up front and center of an otherwise perfect creation.)

You can tell a lot about a fabric by the way it hangs on the bolt. If it falls freely and smoothly, it will probably hang well on you. If in doubt, give the cloth one more once-over. The fabric should lie flat on the cutting counter when folded in half. If it doesn't it will give you nothing but grief. Even if your heart is set on this fabric, don't buy it if it is difficult to manage on the cutting counter.

Watch carefully as the salesperson cuts the fabric from the bolt. If the fabric is not cut straight there might not be enough yardage. Avoid this frustration. Pay close attention and if the first end of the fabric isn't cut on grain, insist that ample allowance be made for this at the other end.

Buying Linings

There is no set rule about whether or not to line. If the garment fabric is sheer, obviously it should be lined. If the fabric is rough and scratchy, line it to protect your tender skin. Sometimes patterns will suggest lining, but more often they don't. The trend in ready-to-wear clothing is away from lined garments. But elegant better-made clothes are always lined, so take your pick. I always line a wool skirt to keep it from bagging and sagging. And when I want to treat myself to the luxury of a garment that is finished as beautifully inside as out, I line.

When you do decide to line a garment, always select a lining that is slightly lighter in weight than the garment fabric. Don't overwhelm your fabric. Also make sure to select a lining that requires the same care as the garment; match up a washable with a washable. If you pick a dry-clean-only lining for your wash-and-wear summer frock the dress won't make it through the first wash.

Linings are available at different prices. Can't afford china silk? Ask the salesperson to show you to the less expensive linings. There's quite a selection and they work very well.

Match the color of the lining with that of the fabric. If you can't find an identical match, come as close as possible. Go lighter if necessary, rather than darker.

A lightweight SiBonne or UnderCurrent is the best all-around lining for most light- to medium-weight garments. A lining is usually unnecessary with knits; if you choose to use one, try a soft Ciao. Ciao is also a great lining fabric to use with clingy synthetics.

Buy slightly less lining than garment fabric. There's no need to line the parts of a garment that are faced—collars, cuffs, waistbands, and plackets (see Sew Easy Guide 13 for directions).

Interfacing: The Shape Makers

Always interface when it is called for on the pattern.

Interfacing is a special layer of fabric used to stabilize critical areas that may change shape with wear and to support collars, cuffs, and openings. The limp, lifeless collar is the sure sign of an impatient seamstress who thinks she's getting ahead by cutting corners.

Interfacings come in woven, nonwoven, and fusable fabrics and in several weights. Use one that is slightly lighter in weight than the garment fabric. Use woven interfacings with woven fabrics and nonwovens with knits and stretchables. The fusables iron into place and are easy to use, but be sure to test with a swatch of your fabric *before* using—the fusables don't successfully stick to all fabrics.

Yardage requirements for interfacing are listed on the back of the pattern envelope along with the fabric yardage.

A Hot Shopping Tip

By far the best time to shop for fabric and patterns is during the dinner hour, between five and seven. Shop at this time and the whole store is yours—you'll never wait hours in line to be helped. And no matter what time of day, shop alone if you can. You need time and privacy to think. Matching fabrics with patterns is a creative endeavor.

Cutting Fabric Costs

The resourceful seamstress can usually whittle away at fabric costs by keeping an eye and ear open.

Yardage stores have sales from time to time: Check the newspapers for ads. Find out if the local fabric store has a mailing list: most of them do. Add your name and address to the list and you will be notified several days before each sale.

Every fabric store has a remnant bin (or table) of unused bolt ends and fabrics that didn't sell. With a little experience anyone can spot a good buy there. Avoid the remnants that appear in large amounts. Most of the fabrics that weren't big sellers didn't sell for a reason—stay away from these. The bolt ends are the true bargains. These pieces, a yard or two in length, are in the bin because there wasn't enough fabric left to keep them on display. You will be hard pressed to get a dress out of a remnant, but there is usually enough fabric there to make a skirt or blouse. Just make sure that the remnant price really is lower than the price per yard on the bolt.

Be sure to find out the composition of the fabric before you buy a remnant. If it's not marked, ask the salesperson to check the bolt end of the same fabric on regular display. Don't leave the store with a piece of fabric you know nothing about. What a surprise when you wash that supposed wool-like synthetic and it shrinks like the real thing. Don't let me scare you away from the remnant bin. Just exercise caution before buying.

Another source of bargain fabrics are ready-to-wear clothing manufacturers. They unload bolt ends and excess yardage after they cut their lines for the season. Look in the yellow pages of the phone book to see if there are any clothing manufacturers in the area. (Some cities have whole garment districts to explore.) If so, give them a call and ask if they have a store that's open to the public (many do); tell them you'd like to be notified when they have sales.

But discipline your bargain buying: Don't buy a piece of fabric unless you're absolutely in love with it. Have something in mind for that sensational textile *before* you buy. The temptation with remnants and discount fabrics is to buy a fabric that's so-so because it's cheap, and maybe there will be a use for it one day. Chances are the fabric will be sitting in a drawer years from now taking up good storage space. Stockpiling inexpensive fabric that never gets put to use doesn't save you a penny.

I break this rule myself occasionally. I sew a lot and can always find a use for cotton knits, denims, and corduroys. They are great for T-shirts and pants, if for nothing else. When I find good buys on these fabrics, I usually take home a small cache for myself.

And finally, a no-cost bargain tip: Never throw anything away. Become a pack rat. Recycling fabrics will save you plenty. (See Chapter 10 for directions on how to restyle old clothes.)

Fabrics Are for Fun

Now that you know the rules of fabric selection, break a few! Take a fantasy trip through the yardage store and let your imagination run wild. Choose the fabric first, but don't have it cut until you select a pattern. That way you'll know exactly the amount to buy. Buying more fabric than you need is costly, and being caught with too little yardage is often disastrous.

Speaking of inspiring fabrics, don't overlook imported fabrics from faraway places. Add a new dimension to your travels—shop for exciting textiles while journeying through foreign lands. I can't tell you what fun I've had creating treasures with Guatemalan wovens, Indonesian batiks, and Indian saris. Have fun with the drapery and upholstery fabrics, too. The large floral prints make wild long-skirts, and the brocades can't be beat for opulent evening wear.

Do something a little daring. Combine fabrics of different textures to create intriguing illusions (See Chapter 11). Cut a dress on the bias (diagonal grain of the fabric) for the slinky, sexy look (see Guide C). Or make a "sporty" jacket in a "dressy" fabric. How about a velveteen blazer?

The rules exist to aid and assist the novice, but they are made to be broken. After a few successes, risk being adventurous. An act of pure nerve could result in a smashing new discovery.

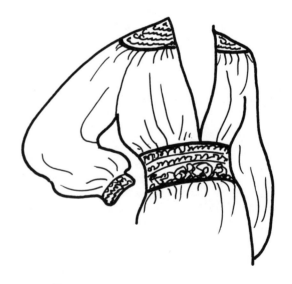

FIGURE 4.7. *Using imported fabrics.*

Chapter Five

Don't Forget the Notions

Now that you've selected a pattern and fabric you are no doubt eager to get home and get to work. In fact, you are already half-way out of the store. But hold on just a minute; you're forgetting something. What about the finishing touches? Imagine how frustrating it is to have to stop in the middle of a productive sewing session and race to the store for a zipper or thread. Plan ahead. Buy *everything* you'll need before you get home and start to sew.

Beginners, you're in luck again. The pattern manufacturers are on your side. They list everything you'll need in the notions department for your chosen pattern. There's no need to worry about what size zipper to use or how many buttons to buy. Look on the back of the pattern envelope. Everything you need to know about buttons, thread, hooks and eyes, bias tape, seam binding, and snaps is listed in the "notions" box underneath the pattern yardage chart. Buy exactly what the pattern calls for and *then* advance directly out the door.

Getting Them Together

There are a few rules to keep in mind when selecting notions. The most important is to make sure that all the trims and accessories for a garment will take the same care as the fabric. Don't use dry-clean-only buttons with wash-and-wear fabric; either the buttons will dissolve in the wash water or the dry-cleaning bills will run a small fortune.

Match zipper, thread, and buttons with your fabric for color. Occasionally you may buy a piece of fabric at a discount house that doesn't have an adequate notions department. If you buy fabric and notions separately, take a swatch of fabric (cut from an end

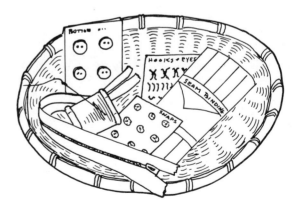

FIGURE 5.1. *Don't leave the store without the notions.*

45

corner) when you shop for notions to guarantee the perfect match. Don't count on being able to remember colors.

As for hooks, eyes, and snaps—those little metal fasteners that polish the look of the garment—use silver ones with light colored fabrics; the black ones are reserved for dark fabrics *only*. Don't spoil a good thing. No matter how expensive the cloth or how fine the sewing, a black snap on that lovely pink frock will make it look like something retrieved from the Good Will box.

Buy nothing but high-quality thread. Poor-quality thread just won't hold up. Thread at half price is no deal if seams separate after a few wearings. After all, the thread has a great burden to bear—it holds the whole works together.

Use mercerized cotton thread with cottons, linens, and wool; silk thread with silk; and polyester thread with synthetics, knits, and stretchables. Do not use mercerized cotton thread with fabric that has a stretch to it. Cotton thread *won't* give with the fabric, so when the fabric stretches the cotton thread breaks.

FIGURE 5.2. *Kinds of thread.*

Sew it right the first time. Use the correct thread and avoid having to repair your newly-made garment. Buy thread that is the same color as the fabric. If you can't find a perfect color match, buy thread that is a shade darker than the fabric.

The next time you go to the notions section, be sure to replenish your supply of sewing machine needles. Sewing machine needles have the habit of breaking, especially if, like me, you are slightly impatient and sew full speed ahead over pins. With a stock of needles on hand, a break is no more than a minor nuisance. Keep a full range of different size needles in the supply box. Use Number 9 needles for delicate fabrics (chiffon, silk, voile, and organdy). Number 11 is for use with the light-weights (batiste, tricot, lawn), and Number 14 is good for gingham, poplin, pique, linen, jersey, and flannel (the medium-weight fabrics). Use a Number 16 with moderately heavy-weight fabrics such as denim, sailcloth, gabardine, tweed, and drapery fabrics; and a Number 18 is fine for the heavies (dungaree, ticking, canvas, and upholstery cloth). Always use a ball-point needle with knits.

A Browse through the Button Gallery

Buttons add the mark of distinction to a garment. They can transform a simple smock into a fancy frock or they can add the professional touch to an elegant gown. But buttons also have the ability to overpower and destroy. The wrong style, color, shape, and size buttons can turn an otherwise stunning creation into a bargain-basement reject.

Buttons are sold in the notions department of most fabric stores on cards or one at a time from boxes of goodies. If you don't find the exact button you seek, try a button specialty shop (listed in the Yellow Pages). The button boutique is a great place to browse. The laces, french ribbons, and fabulous trims you'll find there will send your mind into imaginative flight.

By the way, there's a button revolution afoot. No longer do buttons merely serve to fasten; they are being recognized as an art form all their own. There are buttons of ivory, bone, and wood, and the innovations in plastic are a true delight. Give kid's togs a happy touch; treat them to ship-shaped buttons for a change.

Remember, take a swatch of fabric with you when you go on a button buy. Match that color! Don't take chances. The disappointment you're risking is your own. The pattern will tell you what size buttons to buy.

Do you like the tailored touch of the self-button (a button covered in the garment fabric)? Easy! Have them custom made through almost any fabric store for mere pennies a piece. Take a one-quarter yard swatch of the fabric to the store a week or so before you'll need the buttons. Or, easier still, buy a kit and cover the buttons yourself. The kits are inexpensive and you won't have to wait impatiently for the buttons to arrive. Covering them yourself takes all of five minutes.

Here's a handy hint for the bargain box: Cut all buttons off those tired togs and frumpy frocks that are fast making their way to the discard pile. Start a button bank. Buttons don't grow on trees these days. Every button retrieved is a dime or quarter saved. You'll have a small fortune in negotiable buttons in no time and a ready reserve of buttons on hand for mending. Save seven or eight look-alikes for a new creation; use the loners for repair work.

Time-Saving Notions

Wander through the notions department sometime when you're not in a hurry. You'll be surprised at the wealth of time-saving and decorative devices that fill the bins and racks. You'll find nailheads, buckles, rhinestones, and lacing hooks; collar stays, eyelets, hooks and eyes, and snaps; belts to cover and self-

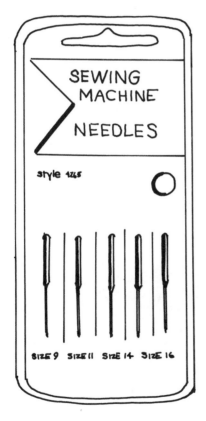

FIGURE 5.3. *An assortment of needles.*

cover buttons; and elastics of every size and color. You'll discover everything you need to make your own lingerie. And comfortable clothes for pregnant ladies are no problem at all with ready-to-install maternity stretch panels (see Chapter 14).

How's this for a great notion—a transparent tape with a guideline to use for top-stitching to perfection? And when it comes to time-savers, you can't beat a pinless spray to hold patterns to the fabric while you cut. For those of you with an aversion to hems there's a fusion material that puts hems, trims, and facings in their place. And there is no need to make patches or pockets anymore—buy them ready-made in the notions department and stitch them into place.

One section in the notions department is usually devoted to the sewing machine. You can buy all you need there for maintenance and minor repairs: needles, lint brushes, oil, belts, light bulbs, and bobbins. You'll also find a selection of those great time- and mind-saving attachments: buttonhole foot, magnetic seam guide, overcast foot, and zipper foot. Don't count on finding everything for the machine in the notions department but definitely depend on it for the essentials.

Chapter Six

Setting the Fabric in Order

Don't tell me, I can read your mind: "This lady's not to be believed. She says it's easy to sew and I'm almost ready to go and then she throws another obstacle in my path. I'm here to sew, not to read a tome on getting ready to work! What gives?"

Exactly this. The goal is to make clothes you will be proud to wear. You want the maximum return for your labor. Making the best use of your energies requires a little forethought and planning, but it's well worth it in the long run.

Home-sewing makes no sense unless you have the feeling that your efforts aren't being made in vain. That's what careful preparation is all about—it is insurance against failure. The price you pay is a little of that precious commodity time. Too high a premium? Consider the guarantee: *Success!*

The Big Shrink

Imagine this: You diligently select a pattern and patiently alter it to fit just so. The fabric costs a pretty penny but it's worth every cent. You sew like a real champ on this one and end up with a terrific creation that's built, like Fort Knox, to last forever. The new frock looks sensational. The women at work make a great fuss over it. Luckily, this masterpiece is washable. Just toss it into the machine after a hard day and it's ready to go. Comes time to give the gang at the office a treat and wear your gorgeous new creation again and—whoops! No, you haven't gained ten pounds overnight; your treasure has shrunk.

Ah, the agony of defeat. Nothing is more exasperating than seeing a product of your patient effort shrink before your eyes. There is not a thing you can do about it now. Give the thing away; the sooner it's out of your sight, the better.

You're not likely to make this mistake a second time—once was enough for me. Remember: *Preshrink all fabric.* Avoid a great disappointment. The preshrink is simple, so there's really no excuse for a shrunken disaster. Before doing anything, snip the selvages (the finished lengthwise edges of the fabric) every four inches or so. These little cuts will keep the selvages from drawing up during the big shrink.

To preshrink the washables, just machine wash and dry. Give woolens an all-over pressing with a steam iron and a damp press cloth. Leave the preshrinking of special dry-clean-only fabrics (silks, velvets, satins, and brocades) to the dry-cleaner. If you're a regular customer, the cleaner may even do it for free.

Some fabrics supposedly need no preshrinking at all and others are said to shrink very little. Be a true skeptic and preshrink everything. And don't forget the linings and the woven interfacings (nonwoven interfacings won't shrink). If you preshrink the garment fabric but forget about the underfabrics, you'll end up with a puckered mess fit for the rag bag. The ribbons and lace trim must be preshrunk too. Remember, if the garment is to be washable, *all* fabrics, trims, and accessories must be washable and all the fabrics and trims must be preshrunk.

Straightening the Grain

Fabric often gets stretched out of shape when it's put on the bolt. You must correct this before cutting to avoid the surprise of a misshapen creation.

Straightening the grain is another one of those simple but critical preparations. Don't even consider skipping this step. Once you get the hang of it, it will take you ten minutes at most to get everything straightened out.

In order to find out if a fabric needs straightening, you must first square off the crosswise ends of the fabric. Square off *woven* fabrics that tear easily by snipping through the selvage near one end of the fabric and tearing across to the other selvage. The fabric will tear straight. Clip through the second selvage. Do the same at the other end of the fabric.

Take wovens that you're reluctant to tear and clip through the selvage at one end of the cloth. Pull a crosswise thread (a thread at right angle to the selvage) until the fabric starts to gather. Cut across the fabric along this thread, pulling and gathering a little at a time as you go (Figure 6.1).

Square off the *nonwoven* fabrics (knits) by cutting each end perpendicular to the selvages. Use the right-triangle ruler to draw cutting lines at right angles to the selvages (Figure 6.2).

To tell if the fabric needs straightening, place the

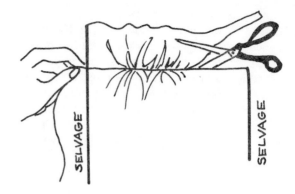

FIGURE 6.1.   *Squaring off woven fabrics.*

fabric on a flat surface and fold it in half, selvages together. Pin the straightened crosswise ends together. If the fabric lies flat when the selvages are together, there is no need to straighten the grain. Otherwise, straighten!

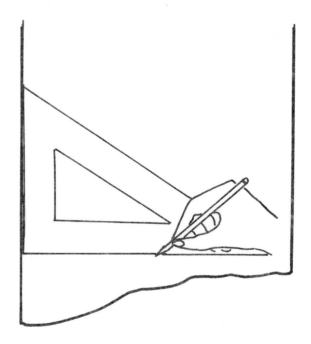

FIGURE 6.2.   *Squaring off nonwoven fabrics (knits).*

Straighten *washables* by dampening the fabric with a sponge and then pulling the fabric on the true bias (the diagonal grain) until the lengthwise and crosswise threads are at right angles to one another (Figure 6.3).

The *nonwashables* can be straightened by pressing with a steam iron. Fold the fabric in half, right sides together (Figure 6.4). Pin selvages together and pin the straightened crosswise ends together with rust-proof pins (one pin every five inches or so). Using a steam iron, press from the selvage to the fold in parallel paths from one end of the fabric to the other.

If a nonwashable fabric resists your straightening efforts, place a wet sheet over the cloth and leave it there long enough to dampen the fabric. You should have no trouble putting the grain straight now.

For the impatient seamstress who is sure that this straightening business is a waste of time, maybe this sounds familiar: Have you ever bought a pair of jeans, washed and worn them a few times and then noticed that the side seams of one pant leg are creeping in a circular fashion around your leg? You tug and tug at the seam in an effort to straighten it, but to no avail. The pants hang off grain and no amount of pulling will ever set them straight.

The only way to guarantee that a garment will hang properly is to straighten the grain *before* cutting the fabric. Clothes that hang off grain don't turn out to be great money-savers; the constant fiddling with cock-eyed seams is more trouble than it's worth.

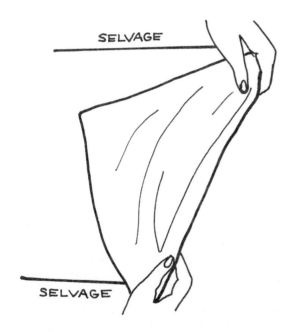

FIGURE 6.3. *Straightening washable fabrics.*

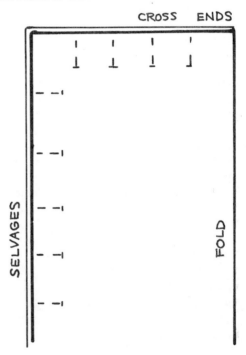

FIGURE 6.4. *Straightening nonwashable fabrics.*

Chapter Seven

Altering the Pattern

Everyone is familiar with clothes that don't fit; we've all been wearing them for years. Few of us can step into a ready-to-wear dress that fits perfectly. Outraged at the price of alterations, we usually make do with ill-fitting garb. But there's no reason to settle for a less-than-perfect fit when you tailor-make your own wardrobe.

The key to the perfect fit is to start with the correct pattern size (see Chapter 3). The next step is to alter the paper pattern.

"Wait just a minute. If I follow the directions and buy the 'right' pattern, why do I have to bother with this alteration stuff? I'm ready to sew!"

Pattern sizes, like ready-to-wear sizes, are meant to fit average figures that hardly ever exist in the real world. Almost everyone who sews has to make some alterations in the pattern to achieve a perfect fit. If you buy the right pattern to begin with the alterations will be minor. But even a minor alteration can make a big difference in fit, *so don't ignore this important step*. Once you get the hang of altering and are familiar with the kinds of alterations needed to fit clothes to your body, altering a pattern will take no time at all.

The procedure has three basic steps, to be followed every time you sew with a new pattern.

1. Compare your body measurements with pattern measurements.
2. Make necessary changes on the paper pattern.
3. Try on the paper pattern and adjust it to fit.

Follow this three-step procedure *before* cutting the fabric. Some alterations can only be made at this stage of the game. Others can be done later by the sew-and-rip method of altering, but that method is guaranteed to have you pulling your hair out in no time. Save yourself and your fabrics from needless wear and tear.

You should have the following equipment at your finger tips before you start altering a pattern: A pencil with a good sharp point; tissue paper; a ruler; a dressmaker's curve; a right-triangle ruler; your cutting board; scissors for cutting paper; an iron and ironing board; scotch tape; a piece of string; a sewing gauge; a tape measure; your measurement record; some blank paper; and, of course, the pattern.

Measure Up!

Okay, you're ready to start. Take the pattern out of the envelope. Read the sewing and cutting directions to find out which pattern pieces you need to make the style or view of your choice. Put the unnecessary pieces back into the envelope for safe-keeping.

You are about to determine whether the measurements of the finished garment will match your own, with a little room left over to make for a comfortable fit. If the pattern is too big or too small, you will find out how much to alter and where.

Trim each pattern piece to the cutting line and iron with a warm iron to remove creases. (A hot iron will cause the pattern to crinkle.) Place the pattern pieces on a flat surface; the cutting board will do fine.

Take out your measurement record (the one you used to select the pattern) and a tape measure. In order to ensure a perfect fit, you need a few more measurements. Tie a string at the waist again to help you measure accurately. Keep a record of the following measurements along with the others in your sewing notebook (Figures 7.1 and 7.2).

Front-waist Length: Measure from the base of the neck straight down to the string at the waistline, along the center front of your body.

Side-bodice Length: Stand with your hand resting on your hip. Measure from the armpit to the string at the waist, along the side of the body.

Shoulder: Measure from the base of the neck, on the side, along the shoulder to the shoulder point.

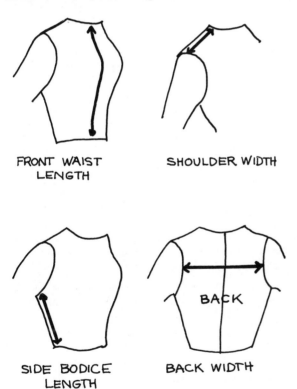

FIGURE 7.1. *Bodice measurements.*

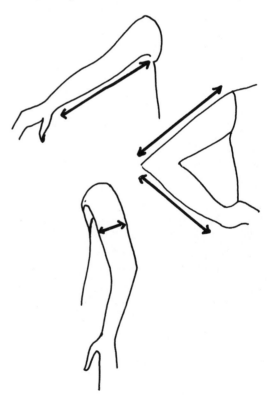

FIGURE 7.2. *Sleeve measurements.*

You'd better measure both shoulders, they often differ markedly.

Back Width: Have a friend help with this one. Put on a blouse that fits well. Measure from one armhole seam to the other, about 4 inches below the neck.

Sleeve Length: You'll need two measurements here. For the inside sleeve length, measure from one inch below the armpit to the wrist. Keep the arm straight while taking this measurement. Now for the outside, bend the arms and rest the hand on your hip. Measure from the shoulder point to the elbow point and from the elbow point to the wrist along the outside of the arm.

Arm: Measure around the bare arm at two places—at the wrist and around the upper arm, halfway between the shoulder and elbow. (Remember the caution about taking honest measurements. A sleeve that's too tight is uncomfortable and wrinkles.)

You will need to compare your body measurements with the pattern measurements at the following points: (1) bust, (2) front-waist length, (3) shoulder, (4) side-bodice length, (5) waist, (6) hips, (7) skirt length, (8) back-waist length, (9) back width, (10) sleeve length inside, (11) sleeve length outside, (12) upper arm, and (13) wrist (Figure 7.3).

When measuring the pattern, be sure to measure only the distance *between* the stitching lines on the pattern. *Do not* include seam allowances (the distance between the cutting and stitching lines—usually ⅝ inch) in your measurements. If the pattern piece is to be placed on a fold and there is no stitching line, measure up to the fold line. Also, pin all darts *before* measuring, or subtract the amount that will be taken up in darts from the pattern measurement. You want the measurements of the *finished* garment.

Remember, you are working with a pattern for half the garment. You will cut the pattern out in double thicknesses of fabric to make a whole garment. Also, some of the alteration points require that measurements be taken on several pattern pieces to find out

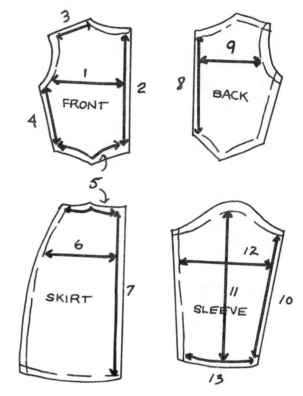

FIGURE 7.3. *Pattern piece measurements.*

the dimensions of the finished garment. To determine what the bust measurement of a garment will be, measure from one stitching line to the other (or to the fold line) across the bust of the front bodice piece of the pattern. Multiply this figure by two since you'll be cutting this piece out double (Figure 7.4).

Now measure across the back bodice piece of the pattern at the same distance from the waist as you took the front bust measurement. Multiply this figure by two and add it to the front bust pattern measurement. This is the distance all the way around the bust of the finished garment (Figure 7.5).

Do the same sort of computation for the waist and hip measurements. (Be sure to take the pattern hip measurement at the same distance below the waist as

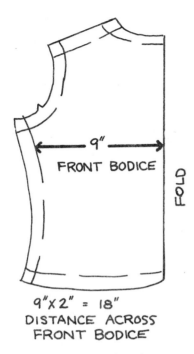

FIGURE 7.4. *Determining front bust measurement.*

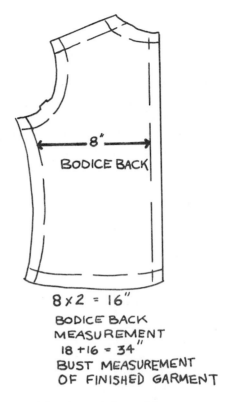

FIGURE 7.5. *Determining total bust measurement.*

you took your body hip measurement—usually seven to nine inches.)

Compare the pattern measurements with your actual body measurements. Don't expect the two sets to match perfectly. Pattern manufacturers allow a little extra space (called *ease*) in the pattern so that you can move comfortably in the finished garment. A little ease is essential to a good fit. We all know what tight clothes do for us—absolutely nothing!

Use this simple formula to determine whether or not a pattern needs altering and if so how much:

Your body measurement + ease = the perfect fit

The difference between the "perfect fit" measurement and the pattern measurement is the amount of alteration needed to make a perfect fit.

The amount of ease is standard for most garments. You want a good close fit in the shoulders, so don't allow any ease there. Allow about 1 to 2 inches ease in the bust and 2 to 3 inches in the hips. The waist should fit a little more closely—add an extra ½ to 1 inch for ease. Add ½ to ¾ inch to the front-waist length and ¼ to ½ inch to the back-waist length. The underarm seam should start 1 inch below the armpit, so subtract an inch from the side-bodice length when comparing it with the pattern measurement.

Take a look at your ready-made wardrobe for hints on sleeve lengths and skirt lengths. Measure the length of a sleeve or skirt that fits just right and use this measurement as a guide to alterations.

Most people have an aversion to charts and graphs, but it makes good sense to keep a record of alterations, and it's easiest to alter a pattern if you go about

PATTERN ALTERATION CHART

1. Body measurement	2. Your measurement	3. Ease	4. Perfect fit measurement	5. Pattern measurement	6. Amount to be altered (+ or −)
Bust		+1-2″			
Front-waist length		+½-¾″			
Shoulder		None			
Side-bodice length		−1″			
Waist		+½-1″			
Hips		+2-3″			
Skirt length		Varies			
Back-waist length		+¼-½″			
Back width		+½″			
Sleeve length— inside		Varies			
Sleeve length— outside		Varies			
Upper arm		+½″			
Wrist		+¼″			

it in an organized fashion. Here is an alteration chart to help you keep track of measurements and calculations. For each measurement add column 2 and 3 to get the perfect fit measurement. Calculate the difference between column 4 and 5 to determine 6, the amount to be altered.

Take a look at the "amount to be altered" column. If you see nothing but zeros, no alterations are necessary—you already have a pattern that fits. But pay attention to the altering procedure anyway. You are not likely to be that lucky all the time.

Changing the Paper Pattern

Making alterations on the paper pattern is a straightforward operation. Adjustments for the horizontal measurements (bust, waist, and hips) are made at the side-seam stitching lines of the pattern pieces. Alterations for the vertical measurements (front-waist length, back-waist length, sleeve and skirt lengths) are made at the adjustment lines printed on the pattern.

Follow these simple directions as you would follow a recipe in a cook book. Don't try to learn the procedure by heart. Let the book guide you through a few alterations; you'll pick up the routine in no time.

The first step in altering is to set up a flat working surface. To save yourself from a splitting backache, place the cutting board on top of a waist-high table.

Horizontal Alterations

Now let's run through alteration number one: Altering a pattern that is *too big around*. You will alter the pattern a little at each side seam (right front, left front, right back, left back), rather than all in one spot. Divide the "amount to be altered" by four. (Don't feel overwhelmed by the thought of working with numbers—this is the only arithmetic involved.)

(Remember, you will cut each pattern section out from double thicknesses of fabric. So, if you take one fourth of the "amount to be altered" off the side

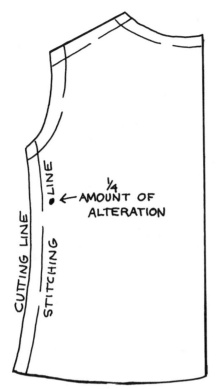

FIGURE 7.6. *Marking a pattern that is too big around.*

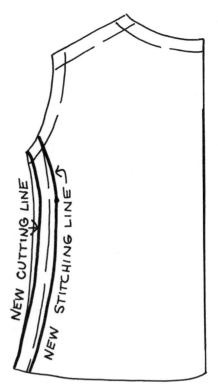

FIGURE 7.7. *Redrawing the lines on a pattern that is too big around.*

seams of the front and back pattern sections [one side seam on a section], and then cut each section out double, you will alter the pattern the total amount necessary.)

Measure the amount (one-fourth of the amount to be altered) from the side seams stitching lines of the front *and* back pattern sections. Mark the amount on the pattern with a pencil (Figure 7.6).

Draw a line from the pencil mark to the pattern stitching line (see illustration). This alteration line should gradually increase to and decrease from the point of alteration to give a smooth stitching line and a neat fit. Draw in a new cutting line ⅝ inch outside of and parallel to your new stitching line (Figure 7.7).

If you are not artistically inclined, use the dressmaker's curve to draw a smooth new stitching line.

Set the sewing gauge at ⅝-inch and use it to measure along the outside of the new stitching line—presto; a new cutting line.

To alter a pattern piece that's *too small around* use roughly the same procedure but increase, rather than decrease, one-fourth of the total amount of the alteration at each side seam. Since the alteration will probably extend beyond the pattern section, tape tissue paper to the pattern to form an extension (Figure 7.8). Cut the excess paper away after drawing the new stitching and cutting lines (Figure 7.9).

If you make a substantial alteration to the hips of a garment, don't join the new stitching line to the old stitching line below the point of alteration. Draw a new stitching line *parallel* to the old one—this will give the finished garment a nicer line.

ALTERING THE PATTERN **57**

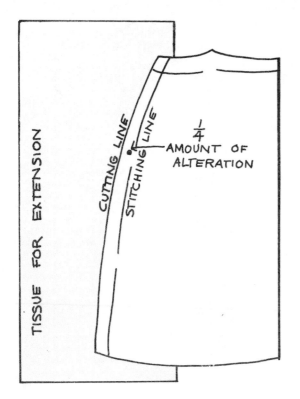

FIGURE 7.8. *Marking a pattern that is too small around.*

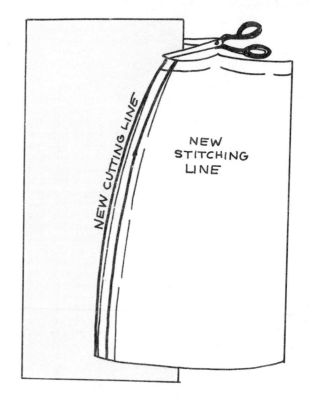

FIGURE 7.9. *Redrawing the lines on a pattern that is too small around.*

Vertical Alterations

Use the adjustment lines printed on the pattern to make alterations in vertical measurements. These lines are clearly marked, "Lengthen or shorten here."

To *lengthen a pattern section*, cut a piece of tissue paper several inches longer than the amount of the alteration and several inches wider than the pattern section. Draw a straight pencil line at right angles to the printed adjustment line at the center of the pattern section. Draw an identical line at the center of the tissue to be used as the extension (Figure 7.10).

Cut the pattern section along the adjustment line. Separate the pattern pieces an amount equal to the *total* alteration. Place the tissue extension underneath the two pattern pieces and center all three pieces using the pencil lines as guides. Double check the new pattern measurement, then pin the pattern to the tissue and secure with tape. Trim away the excess tissue (Figure 7.11). Remember, when altering a skirt length allow for the hem—usually 2½ to 3 inches below the finished length of the skirt.

Shortening a pattern section is a simple operation. Draw a pencil line parallel with the adjustment line at a distance from the adjustment line equal to the amount of the alteration (Figure 7.12). Fold the pattern so that the adjustment line meets the pencil line. This fold will make a tuck in the pattern equal to the amount of the alteration. Check the new pattern length and tape the fold into place along the pencil

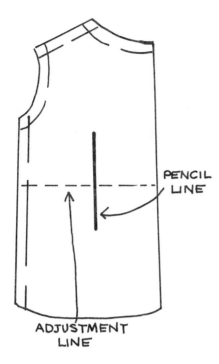

FIGURE 7.10. *Marking a pattern to be lengthened.*

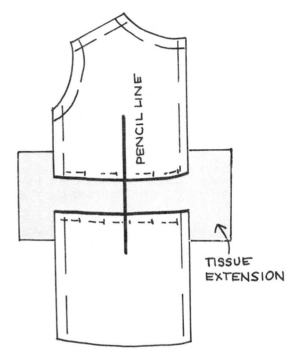

FIGURE 7.11. *Cutting and extending a pattern to be lengthened.*

line (Figure 7.13). If shortening disturbs the stitching line, draw a new stitching line, tapering it into the original stitching line. And a new stitching line requires a new cutting line.

Watch out for buttonholes! If you alter the length of a garment that has buttons evenly spaced down the front, be sure to respace the buttonholes after altering the pattern to fit.

The Pattern-Fitting Session

It's time to put your alterations to the test. Paper hardly has the hang of fabric, but trying on the pattern will give a general idea of the fit.

Pin all tucks and darts marked on the pattern. Then pin pattern pieces together along the seam lines. (Pin all seams and darts *on the outside* of the pattern for easier fitting.)

Put on the lingerie that you would normally wear with this garment and try the paper pattern on the right side of your body. (Remember, you only have a pattern for half the garment.) Check the pattern for fit, starting with the shoulders. The shoulder seam should rest directly on top of the shoulder. The side seams should hang straight from the armpits.

The fit across the bust is critical. The bust dart should end at the tip of your breast. Don't panic if the dart is too high or low. It's easy to alter a bust dart to fit: Unpin the pattern dart and the side seam on either side of the dart. Be sure the pattern is still pinned at the waist and at the underarm. Mark your bust point on the pattern with a pencil. Pin from this point to the side seam, taking up the fullness to create a new bust dart as you go. Don't fit too tightly. Repin the side seam and there you are—a perfectly tailored bustline.

ALTERING THE PATTERN **59**

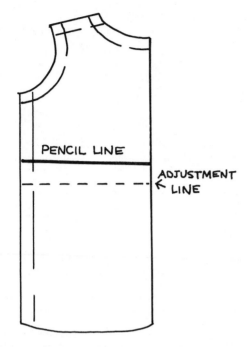

FIGURE 7.12. *Marking a pattern to be shortened.*

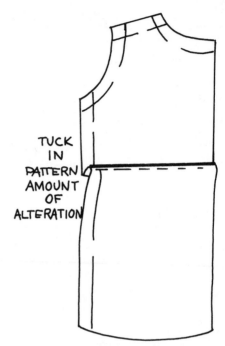

FIGURE 7.13. *Folding a pattern to be shortened.*

Take a good look at the overall fit of the garment. Wrinkling at any spot means the pattern is too big at that point. To correct, take a tuck in the paper and pin out the excess fullness (Figure 7.14).

Wherever the pattern is too tight mark with a pencil. Take the pattern off and slash the pattern at the pencil mark. Open the pattern up along the slash line to allow enough room for a comfortable fit and make an extension with tissue paper to fill in the gap (Figure 7.15). Secure all alterations with tape after double checking for the perfect fit.

Need more room at a seam? Make a tissue extension and add on the required amount. Be sure to add one-quarter of the required amount at each side seam. If too much pattern is the problem, move the pins in from the stitching line until you get to the perfect fit, again altering one-fourth the total at each side seam.

Be sure that alterations on seams and darts are

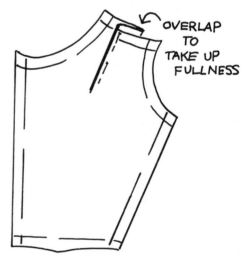

FIGURE 7.14. *Taking a tuck and pinning out excess fullness wherever the pattern wrinkles.*

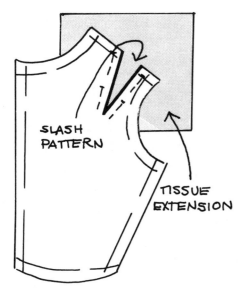

SLASH PATTERN

TISSUE EXTENSION

FIGURE 7.15. *Slashing a pattern wherever it is too tight and reinforcing with tissue.*

clearly marked in pencil on the pattern before you unpin the pieces. And don't forget: A change in a stitching line requires a change in a cutting line.

When all alterations have been made, unpin and repress the pattern pieces. The altered pattern should lie flat on the cutting board. If the pattern bulges in places, fold in the surplus paper and tape it into place.

Congratulations. You have successfully altered your first pattern.

Finally—Pants that Really Fit!

No kidding; it's easy to make pants that fit as long as you take time to check the pattern measurements and make the necessary alterations *before* you begin to sew.

Always buy a pants pattern according to your waist measurement *unless* your hips are larger than the hip measurement for this size. Then buy the pattern according to your hip measurement and alter the waist.

Compare your measurements with the pants pattern measurements as you would with any pattern. Be sure to allow for ease: one-half to one inch at the waist; two to four inches at the hips; and one inch around each thigh at the fullest part. Make up a Pattern Alteration Chart; then make the necessary alterations in the horizontal and vertical measurements according to the procedure outlined above.

Pants must fit well in the crotch. Some alterations can be made after the fabric is cut, but crotch length is one of those measurements that *must* be altered *before* cutting. An error here cannot be corrected. But there is an easy, fool-proof way to check and alter the crotch measurement. Sit erect on a chair. Have a friend measure from your waist to the seat of the chair. This is your crotch length (Figure 7.16).

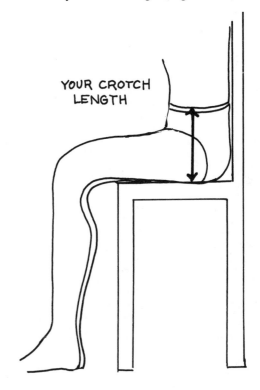

YOUR CROTCH LENGTH

FIGURE 7.16. *Determining crotch length.*

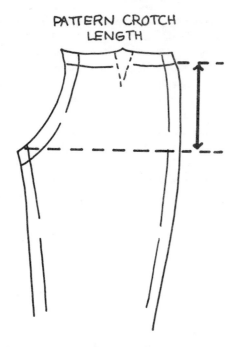

FIGURE 7.17. *Determining pattern crotch length.*

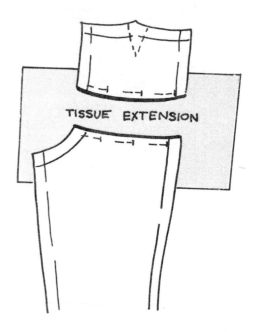

FIGURE 7.18. *Lengthening the pattern crotch.*

Draw a line on the pants-front pattern section from the lowest point of the crotch straight across to the side seam. Measure from this line to the waistline of the pattern. This is the *pattern* crotch length (Figure 7.17).

Your crotch length plus three-fourth inch for ease should be equal to the pattern-front crotch length for the perfect fit. If the pattern is too long or too short in the crotch, alter at the adjustment line, (crotch length is a vertical measurement) using the procedures described above for shortening or lengthening a pattern piece (Figures 7.18 and 7.19). Alter the back pattern section the same amount as you altered the front pattern section.

Be sure to fit pants as you sew. Even if the pattern has been altered, fabrics vary and so does your body; every pair of pants will be slightly different. Stitch the crotch and inside seams first. Pin-fit the outside seams before doing the final stitching.

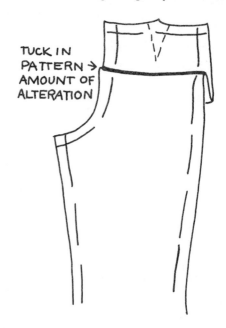

FIGURE 7.19. *Shortening the pattern crotch.*

Make It in Muslin

If you are working with a tricky pattern that calls for detailed seaming and subtle style lines, it may be worthwhile to make a mock-up in muslin and double-check that fit *before* you cut the fine, high-priced fabric. Balk at the extra work all you want. Some fabrics won't allow alterations—ripped-out seams leave tell-tale marks on velvets, velveteens, suedes, silks, and satins. It's better to spend a few minutes now and have a sure fit than to forge ahead and end up with another closet-case disaster.

Always use high-quality muslin for fitting—the more threads to the inch, the better. Poor-quality muslin will stretch and your fitting will be inaccurate.

There is no need to make the whole garment in muslin. If in doubt about how the bust will fit, just stitch up the bodice. Forget those fancy finishes—simply sew the seams and darts and check for fit.

Fit the muslin to your body as you would a paper pattern. Start with the shoulders and gradually move down from there, altering one seam at a time; pinning and slashing as you go. Mark alterations on the muslin with pen or pencil. Undo the seams and darts with a seam ripper (see Chapter 9 for details on ripping) and press the muslin flat. Transfer all alterations from the muslin to the paper pattern. And remember, if you change a stitching line, change the cutting line too.

Chapter Eight

Pinning, Cutting, and Marking the Fabric

Here is the moment you have been waiting for: the fabric has been straightened and the pattern fits. Now, the two finally come together.

The first step in constructing a garment is to pin the pattern pieces *very carefully* to the fabric. The importance of this step is too often overlooked. Accurate pinning, cutting, and marking is absolutely critical to the success of a sewing project.

Preparing the Layout and Reading the Pattern

After giving the altered pattern a touch-up with a warm iron and pressing out all the creases and wrinkles in the fabric, find a flat surface large enough to hold the entire length of the fabric. Lay the fabric out flat and then carefully study the cutting guide that comes with the pattern. Select the right layout for the view you are working on and circle it with a red felt-tipped pen so you don't start following the wrong guide by mistake.

Your pattern is the blueprint for this build-a-dress project. *All* the pattern symbols are instructions that will make the construction job easier and more precise. Here is a key to pattern symbols:

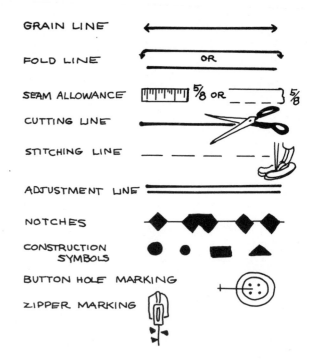

NOTE: Notches and construction symbols—those little dots, squares, and triangles—help in joining pattern sections to one another. Though small they are critical. In addition to these symbols there is usually a box on each pattern piece that carries special information on cutting, interfacing, lining, and underlining.

Here are several more things to keep in mind when laying out the pattern and fabric:

When sewing on those furry favorites (velvets, velveteens, corduroys, and velours), be sure to use the cutting layout designed for fabrics "with nap." The pattern pieces *must* be laid out in one direction. Napped fabrics are one color when the nap is up and another when it's down. If you combine the two unintentionally, the effect will be somewhat less than sensational, to say the least.

Most pattern pieces are cut from double thicknesses of fabric. Fold the fabric so that right sides are together, and pin the selvages to one another every inch or two. (If the selvages weren't snipped before preshrinking, do it now.)

Occasionally a pattern requires that some pieces be cut double and some single. Plan to cut the doubles first, then unfold the fabric and cut the singles. When cutting from single thicknesses of fabric, be sure that the fabric is right side up on the cutting board.

That pattern should be looking you square in the eye—as you work—always pin the pattern with the right side up, unless instructed otherwise.

And here's the "otherwise": When cutting a pattern from a single thickness of fabric, be sure to turn the pattern over (right side down to the fabric) to cut the piece for the other side of the body. If you ignore this rule, you may wind up with two right sleeves and perhaps not enough excess fabric to cut a left one. See how fast that jacket turns into a vest then!

The Layout

To begin the layout, fold the fabric according to the layout diagram. Separate the pieces that are to be placed on the fold from the rest. Position the on-the-fold pieces first. Arrange the others according to the diagram. Don't pin a single piece until every piece is arranged. Avoid the hassle of pinning and repinning.

Check all grain lines. Grain lines are clearly marked on all pattern pieces (except for those that are placed on the fold). If the pattern piece is to be placed on the lengthwise grain, the pattern grain line should be parallel to the selvages. Measure the distance between the grain line and the selvages at several points to be sure the pattern is on the straight of the grain (Figure 8.1). If the pattern section is to run crosswise on the fabric, place it parallel to the squared-off cross ends.

After double-checking the grain lines and the position of the pattern sections, pin each piece into place. Try not to move the fabric while pinning and don't pin right to the selvage edge. Place pins parallel to the cutting line, and not across it.

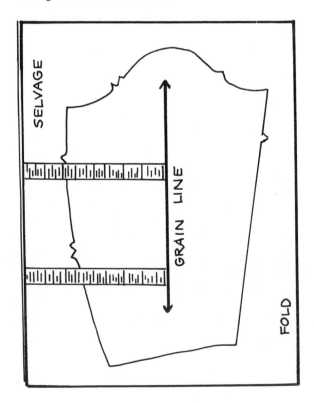

FIGURE 8.1. *Checking the grain line.*

Pick up only a few threads with each pin—just enough to hold the pattern in place. Pins leave marks on some fabrics (silks, satins, velvet). Check this out first on a scrap of fabric. If pin marks won't press out with a little steam, carefully pin *within* the pattern seam allowances so as not to mar the finished frock.

Do not cut until all pieces are pinned into place. If you cut as you pin, you may find too late that there's not enough fabric to go around.

Matching Patterned Fabric

Plaids, checks, and stripes aren't hard to work with; they merely require a little extra care. Here are some hints for working with patterned fabric:

Fold striped and checked fabric exactly half-way through a stripe or check; the two halves will be lined up perfectly. To guard against a mismatch, pin the two layers of fabric together at intervals, making sure

that stripes and checks are right on line (Figure 8.2). Now it's okay to cut two pieces at once; the stripes and checks will match at the seams.

Uneven stripes and plaids are best cut from a single thickness of fabric. Use those numbered notches on the pattern pieces to match the fabric design along the important seams (Figures 8.3 and 8.4). Be sure to match *seam* lines, *not* cutting lines.

It is usually impossible to match every seam: Give priority to front seams over back ones, and to horizontals over verticals. Avoid a costly mistake: Don't cut anything until all the pieces are matched. For a sure match, make a duplicate of each pattern piece and lay out all the pieces on a single thickness of fabric. Don't forget the notches!

Watch out for the large floral prints—they can be real trouble-makers. A rather unpleasant surprise

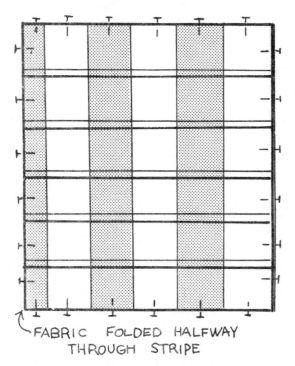

FIGURE 8.2. *Matching stripes, plaids, or checks.*

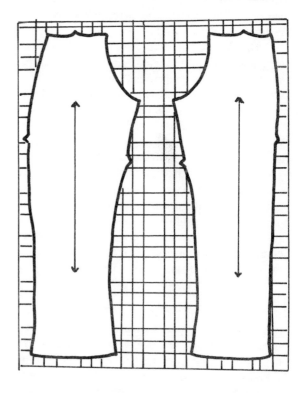

FIGURE 8.3. *Matching uneven stripes or plaids.*

awaits anyone who forgets to match flowers when they fall on a center-front or center-back seam. And give a second thought to how you will look in those posies. Do you really want two beautious begonias hugging the bust or a brightly colored daisy sprouting from the derriere? It may be cute on the back of jeans, but how will it look at the next garden party?

Do something exciting with prints. A border print makes a smashing hemline. Place the pattern pieces vertically on the crossgrain (Figure 8.5). Result: instant fashion. (Be sure the hem is a straight-edged one.)

Go a step further. Some Indian and African prints have borders at the edges and large design motifs in the center. Use the borders to cuff and hem a new shirt. Position a circular design around the neckline to simulate a collar or yoke and one at the center back for kicks (Figure 8.6).

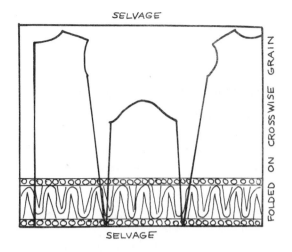

FIGURE 8.5. *Using a border print.*

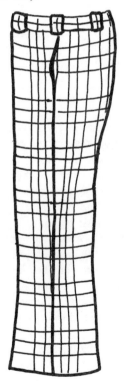

FIGURE 8.4. *The matched plaid.*

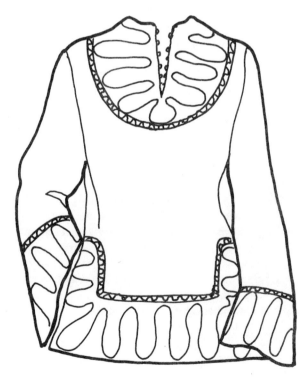

FIGURE 8.6. *Incorporating a print into the total design.*

PINNING, CUTTING, AND MARKING THE FABRIC **67**

Don't overlook the bias-cut for an interesting twist to the stripe affair (see Guide C). Garments laid out on the bias will be cut in single thicknesses of fabric at a time.

Go Ahead and Cut!

Just a few things to remember here for a precision cut. First, *never use pinking shears* to cut out a garmet. The professionals shudder at the mere mention of these saw-toothed monsters. They are impossible to keep sharp; consequently they have a tendency to chew the cloth rather than cut clean through. This not only makes for ragged seams; it can throw the grain line of the whole garment off.

Use seven to eight inch bent-handle dressmakers shears, and *keep them sharp*. The lefties should treat themselves to left-handed shears. Why struggle with scissors made for the ordinaries? You're special.

Have a small pair of scissors handy for cutting notches. The notches along the cutting lines are to help in constructing the garment. They are numbered in the order in which they are to be used in assembling. Cut notches outward from the cutting line; otherwise the seam allowance will be weakened. Cut double and triple notches as in Figure 8.7. *Accurate construction depends on carefully cut notches.* Don't risk the sleeve-on-backwards syndrome—the inevitable consequence of a missed notch or two.

Do not move the fabric while cutting. Leave the fabric flat on the cutting board and cut with the scissors-edge resting on the board. Cut along the cutting lines with long strokes, and don't close the scissors all the way to the point between each cut. This cutting style will prevent ragged edges.

To cut two intersecting straight lines so that you get a true sharp angle, rather than a gnawed corner, cut along one line until you reach the point. Pull the shears out and cut along the second line. Don't try to round the corner in one cut.

Cut out all the pattern pieces at one sitting. Do not unpin the pattern from the fabric until you have transferred *all* pattern markings to the fabric.

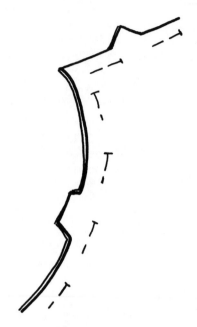

FIGURE 8.7. *Cutting notches.*

Transferring the Pattern Markings

Carbon and the Tracing Wheel

The quickest and easiest way to transfer pattern markings is to use dressmaker's carbon and a tracing wheel. But never use these tools without trying them out on a test-scrap first. Carbon markings show through to the right side of some fabrics. If your test shows this to be the case, use pins and chalk or tailor's tacks (see next section).

Use light-colored carbons with light-colored fabrics and dark carbons with dark fabrics. Never use a dark carbon on light fabric on the rationale that it will show up better. It will do that—but probably well enough for everyone else to see too.

To use the carbon and wheel for transferring markings to fabrics folded double unpin the pattern just enough to slip a piece of carbon, carbon side down, between the pattern and the fabric. (The fabric should be folded with right sides together.) Repin the pattern into place. Now, slip another piece of carbon between the cutting board and the bottom layer of fabric, carbon side up (Figure 8.8).

Double-check to be sure that you are transferring markings to the *wrong* side of the fabric. There is no remedy if that blueprint shows front side up on a stunning piece of cloth.

Use firm, forward-moving strokes of the wheel to transfer pattern markings (Figure 8.9); never run the wheel backwards. Use a pencil to mark X's through the construction symbols. Trace over the pattern markings that will aid in constructing the garment. Mark darts, center fold lines, buttons and buttonholes, and construction symbols—those little circles, squares, and triangles. If you have cut the pattern precisely there is no need to transfer the stitching lines; you will be able to depend on the seam gauge to guide in sewing.

To mark a single thickness of fabric, slip the carbon paper, carbon side up, between the cutting

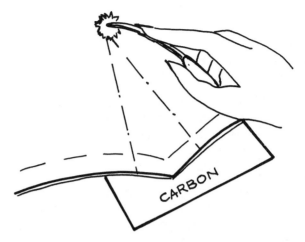

FIGURE 8.9. *Using the tracing wheel.*

board and the fabric, and wheel away. Since the fabric is right-side up, the wrong side will be marked.

Some markings should show on *both* sides of the fabric. How will you know where to place that pocket or buttonhole without a guideline on the front to follow? Simple! Baste over the markings on the wrong side of the fabric—instant transfer! This technique is called "thread tracing."

Pin and Chalk

Sometimes a fabric just won't take the tracing wheel. Perhaps the carbon is too dark or the mere pressure of the wheel on the fabric is enough to mar it permanently. In these cases use the pin-and-chalk method to transfer markings. Don't forget to give the chalk a trial run on a fabric scrap before forging ahead.

Pin through the pattern and both layers of fabric at all construction symbols. Turn the work over and chalk over each pin on the wrong side of the fabric. Remove the pattern by pressing each pin-head carefully through the pattern. Chalk over the pins on the top layer of the fabric and remove the pins (Figure 8.10).

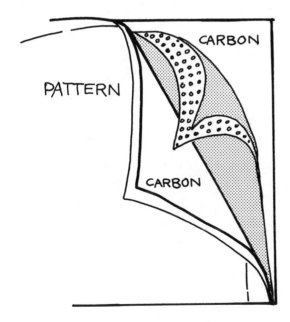

FIGURE 8.8. *Positioning the carbon paper.*

PINNING, CUTTING, AND MARKING THE FABRIC **69**

FIGURE 8.10. *The pin and chalk method.*

Chalk may rub off some fabrics very easily. If the marks fade fast, baste through each chalk marking immediately or you might be witness to a great disappearing act.

When All Else Fails, Tack

A few delicate fabrics can't be marked successfully with either carbon or chalk. Use tailor's tacks to transfer markings to these temperamental materials.

To make tailor's tacks, start with a long, unknotted, double strand of thread. Take a stitch through both layers of fabric and the pattern at each construction symbol, leaving an inch-long thread end. Take another stitch in the same place, leaving a loop of thread on the pattern side. Clip the thread, leaving another inch-long thread end. See Figure 8.11.

Raise the upper layer of the fabric and clip the threads between it and the bottom layer of fabric. This leaves tufts of thread marking each critical spot (Figure 8.12). Carefully remove the pattern by pulling the threads through the pattern.

If a lot of tacks are needed in an area, as with darts for example, move directly from one tack to another without clipping the thread after each one (Figure 8.13). Clip the thread in between each tack after completing a group.

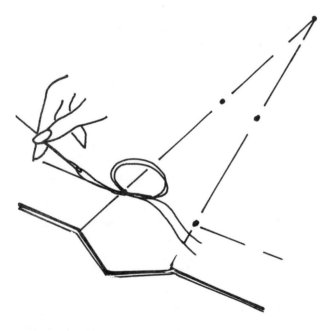

FIGURE 8.11. *Making loops for tailor's tacks to transfer markings.*

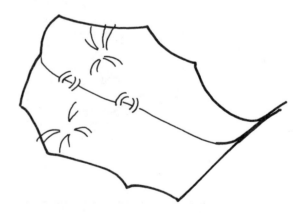

FIGURE 8.12. *Clipping the loops for tailor's tacks.*

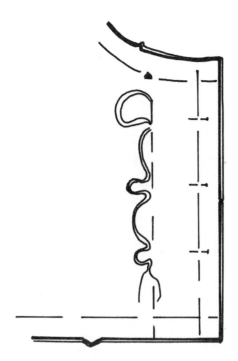

FIGURE 8.13. *A series of tacks, unclipped.*

Chapter Nine

Tricks of the Trade

You are now at the "assemble and sew" stage of your build-a-garment project. Take some advice: *Sew only when you are in the mood.*

If you don't follow this advice, sewing will become drudgery. You'll begin to hate what you're doing, you'll rush to get through it, and inevitably you'll skip a step or two. One mistake after another will appear to haunt and harrass you, and finally that old friend patience, who probably wasn't much in evidence to begin with, will split the scene entirely, leaving you and the seam ripper alone to battle it out with that poor, unsuspecting piece of cloth. A few sessions like this and you'll swear off sewing forever.

Stay relaxed but determined. Work on your project until it's just right. Settle for nothing less than the best. But don't let a silly mistake spoil your day. There is no need to have the dexterity of a baton-twirler or the brains of a genius to sew. The only prerequisite is *patience*.

Following Instructions

This chapter is designed to guide you through the basic sewing procedures required to assemble a garment. At this point, each pattern piece is carefully cut and marked. Now all you have to do is read this chapter and follow the pattern instructions very carefully and your garment will be sewed. It is impossible to overstate the importance of following pattern instructions. Friends have marvelled at my hand-made clothes for years. The secret of my success is so simple I'm embarassed to admit it. I simply follow the instructions *to the letter*, every stitch of the way. At this stage it pays to play dumb. Even after making the same dress over and over, I never assume that I know the directions by heart. I take out the instructions, tack them in clear line of sight, and refer to them one step at a time.

And why not? It takes off the burden of trying to figure out what step comes next. Someone else has already taken the time and energy to find out the easiest way to get the job done. Follow the instructions and you are left free to just sew.

Read *all* the instructions *before* beginning to work. Get a sense of what lies ahead.

Remember that patterns usually contain instructions for several *views* which are variations on a basic style. This means that there are likely to be directions you have no use for. *Underline* the instructions pertaining to your choice with a red felt-tipped pen.

Be sure to follow the construction order (each step is numbered). Skipped steps spell disaster. And don't fear being led astray. In all my sewing years I have never found a serious error in a pattern instruction.

Don't panic if you feel more confused than enlightened by a direction. Use the Guides at the back of this book. *Always* look up any term you don't understand in Guide A (Glossary of Sewing Terms). Check to see whether the fabric you are working with is discussed in Guide C (Sewing on Special Fabrics). Depend on Guide H, the Sew-Easy Guide for detailed instructions on how to get through tricky procedures: seam finishing, facing, interfacing, buttonholes, zippers, collars, waistbands, etc. Look up each step as you come to it in the pattern instructions. The sewing techniques are listed in alphabetical order, and simple but complete instructions accompany each procedure. Follow them, one step at a time, just as you would follow a recipe in a cookbook. The directions are easy to understand particularly if you're doing while you're reading.

The Trial Run

Well, you finally made it. You are actually ready to sew. Wind the bobbin, thread the machine, and take a trial run. Sew a few rows of stitching on an extra scrap of fabric to determine which stitch length will give the best results. Delicate fabrics usually require short, fine stitches; the heavy ones go for a longer stitch. If the fabric puckers along the stitching line, increase the stitch length to get a clean, flat look.

Make a tension check. Remember, you are after an even balance in tension between the needle thread and the bobbin thread. The threads should be drawn into the fabric to an equal degree. Test the tension using a stitch length of between 10 and 12. Carefully inspect the line of stitching. If either top or bottom thread is pulled too much to one side or the other, adjust the tension (see Chapter 2). A seam sewn with balanced tensions is twice as strong as one sewn with unbalanced tensions.

Experiment every time you come across a new procedure. Test-iron a scrap to find the correct temperature for pressing; stitch up a buttonhole on an extra piece of fabric; and find out in advance how the fabric reacts to ripping.

Time Out for Fitting

Break up the sewing routine with a few fitting sessions to see how the garment is shaping up. Major changes are rarely needed at this stage. After all, the pattern has been altered to fit. A minor alteration is no problem at all as long as it's taken care of as soon as the problem arises. If you wait until the garment is complete, you'd have to have the patience of a saint to rip the whole thing apart to get at a dart.

Fit the garment to the body as you did the pinned pattern. Start with the shoulders and fit from there down. Pinch in seams where there is too much fabric and let them out where there is not enough.

Even if the pattern has been altered to fit before, it's a good idea to fit on the way. Fabrics behave differently from one another and this often shows up in the fit.

The Art of Seam Ripping

So, you have to rip out a seam. Big deal! Don't take it personally. It happens to the best of us.

Virtually every mistake I ever made in sewing was correctable. With the help of a little patience and the faithful seam ripper, I was on my way again in no time. You can fix most errors without leaving a trace—if you're careful. A good seamstress isn't one who never makes a mistake, but one who corrects her sewing errors as they show up. By the way, ripping is not drudgery; it's a quick and easy way to correct a mistake.

The first step in seam ripping is, as usual, to test the fabric. Some fabrics are permanantly marred by ripping; among them are silks, taffetas, satins, velvet, velveteen, corduroy, and leather. Sew a seam on a

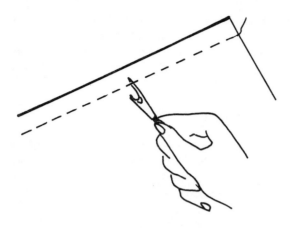

FIGURE 9.1. *Ripping a seam in woven fabric.*

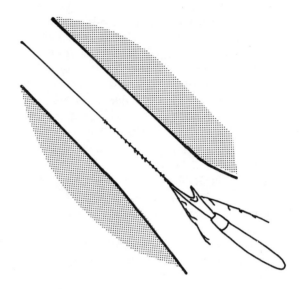

FIGURE 9.2. *Ripping a seam in a knit fabric.*

test swatch and then rip it out to see how your fabric reacts. (If ripped out seams leave marks on the fabric, baste all seams and sew slowly and carefully to avoid mistakes.)

To rip a seam, use a seam ripper and cut the thread every inch or so on one side of a row of stitching. Slide the pointed end of the ripper under a stitch and cut the thread on the sharpened edge. Pull out the thread on the other side of the seam and pick out any remaining bits of thread (Figure 9.1).

Rip seams in knit fabrics by spreading the seam open and cutting the thread with the ripper. Continue down the seam spreading and cutting in this fashion (Figure 9.2). Use your most delicate touch with the ripper and never yank or pull impatiently to get threads out.

Machine-basting (with long machine stitches) is the answer to perfectly fitting clothes. The sewing goes fast and ripping is a snap, if the garment needs altering. As always, test this technique before you use it.

Press as You Sew

Shape up those pressing skills! The pressing can make or break the look of a garment. A skillfully sewn frock will look like an amateur-hour reject if the pressing is inadequate. And minor sewing errors can be made to disappear with a skillful touch and a little steam.

Press seams and darts as you sew to achieve a professional look. A seam must be pressed open *before* another seam is sewn across it; otherwise lumpy intersections result. Press with an up-and-down motion; never go round and round. And don't drag the iron across the cloth.

When working with wools or delicate fabrics, use a press cloth or a piece of heavy brown paper cut from a clean shopping bag. Iron on the wrong side of the fabric as much as possible. Sometimes you are forced to press on the right side; then place a piece of fabric between the iron and the garment to prevent an ugly shine from developing.

Here are a few pressing techniques to remember:

1. Always press *with* the grain of the fabric.
2. Press a seam first as it was sewn (seam allowances together). Then, press the seam open (Figure 9.3).
3. Press darts and curved seams over a tailor's mitt or tailor's ham to mold into shape (Figure 9.4).

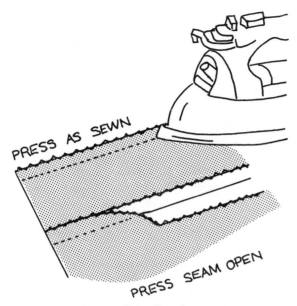

FIGURE 9.4. *Pressing seams.*

4. Press bust darts down and skirt darts toward the center of the skirt (see Figure 9.5).

5. Press waist darts and shoulder darts toward the center of the bodice (Figure 9.6). Press elbow darts down.

6. On very wide darts of heavy fabrics, slash the dart to within an inch of the dart point. Press the dart open and press the point toward the center (Figure 9.7).

7. The armhole seam is pressed toward the sleeve (see Figure 9.8).

8. Never press over pins; and press over bastings *only* if silk thread is used.

And here's a hint for pressing polyester double knits. A sure way to crease these easy-care favorites is to use a press cloth dampened in a mixture of one tablespoon white vinegar to a cup of water.

FIGURE 9.4. *Pressing darts on a tailor's ham.*

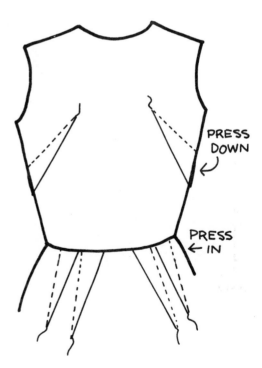

FIGURE 9.5. *Pressing busts and skirt darts.*

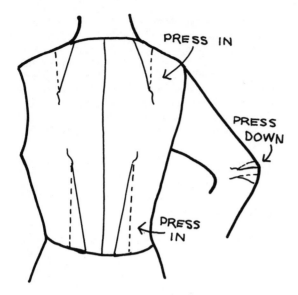

FIGURE 9.6. *Pressing shoulder and waist darts.*

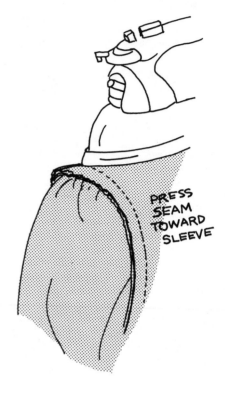

FIGURE 9.8. *Pressing the armhole seam.*

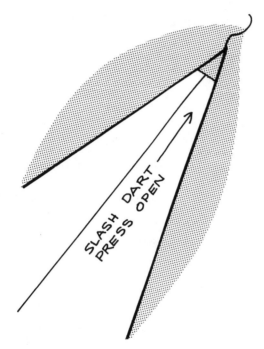

FIGURE 9.7. *Slashing wide darts or darts on heavy fabrics.*

Spots on the Fabric

Need I have mentioned that sewing is best done in an antiseptic environment? I'll never forget the time I sewed at a friend's kitchen table and wound up with a huge butter stain on my beautiful new dress. Occasionally these disasters do happen. So, what's to be done?

Keep a gum eraser handy (the kind artists use) to lift slight soil marks that aren't yet worn in.

Don't use cleaning fluid on a water spot. Let it dry; then rub the edges of the spot until those edges disappear.

Sewing machine oil is sure to be the culprit sooner or later. Press the fabric immediately between two pieces of clean blotting paper with a warm iron. Use talcum powder to absorb some of the oil, but on light-colored fabrics *only*.

Ah, the inevitable pin-prick and the tiny blood spots everywhere. No need to soak the life out of that frock. Roll a long piece of white thread into a ball and chew it for a minute or two. Rub the damp thread hard over the spot and the stain will disappear.

The Tricks that Save Time

Now that you're taking this sewing business seriously, it's time to introduce you to some time-saving tricks. Don't get me wrong, I'm not suggesting you rush. The time saved by the speedy seamstress is usually spent in ripping, repairing, and repenting. It hardly seems worth it. On the other hand, why spend more time sewing than is necessary? Incorporate these suggestions into the sewing routine, and lighten the work-load by hours.

First, don't even consider sewing unless there are no distractions. Invite friends to come over and chat while you're putting the finishing touches on that gorgeous gown, but insist that they stay away while major construction is under way. As for those kids, sew while they're at school when possible.

Set a definite time for sewing. Plan to work in blocks of time. Divide up the work but don't get into the habit of sewing for less than an hour at a time. Sew long enough at one sitting to get a feeling of accomplishment. If you don't see progress, you're likely to lose interest. A three-hour sewing project may never get done if worked on only fifteen minutes at a time.

Construct a garment in sections. Complete sleeves, bodice, collar, and skirt each as separate units before joining them into one complete garment. Work with small, easy-to-handle parts. Combine this idea with the blocks-of-time idea for a neat sewing schedule. Complete one of those sections at a sitting. Add another session to pull the whole thing together, and there's that new dress you've been wanting.

Take a tip from the professionals. Dress manufacturers save time and money by making more than one garment at a time. Take the hint. The time saved by cutting out several garments at one sitting is astounding. A friend of mine sets aside the first two weeks in September of each year for a sew-athon. She sews ten to fifteen small-fry frocks at once. No back-to-school-clothes shopping for this smart lady. Her kid's togs come hot off the machine.

Apply this plan-ahead principle even when sewing on just one garment at a time. Organize the work: Sew several seams at a time, and then press them all at once. The sew-one-seam, press-one-seam method means a constant back and forth between the machine and the ironing board.

The last hint which will help save money and peace of mind as well as time, is more of a command than a suggestion: *Don't cut corners when you sew.* The results of impatient and hasty sewing are usually inadequate. They look home-made, and that means they won't be worn. Time, money, and energy have gone down the drain. Remember, you'll save money by turning out professional-looking clothes that are worn and worn. Don't be fooled: Cutting corners costs dollars.

Part Two

Using Your Sewing Skills

Chapter Ten

Sewing on a Tight Budget

There is no need to convince you that sewing saves dollars; the proof is in the making. And now that you are familiar with the basics you can keep on sewing and stay well dressed no matter how tight the economic pinch.

Economical Patterns

Check the yardage requirements of a style *before* buying. The less yardage required, the lower the cost of the finished garment. If the fabric you have in mind costs only a dollar and a half per yard, an extra yard or so isn't too important. But if the fabric costs seven or eight dollars a yard, the difference is considerable.

The following style features greatly increase fabric requirements: large collars and hoods; long, full sleeves; gathered and circular skirts; and skirts with pleats. Styles with *low* fabric requirements include A-line skirts and dresses; sleeveless or short-sleeved garments; sheaths; and slim-sleeved blouses and jackets. Stick to these styles when trying to economize.

You'll often find that two very similar designs with almost identical lines require different quantities of fabric. For example, the two A-line dresses in Figure 10.1 are very similar in style. But the one with the long sleeves and inverted pleat requires at least one and a half yards more fabric than the other dress. If you are using a nice wool gabardine selling for, say, six dollars a yard, the difference to your pocketbook is a significant nine dollars. Do a little comparative shopping in the pattern catalogue before making the final choice.

Get the most for your money by selecting the pattern that provides the largest selection of views or styles. If one pattern offers an A-line skirt in short and long lengths, and another offers the same skirt with a blouse and slacks to match, is there any question as to which is the best deal?

Remaking Old Patterns

Time is worth money to most of us these days. By this reasoning, a garment that takes less time to construct costs less too. A pattern that has been used is already custom-tailored to you. You save in alteration time and you save, of course, the cost of a new pattern as well.

81

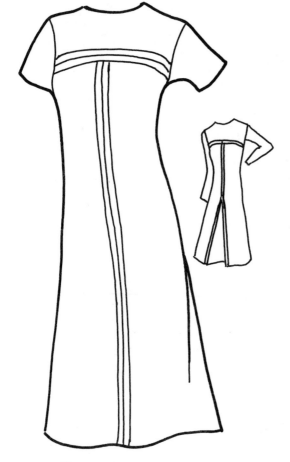

FIGURE 10.1. *Cost comparisons.*

Beware, though, of falling into the monotonous-wardrobe rut. If the closet is boring, the clothes don't get worn.

Modify a collar or cuff and make the sleeves puffed this time, instead of wrist-length. Try another view: Stitch up the tunic and pants for a change and repeat the dress later on.

It's surprising how different a winter suit will look made up in a summer-weight fabric. Shorten the sleeves for a cool touch and no one will notice your penny-pinching caper.

Don't repeat a style too frequently, but never throw a pattern away. A style rarely goes out for good. Save those outdated favorites for a timely revival.

For the Seamstress Short on Time

Don't overlook those easy-sew patterns; they are not for beginners only. These designs are simple to make and are great time-savers for women in a hurry. Cutting construction time down means hours left over for making more clothes. You can update your whole wardrobe in a matter of weeks if you use easy-sew patterns.

Stick to loosely fitting dresses, jackets, and coats. Forget the linings and avoid buttons when possible. Wrap it around if you have the chance. Coats, jackets, vests, skirts, and dresses all look great as wrap-arounds. Raglan sleeves and elasticized waistlines give casual comfort and are simple to make.

Easy-sew garments are clearly marked in the pattern catalogues. They consist of a minimum number of pattern pieces. The fewer separate pieces, the shorter the time needed to put the whole thing together. Casual and loose-fitting, they present no fit problems to stymie the sewer.

There is no need to sacrifice style to save time. You can look chic in a wardrobe of easy-to-sews. Simple designs transform into elegant creations when combined with sensational fabrics and trims (see Chapter 11). Top-stitching style lines give a high-fashioned finish (see Sew-Easy Guide 21).

Coordinating Your Wardrobe

To get more style for your money, coordinate your wardrobe around a central color scheme and make separates to mix, match, combine, and recombine. Choose a coat, suit, dress, and pair of shoes, and hand bag in a basic color. Vary the tone, intensity, and texture to relieve monotony. Now, jazz up the basics with a collection of interchangeable separates and accessories.

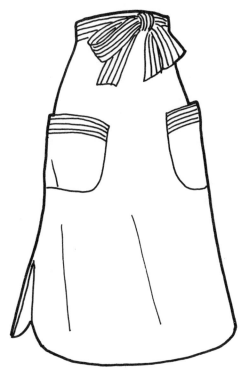

FIGURE 10.2. *Several rows of top stitching for trim.*

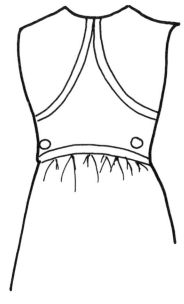

FIGURE 10.3. *Top-stitching.*

FIGURE 10.4. *The decorated T-shirt.*

Last year I had fifty dollars to spend on updating my wardrobe for fall. I could have made three dresses, but instead I scouted out a few fabric bargains and was able to make a three-piece plaid suit, two blouses, an extra skirt, and a matching jacket. Everything was color coordinated so I could play the mix and match game. I've come up with eight new outfits so far without having to fill the closet with wall-to-wall clothes.

This strategy results in more variety with fewer garments. It doesn't take any fancy arithmetic to figure that you stand to save time and money using this approach.

The T-shirt is a separate that will work wonders on any wardrobe. An incredibly versatile item, it adds variety without expense. T-shirts are great with long skirts, short skirts, pants, jeans, shorts, and culottes.

Dress up a T-shirt with sequins, satin, rhinestones, and lace for a flashy twist to a casual affair.

Load up on skirts. They come in an infinite variety of styles and lengths. They dress up or down to go just about anywhere. And skirts are simple to make; use them to revitalize a stagnating wardrobe.

Altering Second-Hand Bargains

Budget-conscious shoppers are getting downright innovative in their search for inexpensive clothing. Thrift shops, second-hand outlets, antique stores, and flea markets are being added to the itineraries of thrifty shoppers. These slightly unorthodox clothing depots are a steady source of good buys and fun garb. And old clothes take the prize when it comes to quality craftsmanship. If the fabric is still holding its own, you might be in for a bargain-buy with a touch of class.

There is only one problem with buying hand-me-down fashions. You're not likely to find a dress to walk away in; old dresses rarely fit. Don't throw away dollars on second-hand bargains that are too small. It's almost impossible to let them out satisfactorily. But a dress that's too big has all sorts of potential. With a box of pins, a little patience, and some ingenuity, a gutsy seamstress can turn an over-sized reject into a form-fitting fashion.

It's a good idea to send a second-hand treasure out to be dry-cleaned before revamping. Don't waste precious time fitting a frock that's permanently soiled. And fabric that disintegrates at the mere mention of dry-cleaning fluid won't withstand much wear. Salvage what you can (trim, buttons, and lace), but forget about remaking this one.

Alter a store-bought garment just as you would alter a pattern or a dress in the making. Try on the new purchase over the undergarments you intend to wear with the dress. Fit the garment to your shape, starting at the shoulders and working down to the waist. Then fit from the waist down the skirt to the hem, and from the armpit down the sleeve to its end.

Use the pinching technique described in Chapter 7 to remove excess fullness. Take in equal amounts on both sides of the garment and don't fit it too tightly. Comfort in action is the key—sit down, cross your legs, stand up, and move around. Put the fit to the test *before* you sew.

Follow the same procedure patiently each time you alter.

Pin-fit first. Then, take off the garment and mark the amount to be altered on each side of a seam with pins. Baste over the pin markings and remove all pins (Figure 10.5).

Carefully rip the seams needing adjustments. Brush off any lint that's collected along old seams and press out the creases. Be sure to trim excess fabric when shortening hems.

Baste seams back together using the thread tracings

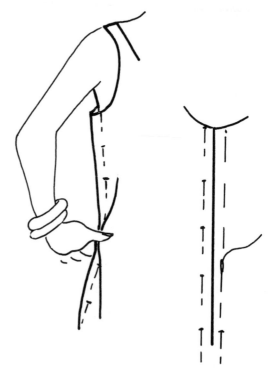

FIGURE 10.5. *Taking in a dress.*

as guidelines. Try on the garment to make sure of the fit. Machine-stitch the corrections and press to a finish.

Have fun and save money searching off-beat boutiques for bargain cover-ups. Add a little fabric funk to the wardrobe.

Seconds

Another source of inexpensive ready-made clothing is the factory-outlet store. These stores carry factory rejects and returned merchandise, commonly referred to as "seconds." Since the garments are less than perfect, they are sold at a discount. The flaws in seconds are usually minor and easily correctable by a determined seamstress.

There are a few things to keep in mind when buying seconds. Most important is to find the flaw *before* making the purchase. Every second has an error or it wouldn't be discounted. Find the mistake first; then decide what it'll take to fix it.

One pair of discounted pants I picked up just lacked a row of stitching to keep a belt loop in place—a simple correction. Another had an almost imperceptible fabric flaw next to the front pocket. A little embroidery took care of this one.

Always try on a second; the error may be in the sizing. If the garment has been cut wrong, you'll never correct it. The misfit will drive you crazy. Pass up the ill-cut bargain no matter how great the savings.

Outlet stores will sometimes carry discontinued lines. These cheapies are discounted because they are out of style. You may find an occasional bargain-buy among these outcasts. A friend bought, for an extremely reasonable price, a pair of slacks that had been put to pasture for the mere lack of belt loops. Since the pants needed shortening, we made loops from the fabric taken off the hem. This minor alteration turned a pair of sad slacks into a real fashion find.

Locate factory-outlet stores by phoning the clothing manufacturers in the area. Ask where they sell rejects and returned merchandise. Check these outlets from time-to-time and buy cautiously.

Restyling

Give new life to those tired old clothes. Refurbish and restyle what you've got before spending a fortune on more clutter for the closet.

You are probably sick to death of yesterday's fashions in your wardrobe. Almost as bad are those old favorites that have been worn until they are threadbare. Whether outdated, worn out, or simply a bore, old clothes offer all sorts of make-over possibilities for sewers who think in terms of reusing rather than removing. The only ingredients essential to successful revamping are raw nerve and a wild imagination. Think big, have fun, and take the risk.

There is a definite procedure to follow when preparing for a major overhaul. First, check the condition of the fabric. If the fabric is too far gone, forget the remodeling plans.

Even when the fabric is worn to its limits, though, there is usually *something* worth saving. Old buttons are collector's items today, and great looking collars, cuffs, sleeves, and trims will come in handy sooner or later. Carefully remove salvagable goodies and put them away for use in future restyling.

Garments that pass the fabric inspection should be immediately shipped off to the dry-cleaner. An old-time favorite that doesn't clean up to spec is usually destined for the discard pile. But a persistant spot or two can sometimes be cleverly disguised or worked around. Use your imaginagion and salvage what you can.

Armed with the ripper and a good light to work under, carefully start disassembling the garment. Remove all trims, zippers, snaps, hooks and eyes, and buttons. Remember, you need patience for ripping, not strength.

Open up all darts and seams and press each garment section flat on the wrong side of the fabric.

Check the grain of the fabric. If the fabric has been

pulled out of shape with wear, straighten the grain according to the instructions in Chapter 6.

A fabric in weakened condition, but not completely threadbare, can be reclaimed by *bonding*. Bonding is a foundation of lining attached to a weakened fabric to give it strength. Try to match the color of the bonding to the fabric and select a weight lining that supports the fabric without making it too stiff (Sew-Easy Guide 13 for directions).

Once the fabric is salvaged, sometimes a minor change is all that's necessary to bring a frumpy old frock up to date. Try new buttons for a subtle change, or add a braid, rickrack, ribbon, or lace. You'll be surprised at how classy that camel coat will look when you replace the old painted plastic buttons with real leather ones.

Sometimes a garment is just too busy. Remove some of the fuss; there is elegance in simplicity.

Or maybe the color is all wrong. Recently, while rummaging through my sister's closet, I found a white jacket that had never been worn. My sister, who wears a nurse's uniform all week long, hated this antiseptic-looking wrap and was going to throw it out. Instead, we dyed it khaki-color and changed the buttons, and voila! a bush jacket. Quite the thing!

Don't be fooled into thinking a garment has to go just because it doesn't fit quite right. Figure out what's wrong with it. A simple alteration in sleeve length can change the whole look of a garment.

Shortening a skirt is the obvious answer to a dowdy dress. Lengthening is a little more tricky, but it's a great pick-me-up for a tired old tog. Ruffles and bias bands are the perfect hem-lengtheners. That old cotton dress will take on the air of romance with ruffles to add length along with a new look (Sew-Easy Guides 12 and 16).

Pay attention to the kinds of fabric you use for additions. Keep in mind two things when making a choice: The old and the new fabrics must be compatible in weight and washability; and the two fabrics must look like they belong together to avoid the tacked-on-at-home look. Within these two restric-tions, you're pretty much free to add what you will. If you like the idea of sticking to one color, vary the texture to relieve the monotony. Print ruffles do wonders for plain cotton dresses and prints go together for a patchwork effect. A smashing combination is a satin band on a plain woolen dress—subtly elegant if the colors are matched (Sew-Easy Guide 12). Take a swatch of the garment fabric (or the garment itself) along to the store for a perfect color match. Add satin collar (Sew-Easy Guide 5) and cuffs (Sew-Easy Guide 6).

One way to insure that additions don't look like afterthoughts is to tie the whole ensemble together by repeating a new touch more than once. A ruffle at the hemline calls for two at the wrists and another to soften the neckline. To add a ruffle at the neckline, carefully remove the neckline facings and pin the ruffle in between the garment and facings along the neck edge. Baste, stitch, trim, and turn.

Do something intriguing to that unflattering neckline—plunge it, scoop it, slash it, or square it. Remove old facings and press front and back bodice sections flat. Draw the new style line on the garment, being sure that the lines are symmetrical and that they match at the shoulder seams. Cut away the excess fabric.

To make a pattern to face that improvised neckline, fold the bodice front in half along the center front. Pin the folded bodice to a piece of tissue paper. Trace along the edge of the new neckline, starting at the center front and ending at the shoulder line. Remove the garment from the tissue.

Add a ⅝ inch seam allowance at the neck edge and shoulder seam. Measure down 2 inches from the neckline edge and draw the outside facing edge parallel to the neckline edge (See Figure 10.6). Place the center line of the front facing pattern on the fabric fold when cutting.

Follow the same procedure for the back bodice section. Be sure to add a ⅝ inch seam allowance to the center back edge (or center front edge) of the facing if the garment has a center opening.

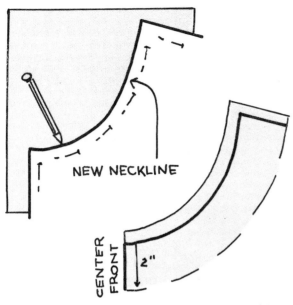

FIGURE 10.6. *Making a new neckline and facing.*

For renovating wool slacks that fit but hardly ever get worn, cut off the pant legs below the knee, gather softly at the edge, and finish with a band. Instant knickers (Sew-Easy Guide 6).

Don't throw out pants that are a little too tight. Open up the side seams and insert a long strip of contrasting fabric extending from the waist to hemline at each side. Widen the insert at the bottom to convert peg-legs to flares.

Turn those tatter-kneed trousers into Bermuda shorts. Cuff them at mid-thigh and add patch pockets made from leftover fabric (Sew-Easy Guide 15).

Practice with simple refurbishing first, then take on more ambitious make-over projects.

Bargain Fabrics

Often you'll find a remnant or a hunk of reclaimed fabric that's *almost* large enough to make what you have in mind. Stretch the fabric to meet your needs by cutting corners where you can—without sacrificing quality craftsmanship, of course.

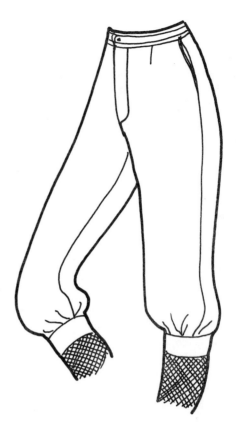

FIGURE 10.7. *Knickers.*

FIGURE 10.8. *Bermuda shorts.*

SEWING ON A TIGHT BUDGET **87**

Piecing where it won't show is an obvious solution —piece in other fabrics in the hem allowance, across a facing, or on the back of a waistband. Redesigning is another alternative: shorten the sleeves, lift the hemline, change the collar, forget the cuffs. Or make collar, cuffs, and hem band in a contrasting fabric to add interest as well as yardage.

Recycling Everything

Implicit in the reuse-rather-than-remove strategy is a commitment to save everything. Don't cast aside anything made of cloth until you are sure it has no salvage potential.

Old drapes, curtains, and tablecloths make into long skirts, shawls, placemats, and pillow covers if the fabric is not faded beyond repair.

Cut frayed towels into six-inch squares and encase raw edges in seam binding to instantly replenish the wash-cloth supply. Or piece towels together to make patchwork beach wear (See Chapter 11 for patchwork).

Recycle leftovers into belts, totes, and creative headcoverings. Check the pattern catalogues—they are full of great ideas and patterns to match for purses, turbans, and colorful cummerbunds (Figure 10.9).

Start a scrap bag of leftover remnants. Exchange special fabrics with friends who sew; that's a great way to enrichen the grab bag. Scraps can be pieced together for patchwork squares, and there's nothing more fun than appliqué with a cache of cloth to create with.

There is no excuse for tossing away clothes just because they are stained, ripped, or torn. Mend all

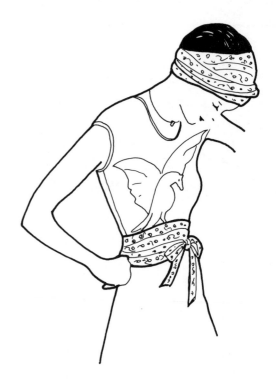

FIGURE 10.9. *Turban and cummerbund.*

rips and tears. Disguise the repair work behind a clever appliqué; cover a stain with a splash of embroidery (See Chapter 11).

And a broken zipper isn't the end of the world. It will take twice as long to find a new pair of pants as it will to replace the zipper. Why not get smart? Recycling is the savvy shopper's golden rule (Sew-Easy Guide 25).

Chapter Eleven

Expressing Yourself

Now is your chance to use your creative energy and brighten up the wardrobe with distinctive and unique clothes that reflect the real you.

Trims

It's amazing what a few rows of rickrack, braid, lace, or trim can do to transform a simple smock into a distinctive dress. As usual when mixing fabrics, choose a trim that requires the same care as the garment fabric: washable trims with washable fabrics, and dry-clean-only trims with the nonwashables. Remember to preshrink the trims and pay attention to pressing requirements. A nylon lace will stick to an iron set to press a cotton fabric.

Don't let the nearly endless variety of trims and braids available today overwhelm you. Follow this simple rule: *Understate rather than over-trim.* An overpowering trim can turn a good idea into a gaudy disaster.

Choose plain and simple trims to accent fabrics with intricate patterns and to decorate garments with detailed and complicated style lines. Save the elaborate trims for adding a touch of elegance and excite-

ment to solid-color fabrics and designs with simple style lines. Some trims are sporty and others dressy. Make up your mind ahead of time as to what effect you wish to create.

Determine how much trim you need by measuring the finished garment at the places where you intend to trim (for example, the circumference of the skirt edge). Allow a few extra inches to finish and turn under the raw ends.

If you want to buy trim at the same time you buy the fabric and pattern, figure out how much trim to buy by measuring the pattern pieces in question. Borrow a tape measure from a salesperson and ask for some unused space at a fabric counter. (Remember to subtract the seam allowances from the measurements to find out the dimensions of the *finished* garment.)

To trim the finished garment, pin and baste the trim, rickrack, or braid into place along the hem edge, sleeve edges, at the neckline, and down the front of the bodice. Stitch into place using an invisible slip-stitch by hand or top-stitch by machine (see Sew-Easy Guide 11 and 21). Turn the trim under one-quarter inch at each end, and overcast or zigzag the edges if the trim frays easily. Rickrack takes one row of top-stitching down the center; most braids and trims are best secured with one row of top-stitching placed very close to each edge (Figure 11.1).

If a trim turns a corner, you must *miter* the corner. Fold the excess trim to the inside as you pin round the corner. Unpin the trim, stitch along the fold, and cut away the excess trim (Figure 11.2).

Prefolded braids and trims can be used to encase raw edges while adding a decorative touch. Pin and baste the braid over the raw edge, with the narrower side of the braid on the top side of the fabric. Machine-stitch very close to the edge of the braid from the top side. Both sides of the braid will be stitched to the garment at once.

Braid is useful for saving jeans that have shrunk. Add a wide braid to the bottom of each pant leg, or lengthen the pants if the hems allow, and add a narrow trim to conceal the old hem mark.

Check the upholstery and drapery-fabric department from time to time. Trims used in home decorating are great pick-me-ups for the wardrobe as well.

Ribbons open up another realm of decorative possibilities. Turn everyday jeans into fun night-time fashion with a fanciful trim of satin ribbons. Run a stripe down each leg or around each cuff or stitch several rows of ribbon in a zigzag design around the bottom of each pant leg (Figure 11.3). Go crazy with color or choose tones that grade subtly one into another.

Create an elegant and unique piece of cloth by sewing ribbons together horizontally. Use this as a piece of fabric and make whatever strikes your fancy (Figure 11.4). Be sure to use simple patterns that keep yardage requirements low. Mix and match silk and satin ribbons; vary the width, texture, and color; or stick to one theme. Introduce a row of lace every so often for an aristocratic touch. Have fun with this project, but take your time. Pick up several ribbons at a time. Hunting through ribbon and trim boutiques is a great diversion from the hum-drum routine.

How about nailheads, rhinestones, beads, and se-

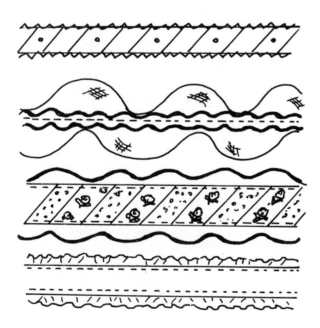

FIGURE 11.1. *Stitching trims.*

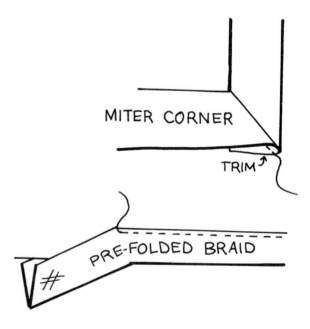

FIGURE 11.2. *Trimming techniques.*

FIGURE 11.3. *Trimming jeans with rows of ribbon.*

FIGURE 11.4. *A skirt made of ribbon fabric.*

quins for a little fashion flash? Nailheads and rhinestones can be installed by hand or by machine. Mark your design on the fabric with tailor's chalk (if you are sure it will brush off completely) or with thread tracing. Poke the prongs of the nailhead or rhinestone through the fabric. Turn the fabric over and bend the prongs down with the end of a screw driver (or tap the prongs lightly with a hammer). If you intend to work with nailheads a lot, invest in a nailhead setter, a staple-gun-type gadget that sets nailheads automatically.

Remember the resalvage and recycle routine. In this case you can use old, outdated necklaces, bracelets, pins, and charms. Disassemble bead necklaces and sew the beads on individually by hand to add a dash of glitter to that new chemise. Use an embroidery hoop to hold the fabric taut.

Salvage beaded design motifs from funky old clothes and appliqué them to a new creation. Use a wide zigzag stitch and carefully stitch back and forth over the strands of beads.

Decorate with sequins for sparkle and fun at minimal expense. Sew each sequin in place with a backstitch from the center hole to the edge of each sequin. See Sew-Easy Guide 11.

Don't forget that simple top-stitching can be used as trim. Accentuate style lines with rows of top-stitching, and try substituting decorative stitches for the simple top-stitch. See Sew-Easy Guide 21.

Lace

A few rows of delicate lace add a touch of femininity to even the most ordinary blouse. Be sure to match the lace to the garment fabric. Use nylon lace on synthetics, fine cotton laces on batiste and lawn, and heavy, crochet-type lace on linen, piqué, and velveteen.

Stitch the lace to the garment by hand or machine, depending on the type of lace. Straight-edged lace can be top-stitched in place by machine; lace with scalloped edges must be sewn on with invisible slipstitches. See Sew-Easy Guides 11 and 21.

FIGURE 11.5. *Top-stitching as trim.*

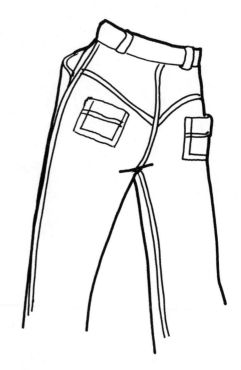

FIGURE 11.6. *Top-stitching to accentuate style lines.*

Pretty up a blouse à la the 1930s with a see-through lace effect and a set of flower-shaped buttons (Figure 11.7). Attach the lace *after* completing the blouse. Baste the lace into place, being sure to miter the square corners (see above, Figure 11.2). Cut the garment fabric underneath the lace half-way in between the bastings. Trim to one-quarter inch, fold back each edge, and press. Top-stitch the lace to the blouse, catching the folded edge in the stitches.

Ruffles can change a plain-jane into a graceful gown (see Sew-Easy Guide 16). Try cutting the ruffles on the bias sometime; they will drape softly rather than stand crisply.

Once you get the knack of how to apply trim, begin to experiment on your own. Combine ribbons and rickracks for different effects. Gather a lace or a trim to make a ruffle (Sew-Easy Guide 10), or sew ribbon,

rickrack, and lace to a ruffle. Just about anything goes these days, so have a ball!

Machine Artistry

The new automatic and zigzag sewing machines are gold mines when it comes to creative potential. Take advantage of the decorative stitches built into the machine. Even older straight-stitching machines can be adapted to do some of the decorative stitches with the help of attachments. Check your local machine shop to see what is available in the way of artistic extras. Explore the full range of decorative effects yourself with scrap fabric and different colors of thread.

FIGURE 11.7. *A see-through lace effect.*

When doing decorative stitching on the machine place typing paper between the throat plate and the fabric to keep the fabric from puckering or getting caught.

Combine rows of different decorative stitches to create a braid-like trim. Liven up kids' clothes with machine-embroidery—stitch a row of stars around the neck, sleeves, and hem edge of a T-shirt.

The decoratively stitched workshirt makes a great gift. Decorate the yoke, collar, cuffs, plackets, and pockets of the shirt. Remove the buttons from the front placket and the cuffs so you can make perfectly uniform rows of stitches. Experiment on a piece of scrap fabric until you decide on a pattern of stitches to use. Practice the pattern until you have the procedure down.

Make two or three rows of stitching along each style line you wish to emphasize. To save time, sew

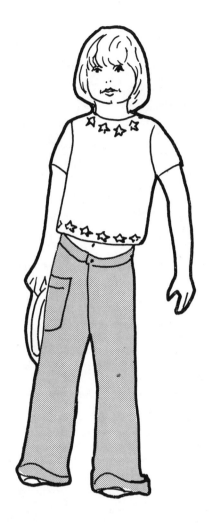

FIGURE 11.8. *Machine-embroidery on a T-shirt.*

one kind of stitch wherever it is to occur on the garment; then go on to the next kind of stitch.

A long A-line dress with center-front, center-back, and high or low waistline seams offers obvious stitching possibilities. Follow the seam lines with fanciful stitches for an effect that's slenderizing as well as unique.

Now you can start to combine machine-stitching

EXPRESSING YOURSELF **93**

FIGURE 11.9. *The decoratively stitched workshirt.*

with the other decorative devices. Use machine embroidery to sew on ruffles, rickrack, lace, and ribbon. If your machine does the feather-stitch, use it and silk thread to sew satin ribbon onto velvet—an elegant and timeless combination.

The Patchworks

Mixing and matching fabrics to form patchwork designs is the perfect way to put leftovers to good use. But there are some rules to remember when combining fabrics:

Match all fabrics for cleaning requirements, and preshrink all fabrics *before* piecing. If you must include a dry-clean-only fabric in an otherwise washable patchwork creation, be sure to dry clean the finished garment. A single machine washing could turn a perfect piecing job into a misshapen hodgepodge.

Make sure that the fabrics to be combined are all the same weight and flexibility; incompatibilities here will distort the hang of the garment. There is no reason to eliminate lightweights or sheers from a patchwork array; just bond them with a suitable lining and they will be compatible for use with heavier weight fabrics (see Sew-Easy Guide 13).

It's hard to do patchwork with ravelly and bulky fabrics, so steer clear of these, especially if you are patching with small, intricate pieces.

Aside from these few restrictions, you are free to piece and patch at will. Combine solid colors to form geometric designs, or piece several conventional prints together for the old-fashioned look. Stick to one color and vary the texture for a subtle fabric collage; or go all out for the crazy-quilt look—solids, prints, plaids, polka dots, and a rainbow of color.

Even the simplest patchwork adds interest, individuality, and intrigue to a garment. Start with a border of patches before attempting to piece an entire creation. The checkerboard patchwork design makes a great border trim. Decide what size the squares will be; then cut a pattern out of heavy paper equal to the size of the square, plus one-half inch on each edge for seam allowances. Be sure to straighten the grain of the fabric before cutting the squares and cut each square on the straight of the grain.

Cut a lot of squares at once to save time. Arrange and rearrange the squares to find an attractive combination or space squares randomly if you are tired of the ordered routine.

Join squares into long strips, machine-sewing right sides together and taking one-half inch seam allowances. Press all seams open and finish the edges if you do not intend to line or face the patched fabric. Join the strips of squares together to form a band of the desired width. Be sure to line up the seams, basting if necessary before you sew, and press the seam allowances open.

Cut a facing equal in size to the patchwork band (the facing will finish the raw edges and cover the patchwork seams). Stitch the facing and band together along one lengthwise edge, right sides facing in. Press the seam open. Sew the ends of the strip, right sides together, to form a circular band. Turn under the facing and baste the raw edges together. Attach the band to the bottom of a skirt or dress following the directions for adding a bias-band hem (see Sew-Easy Guide 12).

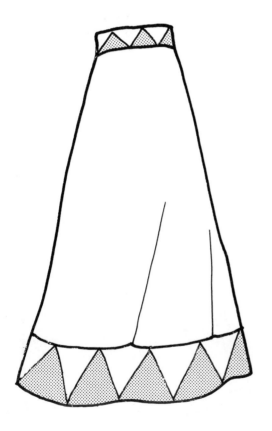

FIGURE 11.10. *A pyramid-patchwork trim.*

Make a pyramid patchwork design by joining triangular pieces into colorful geometric strips—a great finish for the waistband and hem of a cotton muslin skirt (Figure 11.10). Make a pattern for the triangle out of heavy paper (Figure 11.11). Draw a line equal to the length of the base of the triangle on a square of paper. Draw a line equal to the height of the triangle at the mid-point of the base line and exactly perpendicular to it (use right-triangle ruler). Fold the paper in half along this line. Connect the tip of the vertical line to the tip of the horizontal line. Measure out one-half inch from the base and connecting lines to draw the cutting lines. Cut along the cutting lines and unfold the triangle.

Join the first two triangles together in the following manner: Turn one of the triangles upside down. With right sides together, stitch the two along a side edge. Add the next triangle right side up; the next one upsidedown; and so on (Figure 11.12). Face the finished strip and attach it to waist, sleeve, or hem edges (See the section on adding a bias-band hem, Sew-Easy Guide 12).

After a few simple patchwork successes, you'll be ready for more complex designs. Browse through the handicraft section of your local library or book store for a book on traditional patchwork designs. Try one of the classic favorites and add a little folk art to your twentieth-century closet.

Work your way up from a patchwork band to an entire patchwork garment simply by adding strips of squares until you have a piece of fabric equal in size to the yardage requirement of a whole garment. Pin and cut the patched yardage just as you would a regular piece of fabric.

Any pattern converts to a patchwork creation. Mix and match several gingham prints. Use a different print for each section of the pattern (bodice front, bodice back, skirt, sleeves, collar, cuffs, etc.). Divide pattern sections into more than one piece for added variety. (Be sure to add seam allowances for every new seam you add.)

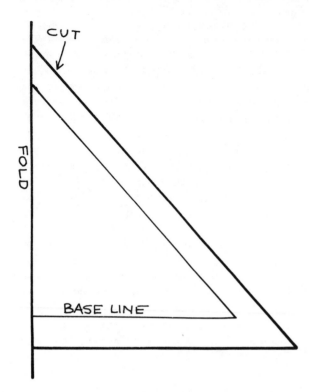

FIGURE 11.11. *Making a pattern for the pyramid patch.*

Here's an idea for what to do with those leftover jean scraps you've been holding onto: Piece them together to make a great looking skirt. Use a plain A-line skirt pattern that fits just right. Draw a straight line down the center of the skirt-front pattern section to form two equal panels (Figure 10.13). Draw a slanted diagonal line across each panel, two-thirds of the way down the skirt. Now, divide each panel in half below each diagonal line. Do the same to the skirt back pattern piece.

Trace each newly drawn pattern section onto tissue paper. Add a ⅝ inch seam allowance along every line that doesn't already have one (along all the newly

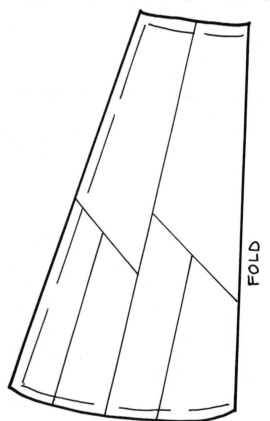

FIGURE 11.13. *Dividing up the skirt pattern for a denim patchwork skirt.*

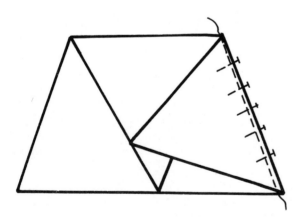

FIGURE 11.12. *Assembling the pyramid patchwork strip.*

drawn lines and along the center front foldline, if there is one.)

Cut each section out *two* times, using a slightly different shade of jean fabric each time, if possible. A nice effect is created by grading one tone into the next.

Join the bottom sections of each panel together first; then add the bottom section to the top section of each panel. Stitch the panels together, being sure to install a zipper between two of the panels so you'll be able to get in and out of this kicky fashion (Figure 11.14). Use this improvised pattern to stitch up other exciting creations: How about a velvet medley, or a batik collage?

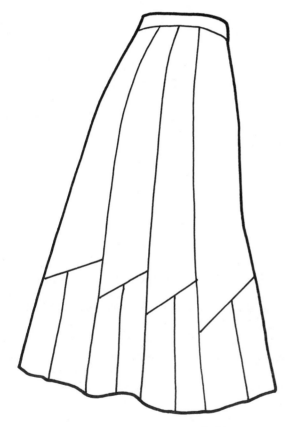

FIGURE 11.14. *The patchwork skirt.*

Hand Embroidery

Even the smallest bit of hand embroidery adds a mark of distinction to any creation. You can create successful embroidered designs using only a few very simple stitches. A basic repertoire of stitches consists of the following: the running-stitch; the back-stitch; the satin-stitch; the stem- or outline-stitch; and the chain stitch. See Sew-Easy Guide 11. Using these simple stitches and an assortment of embroidery thread it's possible to reproduce virtually any design imaginable in full living color.

Follow these rules for perfect hand embroidery:

Use an embroidery hoop for best results. The hoop (a double-ringed frame with a thumb-screw to tighten it) keeps the fabric taut while you work. Be sure that the lengthwise and crosswise grains of the fabric are at right angles to one another in the hoop, and remove the fabric from the hoop after each work session to avoid permanently marking the cloth.

Keep the tension of the stitches even. Stitches that are too tight will pucker the fabric and stitches that are too loose look uneven.

Knot each strand of thread on the wrong wide of the fabric and finish off a strand with small back-stitches on the back side of the design. See Sew-Easy Guide 11.

Delicate embroidery calls for a fine needle and a strand or two of embroidery thread. It looks best on a closely woven fabric. Large embroidery looks best on coarse and open-weave fabrics and calls for a larger needle and crewel yarn.

The beauty of embroidery is that it can easily be corrected if you make a mistake. To rip out, snip the back of the stitches with a small pair of scissors and remove the threads from the wrong side of the fabric.

You'll find patterns for embroidery designs in needlecraft magazines and at the back of some of the pattern catalogues. Check the women's magazines from time to time; they often suggest an embroidery project or two.

Making up your own embroidery patterns is easier

than you might think. First you must decide on a design. No problem here, as long as you use the right strategy. It's impossible to create in a vacuum, so provide yourself a little of the right kind of stimuli. Become an avid peruser of art books. Look at books on folk art, ethnic art, op and pop art, art deco, art nouveau, and treasures from the Orient. There are even whole books devoted to design motifs alone. Look for inspiration in other art forms: sculpture, jewelry, architecture, and furniture. Write down or sketch design ideas in your sewing notebook as they occur to you. Keep clippings from magazines and newspapers.

Don't overlook the artistic possibilities contained within the fabric itself. Embroider over a design motif in the cloth or blow up a pattern to a larger size, and embroider this on a collar or cuff.

Enlarging or reducing a design is really no hassle. Simply draw a grid of squares over the motif (Figure 11.15). Be sure that the size of the squares is in proportion with the size of the design: quarter-inch squares for small designs and one-inch squares for larger ones. Enlarge a design to three times its size by drawing a grid of squares three times as large as the first set of squares on a sheet of paper and duplicate the pattern, one square at a time. Use this process in reverse for reducing designs.

The easiest way to transfer a motif to the right side of the fabric is with a tracing wheel and dressmaker's carbon. Be sure to cover all the carbon markings with your embroidery stitches.

To transfer a small, intricate pattern that can't be transferred with a tracing wheel, pencil the design onto a piece of tracing paper. Pin the paper to the top side of the fabric and secure both the fabric and paper in an embroidery hoop. Embroider right over the paper, carefully following the pencil guidelines. The excess paper will easily pull away from the stitching when the design is complete.

A word of advice on hand embroidery: If you are working on one of those complicated designs made up of tiny little stitches, take your time. A few inches a day is just the right amount; you can see progress

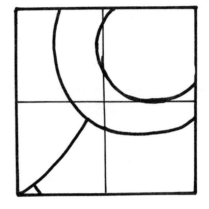

FIGURE 11.15. *Using a grid to enlarge a design motif.*

without becoming exhausted by the tediousness of the work. Still, people in a hurry needn't eliminate embroidery from their lists. Use six strands of embroidery thread at once and a large size needle and work in large stitches. Choose simple designs with strong lines. You'll be surprised how fast the work goes.

Hand-embroider to give life to old favorites, but don't waste your time and energy embroidering on threadbare cloth. Test the fabric before you start; if it rips under the slightest pressure, forget those restoration plans.

By the way, embroidery is a great diversion for dedicated sun worshippers. Get a little work done while basking in those brilliant rays.

The Added Dimension: Appliqué

Appliqué, which is no more than stitching one piece of fabric onto another, is a traditional mode of self-expression through needlework. And it's another great way to use up the leftover scraps.

Appliqués can be attached to a garment either by hand or by machine. No matter which technique you use, the beginning procedures are always the same: Decide on a design; make a pattern; and transfer the design to the appliqué fabric. (You'll find patterns for appliqué at the back of the pattern catalogues, but just as with embroidery, it's fun and easy to design your own.)

Designs with simple lines are the easiest to work with; plan to add detail with a few hand embroidery stitches. Check children's coloring books for design ideas that will help you add a little fun to a nursery-school wardrobe. Or use one of your youngster's paintings from school as an inspiration.

Don't forget the ready-made appliqué patterns contained within print fabrics. You can turn a slightly tattered workshirt into a work of art by cutting flower motifs out of some leftover fabric and stitching them over the rips and tears.

Make a pattern for your appliqué by drawing the design onto a piece of heavy paper. Add a quarter-inch seam allowance around all hand appliqué designs and cut out the pattern. Pin the pattern to the appliqué fabric and trace around the design with a pencil or chalk. Transfer any lines contained within the design with a tracing wheel and dressmaker's carbon.

Machine-stitch around each hand-appliqué design one-eighth inch from the outer edges to prevent ravelling (Figure 11.16). Turn the edges under one-quarter inch and press. Miter all corners (Figure 11.2), clip inside curves, and notch outside curves (Sew-Easy Guide 22).

Pin and baste each appliqué into place on the garment. Create a quilted effect by stuffing the appliqué with cotton batting just before it is completely basted to the garment.

Stitch the appliqué carefully into place using an

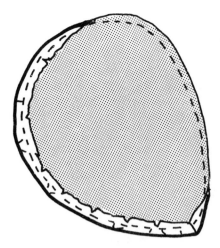

FIGURE 11.16. *Preparing the hand appliqué design.*

invisible slip-stitch, a tiny back-stitch, or buttonhole stitches spaced one-eighth to one-quarter inch (Figure 11.17; Sew-Easy Guide 11). Space stitches evenly, pull the thread firmly in between each stitch, and secure each thread end on the wrong side of the garment with several back-stitches. Be sure to hand wash or dry clean your hand appliqué work.

Machine appliqué has more immediate rewards than the hand-done variety—it's easy, quick, and has the added attraction of being machine washable.

Make a pattern for the design as you did for hand appliqué but *don't* add the quarter-inch seam allowance.

Pin the appliqué to the garment. Place a piece of typing paper between the garment and the throat plate of the machine and machine-baste the appliqué into place. The paper will keep the appliqué from rippling and puckering during the final stitching.

For the final stitching use a machine zigzag stitch, with the stitches spaced very close together (called the *satin-stitch*) (Figure 11.18). If one appliqué overlaps another, don't satin-stitch over the lines that will be covered by the second appliqué.

To machine appliqué around a corner, leave the needle in the fabric, raise the presser foot, and pivot the fabric on the needle. Curves require an extra ounce of patience. Stop the machine on the outside of

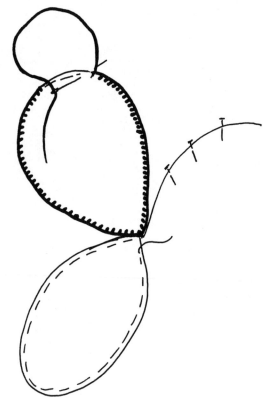

FIGURE 11.17. *Pinning, basting, and stitching the hand appliqué.*

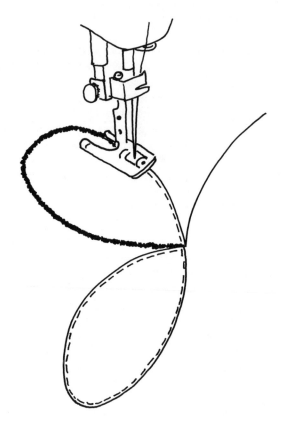

FIGURE 11.18. *Machine-stitching the appliqué.*

a curve; turn the fabric a little; and take a few machine stitches—turning the fly wheel by hand. Repeat as necessary to finish the curve.

Stitch all the appliqués into place, tie off the thread ends (Sew-Easy Guide 19), and tear the paper from the back of the garment.

The quickest and easiest way to appliqué by machine is to use a new iron-active bonding agent to hold the appliqué into place for the final stitching. Be sure to test this product on scrap fabric before applying it to the garment—it doesn't work well with all fabrics.

There is no reason why you shouldn't really enjoy yourself with machine appliqué. It's fast, easy, and mistakes are no problem for a careful ripper. You're

playing with leftovers, so what have you got to lose? One rainy afternoon, while messing around in the scrap bag, I came up with a denim slack suit with a flower appliqué on one pant leg—and all washable, for easy care.

Don't forget about the patch-up possibilities machine appliqué has to offer. Worn-out jeans are easily revived by a tuned-in seamstress.

Start combining machine appliqué with decorative machine-stitching, patchwork, ribbons, and trims. One of my more successful attempts was to decorate a jean jacket by sewing ribbons over seams using decorative stitches. A little piecing, a little patching, and a little machine appliqué resulted in a great Christmas gift for my sister.

Borrowing from Tradition: Quilting, Tucking, and Needlepoint

The age-old art of quilting is easily updated to match our modern tastes. Quilt by machine to add sensual textured effects to skirts, jackets, vests, and dresses.

Quilting requires a top layer of fabric, a middle layer of cotton or polyester filling, and a bottom layer of fabric. The top layer can be pieced, patched, printed, appliquéd, or simply any medium weight but firm fabric. The backing layer is usually a plain cotton.

Quilt the fabrics before cutting out the garment or garment sections. Pin and baste the three layers together around the outside edges and along the lengthwise grain every two inches or so to keep the layers from shifting. Transfer the quilting lines to the right side of the fabric with chalk or thread tracing.

Criss-cross quilting is done by stitching intersecting lines on the diagonals (the bias grain of the fabric) (Figure 11.19). Stitch one set of lines first, working from the center to the edge of each line. When one set of lines is finished, stitch the intersecting lines. For best results, use a quilter foot—it makes sewing on padded fabric easier—and an adjustable space guide. The quilting lines should be one to two inches apart.

Quilt a floral pattern by choosing a floral-print fabric for the top layer and using the print design as your quilting guide.

When the quilting is complete, cut out the pattern sections. Reduce bulk by trimming the filler away at the seam allowances and darts. Quilt whole garments such as skirts, jackets, jumpers, and vests; or use quilting to accent collars, cuffs, and bodice inserts. (See Chapter 12 for patchwork quilts and Chapter 14 for baby quilts.)

If you like quilting but are really pressed for time, take advantage of the prequilted fabrics available at most fabric stores. The choice is limited and the cost

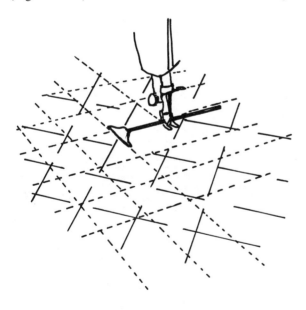

FIGURE 11.19. *Criss-cross quilting by machine.*

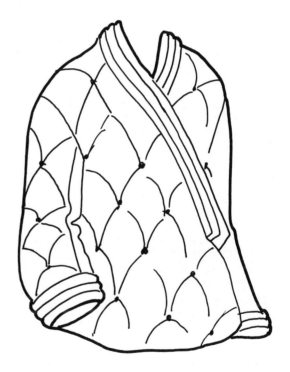

FIGURE 11.20 *A quilted jacket.*

FIGURE 11.21. *Tucking for an old-fashioned style.*

And you needlepoint enthusiasts should not overlook the decorative possibilities in this department. A small insert of needlepoint or petit point at the bodice of a long, flowing gown makes a smashing creation—and you won't see yourself all over town in this one.

FIGURE 11.22. *A needlepoint panel in the bodice of a dress.*

Using Unusual Fabrics

The bodice insert is a great way to make use of treasures you pick up at second-hand shops—especially the Chinese silks and antique embroideries.

Fringed piano shawls transform into sexy blouses and slinky skirts. And imported prints and tapestries make up into unusual caftans, ponchos, and shifts. If there is not enough fabric to make an entire garment, try a panel down the front of a skirt or a caftan. Choose a fabric for the garment that will enhance the intricate design. By the way, a panel insert running the length of a skirt or caftan creates a slimming illusion—a bonus for the diet brigade.

Creating with Patterns

Another way to add individuality to your wardrobe is to improvise with printed paper patterns.

is sometimes high, but you might find an occasional gem if you keep your eyes open.

Tucking is another one of the traditional needlework favorites. It adds a dainty touch of finery to blouses, dresses, and skirts. Tucks can give a real old-fashioned-camisole look to the bodice of a cotton jumper. Add a few tucks on the crosswise grain near the bottom of the skirt for a summertime beauty that can't be beat (See Sew-Easy Guide 23 for directions).

FIGURE 11.23. *Using a second-hand fabric as a bodice insert.*

We discussed restyling patterns in the last chapter and many of the one-of-a-kind creations discussed in this chapter require some innovating with your library of store-bought patterns.

Some styles are easier to create with than others. Simple A-line styles are the best choice for adding panel inserts. Remember to add seam allowances to any style lines drawn within a pattern section. Gathered skirts go well with patchwork and border prints, and bodice inserts are the perfect addition to a simple caftan.

Try mixing parts from different patterns for a real creative adventure. It's a good idea to test combinations in muslin before cutting into the garment fabric. Keep these common-sense rules in mind when combining:

1. Don't mix parts of patterns designed for different figure types (Juniors and Misses, for instance); the proportions are different so the pieces won't mix well.

2. Be sure the pattern pieces are altered to fit before you start combining.

3. The openings of the pattern pieces to be combined must correspond (they should be within a half-inch of each other) and the seam lines should be

FIGURE 11.24. *A full-length panel of imported print fabric.*

similar. Shoulder, underarm, and waistline seams must match.

The novice pattern-mixer will want to start small—change a collar or cuff here and there before taking on major restructuring jobs. Soon you'll be switching pattern parts with confidence, and in no time you'll become your own dress designer.

Chapter Twelve

Sewing for Others

The money-saving aspect of making clothes for others is obvious. The more people you sew for in the household, the greater the savings to the family pocketbook. But the real joy is in the pleasure you give when you make something for someone else.

Sewing for Kids

The easiest way I know to have money left over at the end of each month is to sew some of the children's clothes. Buying clothes that are out-grown in no time is like throwing money away.

Most kids' clothes require very little fabric, so they offer a good opportunity to put salvaged scraps and remnants to use. And sewing small-fry frocks has immediate rewards; you can make a fine miniature garment in almost no time at all.

The key to success in sewing children's clothes is to buy the right pattern. Always buy children's patterns by the size and *not* by the age. A baby pattern size is determined by weight and height. If the baby's weight and height fall into different sizes, let the weight determine the size. The chest and height measurements are critical in selecting the post-toddler pattern size. Buy a pattern for a child that will fit through the shoulders and chest; alter the waist to fit. Buy pants and skirt patterns by the waist measurement (see Guide F, Pattern-size Charts).

Select simply styled garments that are quick to make, easy to fit, and simple to lengthen and let out as your child grows. Expand a child's wardrobe without breaking the family bank by loading up on interchangeable separates.

Don't even consider pinching pennies on fabric for kids' togs. Bargain buys—yes; but cheap, sleazy fabrics that won't hold up under the pressure of hard wear and continual washings—no. Buy sturdy wash-and-wear fabrics for easy care. Corduroys, washable wools, and wool blends are great for winter. Denim, seersucker, cotton knits, and cotton blends are the summertime favorites.

When making kids' clothes follow these two sensible rules: Make them to last; and make them to fit. Even though kids outgrow clothes quickly, if their clothes aren't made to last, you will be continually mending and repairing. Always finish off seams and raw edges. Top-stitch to give seams added strength and double-stitch crotch seams and armholes (Sew-Easy Guide 19 and 21).

Don't make a child's clothes too big with the idea

that he or she will grow into them. Clothes that don't fit are uncomfortable and unattractive and they will probably look awful by the time they're grown into. Fit children's clothes with enough ease to allow for comfort in action, but don't make them baggy.

Clothes that Grow With Your Child

Build in grow-with-you features whenever possible. This strategy will increase the life of children's clothes and save you dollars. Tucks, deep hems, and elasticized waistbands are all easy-sew tricks that add mileage to kids' clothes. If you combine these tricks with simple-to-sew styles, you will have no trouble at all keeping your child well-dressed.

Always add several inches to the lower edges of skirts, dresses, and pants when cutting out a garment. Take a tuck on the inside of the hem of a skirt, or behind the cuff on little boy's pants. (See Sew-Easy Guide 23 for tucks). Use extra-long machine stitches to sew the tuck. When it comes to lengthening time, just rip the seam and the garment is altered instantly. Hide the old hem-mark behind trim, braids, rickrack, or a few rows of decorative machine stitches. Repeat the added touch on collars, cuffs, or around the waistband and turn a simple alteration into a brand new creation.

Face a hem that has no extra fabric for lengthening. If the dress has a straight skirt, cut the facing on the straight of the grain; otherwise cut it on the bias. And jazz up that dress a bit; face the hem with a print.

Tucks on the outside of a little girl's skirt or dress decorate while they provide room to grow. Every half-inch tuck holds an extra inch of fabric. Repeat the tucks on the sleeve and the result is another great grow-with-you fashion.

Tucks can be used in other places on the garment to build in excess fabric. Tuck a bodice horizontally so that it can be lengthened when necessary; this trick is particularly effective on a dress with a waistline. Tuck a simple A-line dress vertically in front and back to make it easy to let out.

A shirt that's too wide in the shoulders can be remedied with tucks along the armhole at the inside of each shoulder. Not only will the garment fit, but it will grow with your child as well.

During those rapid-growth years it really doesn't pay to make anything without an elasticized waistline. Refer to Sew-Easy Guide 24 for instructions on how to put in a super-sturdy elasticized waistband.

Several piecing tricks will help you remake a dress that's too small. If a child needs a little more room over the stomach, slash the dress from the neck to the hem and insert an inverted V-shaped panel. Bind the neck in the same fabric, and remove old collars and pockets if they contrast with the new additions.

To provide more room all the way around, slash the garment from neck to hemline on both sides of the center, front and back (Figure 12.1). Insert strips of contrasting fabric and cover the new seams with rickrack, ribbon, or decorative stitches.

A bias-band hem (Sew-Easy Guide 12) is an obvious solution to the short skirt that has no built-in room to grow. Add collar and cuffs that match the new hem for a sensational remake.

Remnants and Recycling

Recycling grown-up clothes into clothes for the kids makes good fashion sense for any economy-wise seamstress. My mother spent many happy and fulfilling hours recycling her old clothes into great little outfits for my sister and myself. The savings were phenomenal and we were the best-dressed youngsters on the block.

Make sure that the fabrics from castaway clothes are suitable for children's wear; bulky tweeds, for instance, look comical on kids. But sometimes the addition of a white collar, cuffs, and buttons down the front can turn a plain grey dress into a great youngster fashion. Just make sure the old thing has some life left in it.

Clean the garment before disassembling; then carefully take the garment apart with the seam ripper.

FIGURE 12.1. *Tucks in a dress to grow with the child; and a dress made larger with a full-length panel.*

(Trying to rescale big folks' clothes without disassembling the original never works. Don't waste your time.) Be sure there is enough fabric for the remake you have in mind *before* you spend hours ripping. If there is more than enough fabric to go around, skip the rip step and move right on to cutting.

Another sure way to cut dollars from the cost of kids' clothes is to make use of remnants whenever you can. Remember the rules for buying remnants: Find out the composition of the fabric, look for bolt ends, and be sure the remnant price is actually lower than the price per yard of the fabric on the bolt.

Scrap fabric can often be combined, pieced, and patched to create cute clothes for kids. And don't overlook the age-old hand-me-down routine. Passing

down children's clothes to a smaller member of the family makes good sense. Give hand-me-downs a new look so the child on the receiving end doesn't feel like he's walking around in his big brother's rejects. Alter to fit and remake if necessary. Then add something new to hand-me-downs: pockets, appliqués, decorative stitching, or a new collar and cuffs.

A Stitch in Time

The best way to keep on top of mending is to repair rips and tears as soon as you spot them. If you don't maintain children's clothes, you are likely to lose them before they are outgrown; this turns out to be a rather expensive proposition.

Replace worn out and popped elastic; restitch buttons before they are lost. Reinforce knees and bottoms with iron-on patches before they are threadbare; and double-stitch fraying buttonholes, crotch, and underarm seams.

Mending kids clothes can actually be fun. Rips and tears aren't just flaws to be repaired; they are invitations to decorate. Cover tears with iron-on tape. Top with appliqué flowers and add a butterfly or bird for a balanced design. Use a squiggle of embroidery to cover small spots and tiny tears. Or cover a rip on the front of a shirt with your child's favorite animal. Appliqué the back of the animal on the back of the shirt. His pals will love him coming and going.

Speaking of having fun with decorative touches, why not make the Halloween costumes this year? You can work magic with discarded garments, excess fabric, old sheets, and a little dye. The pattern companies offer a selection of costume patterns to choose from. For a real adventure, improvise and create your own.

Sewing for Men

It's finally becoming worthwhile to sew for the men in your life. The pattern companies are responding to the home-sewer's needs with good patterns for

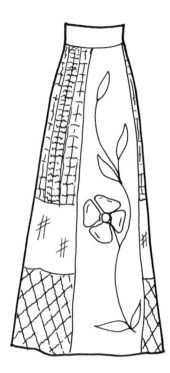

FIGURE 12.2. *A quilted skirt as a special gift.*

men. A quick scan through almost any pattern catalogue yields an ample list of men's wear patterns to choose from. You'll find lined, unlined, sport, and dress jackets; pants; vests; sweaters; coats; caftans; bathrobes; pajamas; shorts; and shirts galore. There are even patterns for neckties (deceivingly expensive to buy but easy to make).

The critical measurements for determining the man's pattern size are the chest and waist measurements. Measure around the fullest part of the chest, and take the waist measurement at the natural waistline over a shirt. Buy shirt and jacket patterns by the chest measurement and pants patterns by the waist

size (see Guide F, Pattern-Size Charts). Then alter each pattern for the perfect fit.

Put the resalvage and recycle strategy to use in the men's wear department and cut clothing costs even further—mend and repair whenever possible. Replace worn elastic in boxer shorts and pajamas, and restitch buttons *before* they work themselves loose and are lost.

A word of caution about sewing for others: Don't waste time sewing in vain. Alter the pattern to fit and sew with an eye to making something that will be worn (or used, if you're sewing for the home). Be sure that you are aware of the taste of the wearer. This goes for children as well as for adults; kids have clothing preferences too.

There is really no trick to discovering what others would like in the clothes line. As soon as family and friends see you sewing for others, they'll let you know only too often what they would like for themselves.

Making It to Last

If you are fed up with the replace-it ethic running rampant throughout our society these days, create something special with an eye toward making it last. Treat yourself and the family to a traditional patchwork quilt. Choose a detailed pattern—they require more patience than a simpler one; not more skill—and plan on taking your time. Do all the cutting at once; then work on a square or a section at a time. Quilting work is portable; work on it in front of the television, or while chatting with friends. The work is relaxing and the rewards at the end are truly astounding. A well-made quilt can be handed down from one generation to the next and cherished for years to come.

Chapter Thirteen

Sewing for the Great Outdoors

Americans have more time on their hands than ever before. And they are spending that free time more and more on sports: skiing, hiking, camping, backpacking, tennis, horseback riding, sailing, and just plain swimming and sunning.

There's only one drawback to the sports mania: Sportswear designed for recreational activities is tremendously expensive. Outfitting a family of four for a ski trip is a major expense. Pants, parkas, sweaters, and T-shirts alone run up a sizable bill.

Well, here's some good news for sports-lovers. Much of the specialized clothing you need to engage in today's favorite sports can be made at home, and the savings are phenomenal.

The Winter Holiday: Ski Clothes

Skiers will be happy to know that patterns now exist for ski pants, jackets, down parkas, vests, turtleneck T-shirts, and sweaters.

Patterns for ski clothes can be obtained by writing to Donner Designs, P.O. Box 6747, Reno, Nevada 89503. Patterns cost three to four dollars a piece, and each one contains several sizes. With one or two patterns you can outfit the whole family.

Contact the management of your local yardage store and ask them to start carrying fabrics suitable for skiwear (wools, nylons, spandex, and stretch fabrics) at least during the fall season. If you can't convince them to do so, go to a store that will.

Make turtleneck T-shirts to match your new ski pants. Luscious cotton knits are available these days in every color imaginable. They are soft, absorbent, and feel great next to the skin. You will find turtleneck patterns in most pattern catalogues, and the knit ribbing to finish the neck and wrists is available in most notions departments.

Imagine this: You can even make the family new ski sweaters this year without knitting a stitch. Buy sweater knits by the yard and stitch up sweaters in record time!

Make a long-sleeved shirt out of nylon to wear between your T-shirt and sweater. Rip-stop nylon is available at most mountain climbing and sporting goods stores. Check army surplus stores from time to time for this miracle fabric. When they do carry it, it is super-cheap.

Did you ever think you'd be able to make down parkas? Take a real do-it-yourself adventure and save a small fortune by making the family's down clothing this year. You can buy pre-assembled kits in which the yardage is pre-cut and the down is pre-measured.

FIGURE 13.1. *Make a complete ski wardrobe.*

wool or corduroy slacks you've been dying to get rid of. Cut them off just below knee length, gather softly (Sew-Easy Guide 10), and add on a band cuff (Sew-Easy Guide 6). Wear these knickers with knee-high argyle socks and see if you're not the rage of the ski slopes. If you're not, cut those rejects off a little shorter for the ultimate late-spring ski fashion. Skiing in shorts is the daredevil's delight.

Junior skiers, who out-grow ski pants faster than you can make them, can start off in jeans treated with water-resistant spray. Turn jeans outgrown by the older children into knickers and shorts for the young-sters. Personalize each pair with a hint of embroidery; and treat younger sister to a new sweater this year so she doesn't feel like a second-hand store on skis.

Once you are outfitted for outdoors, start thinking about what to wear indoors on your winter holiday. Warmth and comfort are the primary considerations, but there is no reason why you shouldn't look your best. Long skirts, warm pants, and knickers make great after-ski wear. Make them out of woolens, wool-like synthetics, single and double knits, velours, and lightweight stretch fabrics. Go crazy with those marvelous fake furs. They make up into the perfect after-ski jackets, capes, and ponchos. And quilted jackets are warm and fashionable. Quilt one yourself or search out a ready-quilted fabric.

Take a long skirt decorated with ribbons, em-broidery, or a few appliqués for holiday parties. Wear it with a sweater, wrap a shawl around your shoulders for warmth, and you're all set for festive occasions.

Back to Nature: Camping and Climbing Gear

Mountain climbing, hiking, camping and back-packing all require substantial, well-designed gear, but the cost of reliable clothing and equipment is often prohibitive. And, inexpensive gear rarely lasts; it often breaks down at the most inopportune times. Save some money without sacrificing quality by mak-ing your own specialized camping equipment.

The capacity of backpacks can be increased with pockets galore. Each new pocket provides a separate

The kits come complete with explicit instructions. Send to Frostline, Dept. SS095, 452 Burbank, Broomfield, Colorado 80020 or Sport Kits, Ltd., 1085 University Avenue, Berkeley, California 94710 for kit catalogues. Down clothing made from kits runs about half the regular price.

Kits are available for down pants, hoods, and vests. A down vest is a real necessity for a spring skier—it keeps the chest warm while the rest of the body stays cool.

Also for warm-weather skiing: Drag out those old

compartment for carrying essentials in an orderly fashion. Buy ready-made pockets at the back-packing store and stitch into place, or make your own pockets out of rip-stop nylon (Sew-Easy Guide 15). Pockets can be put on top of other pockets, they attach to the front and sides of the pack, and they stitch easily into place on the flap.

Ready-made mountain-climbing shorts sell for over twenty-five dollars. Make your own out of corduroy, denim, or a cotton-polyester blend. (There are patterns in most catalogues for these gems.) Or convert cut-offs into super hiking shorts by adding roomy pockets with flaps that button shut.

A good backpacking tent will run over a hundred dollars. There's a real savings here if you make your own. Send to Frostline or Sport Kits, Ltd. for tent kits (see p. 109 for addresses); you can order kits for making down clothing (vests and jackets) and sleeping bags from Frostline as well.

Hard-core do-it-yourselfers might get a kick out of making tents, sleeping bags, and down clothing without the kits. Books on how to make camping equipment from the ground up are available in most libraries.

Tennis Wear

Plenty of ready-made tennis togs are available, but have you checked the prices? Why should you have to spend a fortune on these tiny cover-ups when they are easy and inexpensive to make? The pattern companies are responding to the tennis player's desire to be well-dressed on the courts. There are wide selections of blueprints for shirts, shorts, dresses, skirts, and warm-up jackets.

Have fun designing and decorating your tennis wardrobe. All white is no longer the rule. The red-white-and-blue motif is definitely in; and pastels on the tennis court are a welcomed relief. A few rows of colorful rickrack will really jazz up a solid white suit.

Tote bags are the perfect accessory for tennis buffs. There are patterns for totes at the back of most catalogues. Decorate with monograms or a tennis

FIGURE 13.2.   *Suit yourself for tennis.*

insignia. What a great Christmas gift for a tennis-loving friend.

Good News for Equestrians

Equestrians can save a substantial amount of money by making their own riding apparel. And mothers of children who are starting to take this sport seriously will be happy to know they no longer have to spend a small fortune on riding habits that are soon outgrown. Two pattern companies specialize in riding breeches and jackets. Send for catalogues of patterns and prices:

Authentic Patterns, Inc.
P.O. Box 4560
Stockyards Station
Fort Worth, TX 76106

Jean Hardy Patterns
2151 La Cuesta Dr.
Santa Ana, CA 92705

Patterns for western shirts and jean-style pants are available in the standard pattern catalogues.

Swim, Sail, and Sun

It's never too soon to start getting ready for summer. The pattern catalogues are full of easy-to-sew fashions for staying comfortable and well-dressed throughout the summer. Help yourself to swimming suits that fit at last. Make bra tops, halter tops, shorts, and culottes, beach cover-ups, terrycloth beach towels, and the totes in which to carry them all.

Appliqué a seascape on one side of a tote. Do the appliqué work first; then assemble the tote according to the pattern instructions.

The ready-to-wear swim suit scene is enough to drive anyone to sew. If you are outraged at paying

FIGURE 13.3. *Appliqué a tote bag.*

twenty-five dollars for a microscopic bikini that doesn't even fit, start sewing your own. Most pattern catalogues have swim-suit patterns. If you don't find the right combination of top and bottom in one pattern, buy two. It's worth the extra dollar or two to have exactly what you want. Once you have a pattern that is altered to fit, you can whip out a new swim suit in an hour or two.

Jog Togs

Parks, playing fields, and athletic tracks are filled with people trying to stay in shape by jogging. If you are one of the healthy multitude, suit up in style. Treat yourself to a set of jog togs. In fact, make two—one for wear while the other is being washed.

Double knits are ideal for sweat suits, and the new elasticized fabrics are perfect for slim-cut exercise pants. Be sure that everything is washable for easy care.

Make the sweat shirt hooded or plain. Personalize each suit with monograms, appliqués, or stripes down the leg.

Sweat pants call for a slimly cut pants pattern with an elasticized waistline; a pattern designed for knits is best. Instead of hemming the pants, make a casing at the bottom of each leg and insert elastic (see Sew-Easy Guide 24). Better still, stitch knit ribbing to the bottom of each pant leg. What a work-out you'll get in these leg warmers!

Take the opportunity to experiment with color. We're all tired of plain steel grey and drab navy blue sweat suits. Why not jog in yellow for a change?

Cyclists can save some money by stitching up shorts for bike riding. Use elasticized fabric and make slim-cut shorts that come to mid-thigh. Match these shorts with a warm-up jacket that zips up the front and you will be all set to polish off a quick ten miles.

The Vacation Wardrobe

It is possible to stay well-dressed with a very small vacation wardrobe. The trick is to make vacation

FIGURE 13.4. *A sweat suit for jogging.*

FIGURE 13.5. *A wrinkle-resistant, color-coordinated vacation outfit.*

clothes in crease-resistant materials and in coordinated colors.

Look for all-in-one patterns that include a jacket, skirt, pants, and a top. Skirts usually come in long and short lengths; pants convert easily to become bermuda shorts. Shorten the jacket sleeves for summertime wear. Make the outfit in summer- or winter-weight fabrics depending on where the vacation will take you. Coordinate your color scheme so that you can mix and match separates. By the way, have an

outfit coordinated around a single color for weekend trips.

Living out of a suitcase is really no hassle if the clothes are made out of fabrics that travel well. Wash-and-wear fabrics are the best bet by far. Jerseys, Qianas, single and double knits, and some of the wash-and-wear blends are practically wrinkle-proof. The few wrinkles and creases that might appear will hang out in a steamy bathroom while you shower.

Chapter Fourteen

Maternity and Infant Wear

Staying well-dressed during pregnancy is a real problem. Ready-to-wear maternity clothes are notorious for poor quality craftsmanship and lack of style, and the prices are often outrageous. Maternity clothes are particularly expensive because they are so short-lived and, as might be expected, they are rarely recycled. Most women are delighted to get rid of unflattering and unimaginative clothes for good after months of having to wear them.

Perhaps you've glanced through the maternity section of a pattern catalogue and noticed that the selection of patterns there wasn't a great improvement over the ready-mades. Admittedly, most maternity patterns are not too exciting, but they are usually for simple styles that are easy to make. Take advantage of this situation. Use these unimaginative but uncomplicated styles as foundations for your personal creations. Buy maternity patterns by your bust size *before* pregnancy. Pay particular attention to the choice of fabric. A unique and interesting textile will add a touch of class to an otherwise shapeless sack. Add decorative touches when the style permits. Accentuate style lines with a row or two of top-stitching. Any detail works—trims, braids, decorative machine stitching, and embroidery used at necklines, cuffs, and hems all draw attention away from your increasing girth (see Chapter 11). Let's face it. As proud as you are, there are times when you would like to look thin again.

Optical illusion is an indespensible ally in the quest for flattering lines. An inverted V-shaped panel in a dark color has a slimming effect in the early months of pregnancy. Stay away from large geometric plaids and forget about stripes. Small overall prints are okay, but avoid creating that too-cute look. (Follow the hints to dieters in Chapter 4.)

This is your chance to get really creative with collars. An interesting neckline enhances the elegance of a simple A-line or princess-style dress, both good styles for pregnancy. And, the bigger the collar, the better. (See Sew-Easy Guide 5).

Non-maternity Styles for Pregnant Women

Don't limit your search for styles to the maternity section of the pattern catalogue. Plenty of dresses throughout the catalogue are perfectly suited for wearing during pregnancy.

113

Any dress that isn't fitted in the waist and has room to spare through the middle is a likely candidate. Many classic styles qualify: princess, A-line, styles gathered on yokes, overblouses, unfitted jackets, jumpers, tunics, and tents. Smocks are perfect; they are fun to decorate and can't be beat when it comes to comfort.

The dress in Figure 14.1 can be worn throughout pregnancy and then afterward if it isn't worn threadbare. Remake this beauty often. Vary the length of the hem and sleeves. Top-stitch the yoke or insert a panel of contrasting fabric or needlepoint. Make it for dress out of velvet or Qiana, or in a lightweight Indian gauze for casual wear.

Buy a non-maternity pattern in your regular pattern size. It's important that the garment fit through the shoulders, so don't decide to buy a size too big because you think you'll need the extra room. These styles are already cut full enough at the middle.

Check the pattern for fit before you cut; add inches to side seams to allow for growth if you like.

Nothing is more graceful than a long flowing gown on a lovely pregnant lady. Let a few of your maternity dresses hang to the floor. Be sure to stick with fabrics that drape. Long maternity dresses in stiff fabrics look more like tents. Besides, those soft, sensual textiles feel so much nicer to wear.

More Recycling News

Before creating an entire new wardrobe for this special occasion, see if there's anything hanging in the closet that will serve for maternity duty. Smocks, loose-fitting tops, and shifts are the obvious candidates. Change collars and cuffs if you are sick of old clothes. Add print pockets to smocks for a decorative and practical touch.

Insert maternity stretch panels (available in any notions department) into the front of old pants. Use the same trick on that favorite pair of jeans. Maternity stretch panels can be inserted into the front of any

FIGURE 14.1. *A nonmaternity style for maternity wear.*

garment that has a waistline (Figure 14.2). Simply open up both side seams of the skirt or pants from the waist to the hips. Draw a line straight across the front of the garment at the hips and cut along this line. (Cut below the zipper on jeans). Stitch the stretch panel to the garment at the hipline. Trim the sides of the panel to fit the opening in the garment. Allow an extra ⅝ inch at each side for seam allowances.

Join the back of the garment to the stretch panel at the side seams. Sew the elastic at the top of the panel securely to the waistband of the garment. This simple alteration is perfect for clothes that probably won't get much more wear—use them for maternity wear, before passing them on.

Get the most mileage out of new maternity clothes by making garments that can be worn after the baby arrives. Choose sturdy fabrics and create clothes you'd love to wear anytime. Garments that are strictly for wear during pregnancy can be passed on to friends or sold at the next garage sale. Or the fabric can be recycled into new clothes for you and the baby.

Sewing for the Baby

If you need something to while away those waiting hours, try sewing. And just think how productive you'll be. You can keep yourself beautifully dressed, and sew for the baby as well.

FIGURE 14.2. *Inserting a maternity stretch panel.*

By the way, the items listed below make great shower gifts. If you are not waiting for a baby of your own, stitch up something special for someone who is.

A Place of One's Own: The Baby's Room

Put some of your creative sewing energy to use in getting the baby's room ready for homecoming. Start with brightly colored curtains. Choose a cheerful print or use a plain-colored fabric and decorate with trims, braids, decorative machine-stitching, or appliqué.

Make a ruffle to match the curtains and attach it to the bottom of baby's crib with tacks. This touch ties the whole room together. (To figure out how much yardage you'll need for a ruffle, measure the distance around the bottom of the crib and multiply by 2.)

A baby quilt is the perfect shower gift. It adds a colorful touch to the baby's crib and there'll be no need to worry about cold nights. Use brightly colored fabrics; combine solids and prints. Stick with one of the traditional favorites, or design your own—piece it, patch it, add a touch of embroidery, and a few appliqués. Baby quilts are just the right size—small enough so that the work goes fast; but large enough for you to express yourself.

Here's how to construct the mini-comforter: Design and stitch-up the top piece, which should measure no more than three feet square when finished. Cut a piece of batting equal in size to the top. Back it with another equal-sized piece of fabric—chintz, gingham, and flannel are your best bets. Baste the three pieces together around the outside edges. Cut a bias strip to bind the raw edges of the quilt, piecing where necessary. Use a contrasting or complimentary fabric for fun. Cut the bias strip at least two inches wide. Fold each raw edge under ⅜ inch and press. Encase the outside edges of the quilt in the binding. Pin, baste, and stitch; being sure to *miter* all corners (see Chapter 11).

Add a little interest to the baby's room by stitching up hangings to adorn the walls. The brighter the colors, the better. Simple geometric shapes, animals, and cartoon characters will be cheerful additions to the baby's environment.

Speaking of environments, here's a nifty idea for adding life to baby's world. Stitch up a mobile or two to hang over the crib. Animals and brightly colored geometric shapes come alive when stuffed with dacron batting.

Cut each shape out double, and cut the length of string or yarn for each piece of the mobile. Vary the string lengths. Fold each string in half and baste the fold to the top outside edge of one piece of each mobile section. Roll up the string and pin to the center of the fabric. This will keep the string from getting in the way while you're stitching.

With right sides facing in, stitch the two sections of each shape together around the outside edges. Be sure to sew across the folded string and leave a space open for turning and stuffing.

Trim the seam allowance to one-quarter inch and overcast the edges (Sew-Easy Guide 17). Turn each shape right side out and stuff tightly with batting. Turn the edges of the opening under and finish with invisible slip-stitches (Sew-Easy Guide 11).

Tie each section to a bamboo rod or a piece of wooden dowling. Another piece of string ties to each end of the rod so that the mobile can be suspended from the ceiling. The beauty of this toy is that there are no sharp edges to worry about, should it happen to end up in the baby's hands or mouth.

You can make a playpen floor-pad that doubles as a lap cover. It will consist of five equal size layers—cotton, batting, plastic, batting, and cotton, in that order. Use gingham or prints on the outside. Bind the outside edges.

What about a baby sleeping bag? Take an inexpensive comforter and cut a 4 foot by 3 foot rectangle from it. (Or use quilted fabric, sold by the yard; and

FIGURE 14.3. *A portable bed for the baby.*

line with fleece, also sold by the yard.) Fold the comforter in half lengthwise. Insert a long skirt zipper in an L-shaped fashion down the open lengthwise side and across one end (Sew-Easy Guide 25). There will be no need to worry about the covers coming off when your baby's wrapped in this beauty.

And now for the answer to the portable bed problem (Figure 14.3). Take a good sized basket with sturdy handles and pad it with foam. Cover the foam with a fanciful print. Turn the raw edges of the fabric under and attach to the basket with slip-stitches (Sew-Easy Guide 11) by making your stitches around a straw of the basket. Glue rickrack, ribbon, lace or a ruffle over the stitches on the outside of the basket and decorate the handle. Bundle the baby into that new little sleeping bag and carry her off in her new baby bed. This basket makes a much appreciated shower gift, too.

Don't forget bibs; every mother needs plenty of these. They make great gifts, are fun and simple to make, and needn't cost a penny. Use up your leftovers. A terry cloth remnant forms the basic bib. Bind the edges and make ties with scrap fabric. Personalize each one with decorative appliqués.

The Baby's New Clothes

Set aside a day or two for stitching up a few baby cover-ups. Choose patterns that won't bind, and use soft, absorbent, easy-to-wash fabrics that won't irritate, scratch, or tickle. Flame-retardant flannelette, batiste, challis, jersey, knit, and stretch terry are your best buys.

Make a few of those wonderful all-in-one play suits—you never can have too many of these. Use stretch terry to allow for maximum mobility.

Long cotton flannel gowns are a must and they are easy to sew. Include a growth tuck so that the gown can be lengthened. Finish the hem and sleeves with draw strings for nighttime-wear that keeps baby warm.

Use smooth finishes on all inside seams—bind raw edges if necessary (see Sew-Easy Guide 19). Be sure to choose trims that require the same kind of care as the garment. This is the perfect opportunity to put those decorative touches to use. Turn the baby's wardrobe into a cheerful experience with brightly colored trims, stuffed appliqués, and machine embroidery.

Chapter Fifteen

Sewing for the Home

Most of the home projects in this chapter are simple and fun; so they are perfect first projects for the novice seamstress. Beginners, help yourself to curtains, drapes, bedspreads, placemats, and zipperless pillow covers. Take this opportunity to give yourself and your surroundings a lift. Create a whole new environment—to be comfortable in and proud of. Choose colors that feel good to you. Decorate different rooms for different moods.

The suggestions in this chapter include making your own pattern if you need one. If you would rather not do-it-yourself to this extent, check the back of most pattern catalogues for home furnishings.

Brighten Your Outlook With Curtains

There is nothing like making a pair of curtains to convince you that sewing is simple, enjoyable, and a real money-saver. Ready-made curtains and drapes are expensive and seldom satisfactory. Either the color is wrong, the fabric doesn't hang correctly, or the kitchen print is just too cute. But there's no need to compromise any longer. Make exactly what you want.

Take the same precautionary steps on these home sewing projects as you would on any dressmaking project. Always preshrink and straighten the grain of the fabric before cutting so that your hand-made home furnishings will be washable. Cutting down on dry-cleaning bills can save you a small fortune each year.

The first step, and the most important, is to take accurate measurements (Figure 15.1). Measure the length of the window from the bottom of the curtain rod to either the sill, the lower edge of the apron, or the floor (to within one-half inch of the floor), as you prefer. Measure the width from one edge of the window frame to the other. Add the depth of the return on the curtain rod (the distance between the rod and the wall) to this measurement.

Determine the length of each curtain panel by adding the following amounts to the window length: 4¼ inches at the top for the heading, casing, and turning; 3¼ inches at the bottom for the hem and seam finish. For a double 3 inch hem at the bottom, add 6 inches rather than 3¼ inches.

Multiply the window width by 2 so that the curtains will have a desirable amount of fullness. Add 4 inches for hems (making a ½ inch double-fold hem on each side of two curtain panels). Divide this figure by 2 for the width of each curtain panel.

Always figure out how much yardage you will need to make curtains. Don't rely on the yardage store salespeople; they aren't always qualified to make accurate estimates, and they usually don't have the time. Cut yardage cannot be returned, so take no chances.

The amount of yardage needed is determined by the *width* of the fabric. Let's say you have to make four curtain panels, each 45 inches long and 40 inches wide. Stay away from 36 inch fabric for this job. Such fabric would not be wide enough to make one panel without piecing. You will need four 45 inch lengths of 45 inch wide fabric, or 5 yards, to make the curtains. (Buy the same amount if you use 54 inch or 60 inch wide fabrics.) Buy an extra 9 inches of fabric to allow for shrinkage and straightening the ends.

Be sure to keep a record of the window measurements; the size of each curtain panel; and the amounts added for hems, casings, headings, and seam allowances. These figures will come in handy when you start cutting and sewing.

Pretty much anything goes when it comes to choosing curtain material. Most of the cottons are great—chintz, gingham, dotted swiss, muslin, polished cotton, or organdy for the sheer look. Check into the polyesters for easy-care curtains. Keep in mind that all-cotton fabrics need ironing!

Use solids, prints, plaids, or stripes. Choose antique satin, silk, taffeta, or corduroy for something rich, luxurious, and a little more formal. Plan to decorate with trims, machine embroidery, or ruffles.

Curtains must be cut *exactly* on the grain in order for them to hang correctly. Lay the fabric on a cutting board and measure the length and width of each curtain panel with a tape measure or yardstick. Seam the fabric, if necessary, to achieve the desired width.

Work at the ironing board to fold, press, and pin the hems and seam allowances. Use the sewing gauge to measure each fold of the fabric. Accuracy here is *very important.*

Finish the side hems first. Turn each side edge under ½ inch and press; then turn under another ½ inch. Stitch each hem very close to the edge of the fold. (Be sure to clip or trim off selvages—they can ruin the hang of your curtains.)

Turn the top edge of each panel under one-quarter inch and press. Turn under another 2 inches; press, pin, and stitch into place. Divide the top hem in half using a gauge and lightly colored chalk (Figure 15.2). Stitch along this line. This makes a 1 inch heading and a 1 inch casing. The curtain will be gathered on to the rod through the casing. (If a 1 inch casing does not allow the curtain to slide freely on the rod, make the casing ¼ to ½ inch larger.)

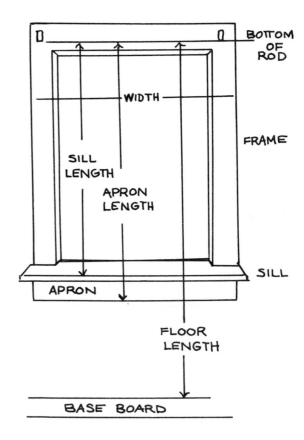

FIGURE 15.1. *Measuring the window for curtains.*

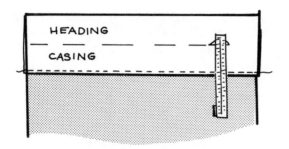

FIGURE 15.2. *Dividing the top hem to make a heading and a casing.*

Turn the bottom edge under ¼ inch and press. Turn under another 3 inches and pin into place. (A double hem requires two 3 inch turnings.) Check the length of the curtain panels on the rod before stitching the hems. Adjust the length where necessary. Take the curtains off the rod; press and stitch.

Café curtains (half-curtains with a separate valance) are the perfect window coverings for kitchens and breakfast nooks; they protect your privacy while letting in lots of sunlight. And if you use easy-to-remove clip-on rings with those café cover-ups, laundering will be a snap.

Determine the length of each curtain panel by measuring from half-way down the window to the window sill. Add 4¼ inches at the top for heading, casing, and turning; and 3¼ inches at the bottom for the hem and seam finish. If you use clip-on rings, there is no need for a heading so add just 2 inches at the top and make a double 1 inch hem to which you can attach the rings. (Sometimes café curtains are gathered onto the rod like regular curtains but without the heading. For these make a double 1 inch hem at the top of each panel and use the hem as a casing through which to insert the rod.)

The width of the curtains should be equal to double the window width plus 4 inches for side hems (a double ½ inch hem at each side of each panel). Divide this figure in half to find the width of each curtain panel.

The valance is made in one piece. The finished length can be anywhere from 6 to 18 inches. Cut a piece for the valance equal to the finished length plus 4¼ inches at the top for heading, casing, and turning; and 3¼ inches at the bottom for the hem and seam finish. (A short valance calls for a shorter hem. And if you want to eliminate the heading on the valance, add just 2 inches at the top for a double 1 inch hem).

The width of the valance is equal to double the window width, plus 2 inches for double ½ inch hems at each side. (If you have to piece the valance, allow an additional ½ inch for each seam allowance.)

Jazz up those café curtains with braid or trim. Before decorating, finish the top and sides of each panel with double ½ inch hems. Then sew vertical strips of trim onto each panel, letting the trim extend four inches beyond the top of the panel. Be sure to space trims evenly and hem the curtains as usual. Finish off the top ends of the trim; fold the trim under two inches; and attach to the top of each curtain with invisible slip-stitches (Sew-Easy Guide 11). The loops formed by the trim substitute for clip-on rings and make for a really unique window dressing.

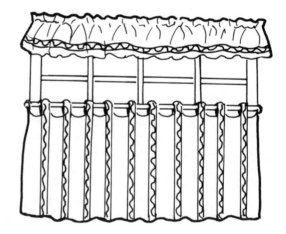

FIGURE 15.3. *Cafe curtains.*

Drapes

Making your own drapes is somewhat more difficult than making curtains and is not recommended for the novice. Once again, your success depends on accurate measurements. The length of each drapery panel is equal to the length of the window, plus 4 inches for the top hem and ½ inch for turning. Add another 6 inches for a double 3 inch hem at the bottom. (A double hem will improve the hang of the drapes.)

The width of each panel is equal to half the width of the window, plus 4 inches for the depth of return at the end, 2 inches for double ½ inch hems at each side, 1 inch for the overlap (of 2 inches) at the center of the window, plus the extra fabric required to make the pleats.

Allow 5 inches for fullness in each pleat and space the pleats 4 inches apart. Let's say each panel must cover 50 inches. Place the first pleat 4 inches from the outside edge and the last pleat 3 inches from the center edge of the panel. This leaves 43 inches that must be covered (4 + 3 = 7; 50 − 7 = 43). The pleats are spaced 4 inches apart so divide 43 by 4 to find out how many more pleats will be needed (11 pleats). Add the two end pleats to this figure to get the full number of pleats needed on each panel (13). Each pleat takes 5 inches of fabric, so add 5 × 13, or 65 inches to the width measurement. To reiterate:

Each drapery panel = ½ window width + 4 inches depth of return + 1 inch for overlap + 2 inches for side hems + (total number of pleats × 5 inches) for pleat fullness.

Most drapery panels will have to be pieced. Place seams just outside a pleat if possible, and allow an extra ½ inch for each seam allowance.

Determine the amount of yardage you'll need the same way you did for curtains. Don't forget to add an extra 9 inches to allow for preshrinking and straightening the grain. Buy extra yardage if the drapery fabric is a one-way or large design that requires matching.

Buy ready-made pleater tape at the yardage store for easy pleating. I wouldn't consider making drapes without this stuff—it makes sewing the custom-made best a snap. Buy a length of pleater tape equal to the combined width measurements of all the drapery panels. (The tape is sold by the yard.)

You'll usually find an adequate supply of drapery fabrics at most local fabric stores. Use the heavier weight fabrics for insulation as well as privacy. Avoid dark colors on windows that are subjected to strong sunlight; they will be sure to fade.

Fiberglass is an excellent fabric for drapes—it lasts forever, is easy to care for, and is sunproof as well. If you choose to work on this great textile, *wear gloves.* Fiberglass is just what the name indicates—a fabric full of tiny glass fibers. Your hands will be a painful mess unless they are protected while you work.

Construct each drapery panel by cutting a piece of pleater tape 2 inches shorter than each panel. Be sure you cut each panel perfectly on the grain of the fabric.

Pin the right side of the pleater tape to the right side of the fabric, ¼ inch from the top edge of the panel. Let the fabric extend 1 inch on either side of the tape. Stitch the tape to the panel, ½ inch from the fabric edge (Figure 15.4). Turn the tape to the inside,

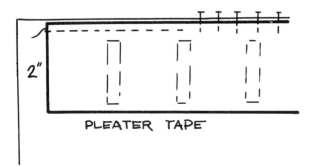

PLEATER TAPE

FIGURE 15.4. *Stitching pleater tape to the drape panel.*

rolling the fabric slightly to the inside so that the seam doesn't show from the front of the drapes.

Pin and stitch the bottom edge of the pleater tape to the drapery fabric. Finish the side and bottom hems the same as for curtains. Using pleater pins and starting 4 inches from the outside edge, make a pleat every four inches across each panel (Figure 15.5).

By the way, don't limit drapes to windows. Hide an extra door that you wish wasn't there behind a luxurious drape panel.

Table Wear

New curtains are the obvious pick-me-up for a tired old kitchen. But why stop there? Four home-made placemats cost the price of one ready-made, and a new table cloth costs almost no effort at all.

Buy ¾ yard of almost any sturdy fabric (explore the gamut from Trigger to Vinyl) to make four standard size placemats. Make a placemat pattern by drawing a 13 by 18 inch rectangle on heavy paper. For an oval mat, fold the pattern into quarters; then round and cut along the outside edges. Cut the mats and sew bias tape around the raw edges of each mat, following the directions for attaching bias tape (see Sew-Easy Guide 17). Another finish suitable for the outside edges of placemats is a machine zigzag stitch. For a smart, decorative touch, trim each end of the rectangular shaped mats with a two-inch wide woven braid.

For matching napkin rings, cut four additional 4 inch lengths of braid; finish the raw edges with a zigzag stitch; and slip-stitch the ends of each strip together. Make four square-shaped napkins to match the mats and you're all set for the next dinner party.

A throw table cloth is easy to make. A rectangular throw consists of three panels sewn together; one for the center of the table, and two side panels. Be sure to match designs along seam lines. Encase the raw edges in bias binding or top-stitch a double quarter-inch hem around the bottom of the cloth.

Here's how to make a paper pattern for the round table throw: Cut a square of paper with each side equal to the diameter of the finished table cloth, and fold the paper into quarters. Attach a string to a pencil as in Figure 15.6. The length of the string should be equal to one-half the diameter of the finished cloth. Pin the free end of the string to corner 1 of the folded pattern. With the pattern perfectly flat, draw a curved line connecting corner 2 of the pattern with corner 4. Cut along this line.

Use this pattern for a throw with a diameter of 45 inches (the width of most fabric) or less. For a larger throw, you must piece the fabric. To make that pattern, follow the procedure used for the smaller throw above. Then make a mark halfway down one side of the folded pattern. Turn the pattern over and

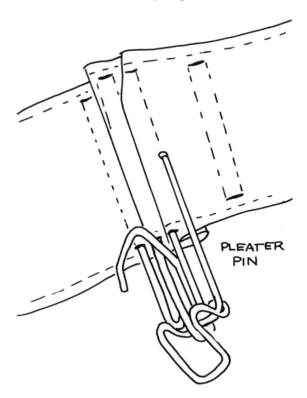

PLEATER PIN

FIGURE 15.5. *Making pleats in drape panels.*

122   USING YOUR SEWING SKILLS

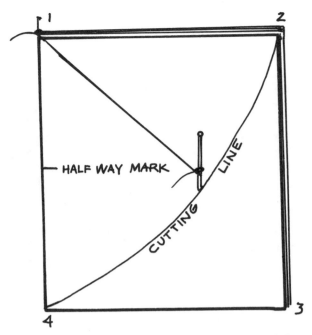

FIGURE 15.6. *Making a paper pattern for a round throw table cloth.*

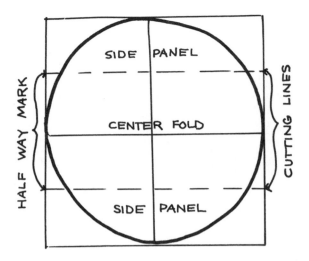

FIGURE 15.7. *Making a pattern for a large round table-cloth.*

mark the same spot on the other side. Unfold the paper pattern. Draw a line parallel to the center fold line, through the two pencil marks. Draw a similar line on the other side of the center fold line. Cut along these lines (Figure 15.7). This makes a pattern with one center section and two side panels. Cut the pattern out with the straight edges on the lengthwise grain, parallel to the selvages, and be sure to add ½ inch seam allowances to each seam line. Piecing the table cloth along the sides this way means there will be no seams running across the table top to disturb your meal.

Spread It Around

The bedspread consists of a width of fabric down the center of the bed and two panels wide enough to complete the overhang on each side. Measure the bed fully made up with sheets, blankets, and pillows (Figure 15.8). The length of the bedspread is equal to the distance from the floor at the foot of the bed to the headboard. Add 15 inches to this measurement to allow for the pillow tuck in.

The width of the center piece of the spread is ideally equal to the distance across the top of the mattress. (It can be narrower than this if necessary). The width of the side panel is equal to the distance from the edge of the center piece to the floor. Add an extra ½ inch for a seam allowance.

You'll need the following number of yards of 45 inch wide material to make a spread: 7 yards for a twin or full size bed, and 10½ yards for a dual, king, or queen size bed.

Once again, just about anything goes in the way of fabric. Keep it washable to save dollars, and wrinkle-resistant for easy care.

Construct the bedspread by stitching the side panel pieces to the center piece, right sides together.

To make a paper pattern for rounding off the square edges, cut a square of paper 9½ inches on a side. Pin the pattern to a square edge of the spread. Tie a 9½ inch piece of string to a pencil and tack the other end of the string to pattern corner 1 (see Figure

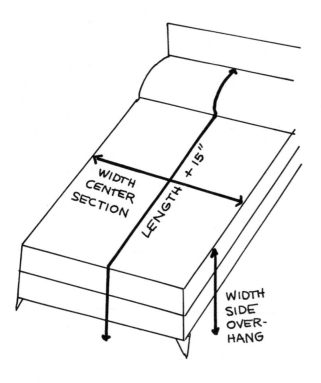

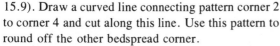

FIGURE 15.8. *Determining the measurements for a bed-spread.*

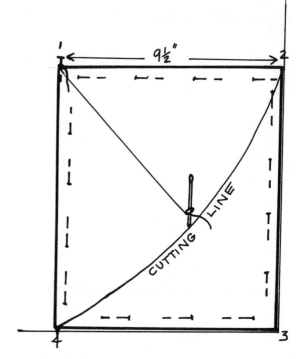

FIGURE 15.9. *Making a pattern to round off bedspread edges.*

15.9). Draw a curved line connecting pattern corner 2 to corner 4 and cut along this line. Use this pattern to round off the other bedspread corner.

Finish the raw edges of the spread with bias seam binding (Sew-Easy Guide 17) or top-stitch a double quarter-inch hem (Sew-Easy Guide 21). (Allow extra yardage for hems.)

Sew-Easy Quilts

Make a quilt that's a spread and a warmer all in one. You'll be surprised how simple it is. Just stitch up two equal sized spreads. Slip-stitch (Sew-Easy Guide 11) strips of dacron batting together until you have a piece equal in size to the spreads. Baste the batting to the backside of one of the spreads, basting one inch

from the outside edges. Trim the batting very close to the bastings.

Pin together the two spreads, right sides together, leaving an opening for turning. Machine-stitch around the spreads, one-half inch from the outside edges. Turn the spreads right side out and close the opening with invisible slip-stitches. Remove the bastings.

Finish off this beauty with tufts of yarn spaced evenly over the quilt. Thread a large-eyed needle with yard and take a few small stitches through all layers at each marked spot. Knot each tuft of yarn on the right side of the quilt.

Piece, patch, or appliqué one side of the quilt for a more unique bed cover (see Chapter 11). Back it with flannel for extra warmth and comfort.

Quilt through all three layers if your machine will

allow. To accommodate the bulky fabric to the right of the needle, roll the quilt tightly under the machine like a bedroll. Continue to roll the quilt as the fabric moves to the right while you sew. Some machines refuse to sew through the dacron batting without making an incredible mess. Take a test-run before taking on a venture like this.

How's this for an effortless way to brighten up the bedroom? Make yourself a friendship quilt. Have each sewing friend stitch up a twelve-inch square. (Provide an instruction sheet that tells exactly what you want.) Encourage them to express their creativity —piece, patch, appliqué, or embroider and the more fabrics and colors the better. Sew the squares together and see what a sensational creation appears.

Here's another bedroom idea that will save you time and money. Buy a cheap satin comforter at the local bargain department store—or make use of the dingy one hidden at the back of the linen closet. Stitch up a patchwork spread on the machine, equal in size to the store-bought quilt. Combine squares and rectangles to create an abstract design (Figure 15.10). Turn the raw edges under one-half inch and top-stitch or slip-stitch the spread to the quilt around the outside edges. How's this for easy quilting?

I'll bet you never thought it would be this simple to make a dust ruffle to go with that quilt. Just stitch up a ruffle that will reach from the bottom of the mattress to the floor and attach it to a sheet (see Sew-Easy Guide 16). Presto—a dust ruffle that's made to order!

Accent on Pillows

Isn't it about time you had some new throw pillows for the living room sofa? Better yet, why not cover those ratty old cushions and save a few dollars? Cover pillows with any sturdy fabric—washable if possible—and be sure to preshrink for easy care.

Make a pattern for the pillow cover out of heavy paper. Find the length of the pillow by measuring from half-way down one side of the pillow (there's usually a seam to use as a guide), across the top, to

FIGURE 15.10. *An abstract patchwork cover on an old quilt.*

half-way down the other side (Figure 15.11). use the same measuring technique to find the width of the pillow. Make the pattern according to these measurements, using a right triangle ruler to be sure that the corners are perfectly square.

Use this pattern to cut two separate pieces. Pin the pieces, right sides together, along three of the edges, leaving one side open for turning. Stitch along the three sides, taking one-half inch seam allowances and pivoting the fabric ninety degrees one-half inch from each corner.

Make a second row of stitching just outside the first row, using a zigzag or machine over-cast stitch. Trim the seam allowances very close to the second row of stitches. Over-cast the raw edges of the seam allowances along the open side. With the edges permanently finished off, there will be no chance of seams unravelling during washings.

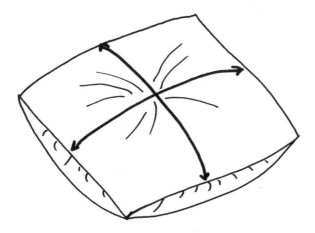

FIGURE 15.11. *Measuring a pillow.*

Turn the pillow cover right side out and push out the corners with an orange stick. Put the pillow into the covering, turn the seam allowances of the opening under, and close the opening with invisible slip-stitches (Sew-Easy Guide 11). When the cover needs washing, just snip the hand-stitching and remove the pillow. Restitch when the cover is clean.

Make washing those pillow covers even easier by inserting a zipper along one side. Select a zipper that's a few inches shorter than a side of the cover and install the zipper *before* sewing up the other three sides: Pin the two pillow cover pieces together along one side. Stitch the ends of the seam, leaving an opening long enough for the zipper. Machine-baste along the zipper opening. Finish off the raw edges of the seam allowances with an over-cast or zigzag stitch. Press the seam open. Working from the wrong side, pin and baste the zipper in place, being sure to line up the zipper teeth with the center of the machine-basted seam. Using a zipper foot, stitch around the zipper on the top side of the fabric. Unzip the zipper.

Pin the remaining three sides of the cover, right sides together. Machine-stitch, finish the raw edges, trim, and turn.

Use those newly acquired piece, patch, and appliqué skills (Chapter 11) to design pillows for every

room. Mix and match leftover scraps for the crazy-quilt look. Choose colors that compliment the rest of the room.

Pick up a design motif from a rug, drapery, upholstery fabric, or even from a carved wood buffet. Appliqué this design motif on a pillow. A little repetition will tie the whole room together. Appliqué a scene onto a pillow for a fun bit of stitchery that's sure to liven up even the darkest den.

Be sure to stitch appliqués to the pillow cover section *before* installing the zipper or sewing the two sections together. There is no point in decorating both sides of the pillow; only one side is on display at a time. Save yourself some work and leave a side plain.

It's easy enough to make your own pillow to cover if you don't happen to have one that's in need of renovation. Use muslin for the inner pillow cover and stuff it with shredded polyester foam—sold in bags at most fabric stores. Cut two pieces of muslin for each pillow. Each piece should be one inch larger on a side than the outside cover. This will make for a full pillow that completely fills out the outer cover.

Pin and stitch the muslin sections together leaving one-half of a side open for turning and stuffing. Turn the cover right side out and stuff with the polyester foam. (The shredded foam is rather messy; stuff outdoors if you can.) Turn the raw edges of the opening under and close the opening with invisible slip-stitches.

Here's a great space-saving idea if you live in one-room apartments. Hide that nighttime pillow in a zippered pillow cover during the day. Decorate this neat cover-up with machine appliqués to transform bedding into colorful throw cushions.

The Convertible Room

You can easily transform a study into a guest bedroom with a little creative stitchery. Cover the extra single bed with a no-wale corduroy spread. Corduroy without the wale has the look of suede—

extra rich and super plush. Cover a couple of bolsters to match and stitch up a few of those pillow cover-ups.

Perking Up Old Chairs

Save yourself a bundle by reupholstering those flea market finds yourself. Straight-back chairs with removable seats can be covered in minutes. Use bargain fabrics and the savings will be even greater.

There is no need to use upholstery fabric, which can sometimes be expensive, as long as the fabric you do use is heavy-duty. All the corduroys are good bets—the no-wales and wide-wale varieties are my favorites for luxurious texture.

To rejuvenate the seat of a standard straight-back chair, cut a piece of fabric on the grain that covers the top of the seat. Add a few extra inches for underlapping. Pad the seat with a thin layer of foam for comfort. Stretch the fabric taut over the seat, being

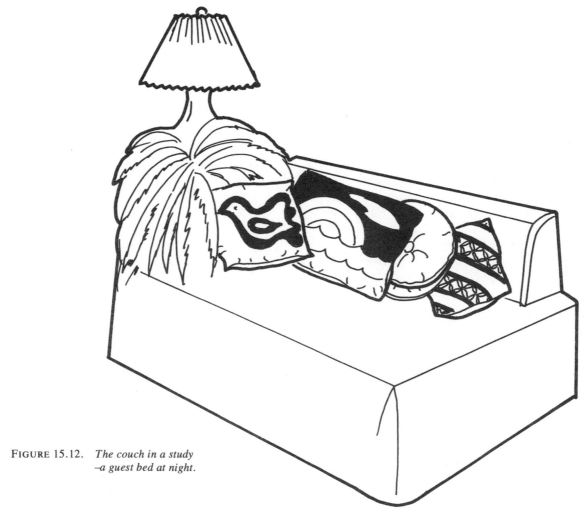

FIGURE 15.12. *The couch in a study —a guest bed at night.*

sure that the grains of the fabric are square with the chair. When all the wrinkles are smoothed out, tack or staple the fabric to the underside of the seat. Replace the seat and screw into place.

Covering Foam to Make Furniture

Here are a few simple do-it-yourself furniture building projects for the energetic seamstress who's short on cash.

Build a wooden platform to fit up against the wall. Cut a piece of 4 inch thick polyester foam the size of the platform and cover it with fabric. A couple of bolsters and a few throw pillows make for a really comfortable couch. Remove the bolsters and the couch becomes a bed.

To make a really professional-looking cushion cover (to cover the foam mattress) measure the length and the width of the cushion, adding 2 inches to each measurement for seam allowances. Cut 2 pieces of fabric equal to these measurements—one for the top of the cushion and one for the bottom.

The depth of the cushion is covered by a piece of fabric cut on the lengthwise grain called a *boxing*. The width of the boxing is equal to the depth of the foam (4 inches in this case), plus 2 inches for seam allowances. Cut one piece for the boxing long enough to cover the front of the cushion and the two sides plus 2 inches for seam allowances. If any piecing is necessary, add seam allowances and place seams at the cushion corners.

Cut a separate piece of boxing 2 inches wider than the first piece, to run along the length of the back of the cushion. Add 2 inches to the length for seam allowances. This piece of the boxing will hold the zippers.

Fold this last piece in half lengthwise and cut along the fold. Pin the 2 pieces, right sides together, along one lengthwise edge. Leaving enough room in the center for two zippers, stitch the ends of the seam taking a 1 inch seam allowance. Machine-baste the zipper opening and press the seam open.

Pin and baste the two zippers into place so that the pull tabs meet at the center of the piece of boxing. Machine-stitch around the zippers on the top side of the fabric, using a zipper foot (Figure 15.13).

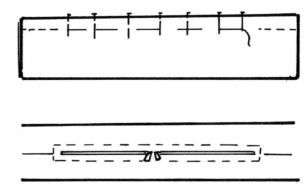

FIGURE 15.13. *Installing the zippers in a cushion cover.*

Stitch the back boxing section (holding the zippers) to the rest of the boxing, right sides together, taking 1 inch seam allowances. Press open the seams and unzip the zippers.

Pin, baste, and stitch the boxing to the outside edges of the top and bottom cushion sections, right sides together, taking 1 inch seam allowances (Figure 15.14). Trim seams, clip curves, and press seam allowances toward the boxing. Be sure to finish all seam allowances so they won't fray during washings. Turn the cushion cover right side out through the zipper opening.

Here's another make-your-own idea that requires no carpentry skills at all. Cover three equal size foam cushions and stack one on top of another. Add a bolster and pillows for a mini-couch that wins hands down when it comes to comfort.

Creative Wall Coverings

Use the decorative techniques discussed in Chapter 11 to create unique tapestries for livening up the walls. Small appliquéd wall-hangings are great fillers

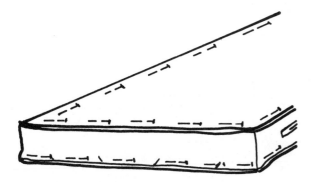

FIGURE 15.14. *Pinning the boxing to the top and bottom cushion sections.*

for odd-shaped spaces. Brightly colored animals, ships, and cartoon characters are ideal for the children's rooms. Kids' rooms are the perfect places to vent your pent-up creativity.

Be bold and brave; design a tapestry to cover a wall—turn dead space into a visual delight. Combine textures for interesting effects. Intersperse ribbons and layered appliqués. Don't forget about dacron batting for creating three-dimensional figures.

The House on Wheels

The weekend camper becomes a home on wheels with cleverly stitched cushions, cheerful curtains, and brightly colored pillow cover-ups. Make everything washable, of course, for easy care. Camperize a van with the same sort of stitching ingenuity. A platform

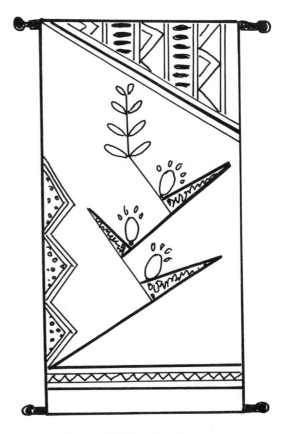

FIGURE 15.15. *A wall-hanging.*

and covered cushion make a great bed. Add curtains to keep out bright lights and the van is transformed into the perfect overnight sleeper. With comfort on wheels like this, why spend weekends at home?

Chapter Sixteen

Needle Profit

Are you looking for ways to boost up the bankroll? With a little ingenuity, patience, and determination, you can turn your craft into a money-making venture. Sell what you sew and watch the family fortune grow.

What to Sell

For years I've supplemented my income seasonally by stitching up wares to sell through boutiques. I've had the most success making and selling items that are unique, but inexpensive. For several years in a row I have sold appliquéd pillows to boutiques during the Christmas gift-buying season. My production costs are low: The pillows take very little fabric and hardly any time at all to make. Keeping my costs to a minimum means that the retail selling price stays within reason. Customers buy a pillow or two without feeling the pinch of a major purchase, and I come out way ahead.

Don't consider making something to sell that is already being mass produced and is readily available to the public. You won't be able to compete with the big manufacturers. To make money by sewing you must capitalize on people's desire to buy fine, hand-crafted, one-of-a-kind goods. Provide an item that is well-made and unique.

Make use of the decorative techniques described in Chapter 11 to create interesting and unusual wares. Appliqué, patchwork, decorative machine-stitching, and hand embroidery are all very popular these days. Garments and pillows made of unusual fabrics are also much in demand: batiks, tie-dyes, and imported woven fabrics are everybody's favorites.

Decorative pillows, quilts, and tote bags are big sellers in the non-garment line. As for clothing that sells, I've had success with halter tops, long skirts, blouses, pants, and long and short dresses.

A reversible halter top is a hot selling item. Use a print fabric on one side; a solid on the other. Appliqué a flower, butterfly, or abstract design on the solid-color side and your customer will get two items for the price of one.

The halter top is a doubly good deal for you too. One size fits all, so you don't have to bother with sizing. And, since every halter you make is cut from the same pattern, you can easily get away with cutting out more than one top at a time. Just make sure your scissors are sharp!

FIGURE 16.1. *Making pillows to sell.*

Halters can be designed to dress up or down. They are as good with skirts as they are with pants; and they can be worn just about anywhere. All these factors add up to make the halter top a sure sell.

Functional Art Is the Way to Go

Make something unique that serves a purpose. The appliquéd throw pillow is my all time favorite, but these other items will certainly sell: workshirts topstitched with decorative machine stitches; skirts with scenes appliquéd around the bottom; dresses with flower gardens growing from the hem; caftans decorated however you like—with an embroidered panel down the front; trimmed collar, cuffs, and hem; or a bodice-insert that's extra special.

Keep these tips in mind when sewing clothes to sell. Shoot for one-size-fits-all fashions. If you must go to sizes, use small, medium, and large rather than numbered sizes. Choose styles that aren't too complex. In fact, easy-sew garments are great. The simpler styles make for faster sewing. The less time in the making, the more money for you. And those easy-sew styles are designed to keep fit problems to a minimum. It's a shame when a beautifully made garment doesn't sell for the mere lack of a good fit.

The following style features will minimize fit prob-lems: halters, wrap-arounds, raglan sleeves, deep hems that can be let down, and elasticized or draw-string waistlines. How about drawstring muslin pants or skirts trimmed with rows of decorative stitches for the next spring season?

Make good use of your time when you sew. The more efficient you are, the higher the profit. Incorporate the time-saving tricks from Chapter 9 into the work regime and watch the per-hour profit soar. Work in blocks of time and make use of mass production techniques to save you time in construction. Cut a batch of clothes at once; stitch seams one after another; and press them all at the same time. Every minute saved is as good as money earned.

Keep the number of different items you're making for sale low. Repeat the same design more than once, especially if your items are to be sold at more than one outlet. The same design takes on a new complexion when the color is changed. Make the same design up in several color schemes; that way you can cut more than one item at a time.

Whatever you can do to keep production costs low will earn you more in the long run. Pass the savings on to the customer and sales will probably increase. If you consider the savings as profit you may sell less, but you'll make more per item.

Shop at fabric warehouses, and buy discount fabrics whenever possible. A trip to a nearby garment district for fabric is particularly worthwhile when you are sewing to sell (See Chapter 10).

Be sure to keep all the receipts for the expenses you run up doing business; such as fabric, notion, pattern costs. These expenses can be deducted from your income tax. The less tax you pay, the more money you earn.

Marketing Your Wares

Now that you know what to make for resale in boutiques, let's consider how to go about marketing your wares. Start by looking up all the local boutiques and specialty shops in the phone book. If your town doesn't support much of this kind of business, consider selling to shops in a nearby town that does.

Organize sales trips to make the best use of your time. Make an itinerary of shops to visit on one business day and move from one to the next in a systematic fashion. Develop a sales pitch so you don't waste time getting down to business. Take a sample of your wares along and photographs of the rest if possible. And don't forget the price list.

Keep the seasons in mind when looking for retail outlets. Some items are perfect for the Christmas gift-giving season (pillows, quilts, long skirts, and blouses); others will sell best at summer vacation resorts (halter tops, simple halter dresses, draw string pants, bathing suits, beach cover-ups, and tote bags.) But avoid trying to sell wares between January and April. This season is deadly for retail sales items—everyone is anxiously awaiting the tax man.

Before doing business with a shop, find out what kind of mark-up system is used. Retail establishments mark the price of each item up from fifty to one hundred percent. The difference between the retail sales price and your price is the fee charged by the shop for marketing your wares. The most equitable arrangement as far as I'm concerned is one in which the shop marks your wholesale price up by one-half. This means that you get two-thirds of the retail sales price on an item, and the shop takes one-third. It also means that the retail sales price is considerably lower than it would be if the shop doubled the wholesale price. The lower the price to the public, the more likely it is that the goods will sell.

Be sure to find out all the particulars about selling prices and mark-up *before* leaving your goods anywhere. If the mark-up is too high, you might be priced out of business. It's far better to find another outlet than to leave your goods at a store where they will never sell.

Try to get retail establishments to pay outright for your wares. Most shops prefer to take items in on consignment (you get paid when the goods sell), at least until your wares have proved themselves as

FIGURE 16.2. *A decorated caftan.*

sellers. Make the best deal possible. Consignment-selling is certainly a way to get started.

Be sure to get a receipt from the shop when leaving goods on consignment. Guard this record with your life; if an item or two were to be stolen or lost, the shop would owe you money. The receipt is your proof of the shop's responsibility.

Pricing Your Goods

Price goods according to the hours spent creating. Pay yourself at least five dollars an hour; add on production costs and the retail establishment mark-up. Compare this price with the going prices on similar items. Is your price competitive? If not, pay yourself a little less and really start organizing the work regime. Remember, time saved is money earned.

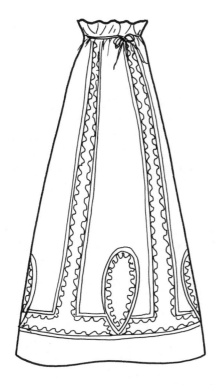

FIGURE 16.3. *A decoratively stitched long skirt.*

Keep this tip in mind when sewing to sell: Inexpensive, unique items that either serve a purpose or make good gifts are the fast, sure sellers. The elaborate one-of-a-kind creations cost more and usually take longer to sell. If you need money now, concentrate your creative energies on the fast-selling items.

Stay on top of what is happening to your product. Find out what is selling and what isn't. If there are a few hangers-on that just can't be moved, consider finding another outlet for them. Move wares around until you find the right outlet.

Craft Fairs, Swap Meets, and Flea Markets

Fairs, meets, and flea markets are fun places to market wares. Not only is the money good, but participating in the marketplace activities is an adventure. These places require that you sell as well as make the goods. Since there's no middleman between you and the customer to mark prices sky high, you can sell wares to the public for far less than is possible through most retail outlets. (Sometimes there's an entry fee to pay, but it is usually a token amount.) Low prices mean that goods will move fast.

Craft fairs usually require that you apply for admittance in advance. Admission to some fairs is competitive; others operate on a first-come first-serve basis.

There's rarely a prior application necessary for swap meets and flea markets—just pay a small entry fee and you're in. These novel shopping centers are packed every weekend with throngs of eager buyers looking for bargains. Offer a good deal, sell easy-to-make but unique items, and you'll clean up for sure.

The Neighborhood Dressmaker

If you are an experienced and self-confident seamstress, set up a part-time or full-time dressmaking business in the comfort of your own home. Run an ad in the local newspaper offering your services to the neighborhood; a card tacked up on the grocery store bulletin board is a handy reminder. Word travels fast, particularly after you have completed a job or two successfully.

It's important that you set aside a substantial work space for yourself—a place where you can work in peace and quiet with no distractions. The only way to really make money at this game is to run an efficient and well-organized operation. Setting equipment up and taking it down between assignments is out of the question; you *must* be able to leave the equipment up at all times.

Be sure to work out the financial arrangements of each job *before* you sew a stitch so there will be no haggling over prices later. Once a garment is complete you'll be inclined to settle for less, rather than be stuck with a garment you have no use for. This rule holds especially with friends. Friends are quick to sell your talents short. They are forever expecting special favors and a "good deal."

Charge no less than five dollars an hour for your work, and keep a meticulous account of the hours spent on each project. Don't cheat yourself out of dollars; your skill is worth every penny.

The one drawback to this kind of business is the occasional customer who will expect you to perform miracles. It's impossible to make a customer look like a rail when she's tipping the scales at 200 plus. Be frank, and do your best—use the tricks of optical illusion to make that customer appear pounds thinner.

If you have no interest in setting up a business but can use some spare change, why not offer your sewing services to a friend. Acquaintances are continually asking me to sew for them: curtains, clothes, bedspreads, etc. Don't price yourself too low; and if you don't like to engage in money transactions with friends, try trading labor instead. The barter system —I'll sew for you, if you'll paint for me—works just fine.

There's Money in Alterations

There is good money in alterations. Make a living at this caper, or work part-time to supplement your income. Offer your services to a local high-quality dress store; they sometimes have a need for a good alteration person. Or set up shop in your own home. Again, the prerequisite is an orderly space where work can progress undisturbed. The drawback to this line of work is that it demands a lot of patience. You won't be creating something new each time you sew; all the work will involve tampering with something that someone else made. The advantage is that you will be providing an invaluable service for customers.

The Last Word

A final note on sewing for money: Whether making items for resale, or opening your own dressmaking business, check with local government agencies to see what licenses or permits are required. Find out what records must be kept, and who is responsible for paying which taxes. Be meticulous about keeping records. Books are available on setting up small businesses; check with your library if you are taking this line of work seriously.

Good luck and happy sewing!

Part Three

Guides to Sewing

Glossary of Fabrics and Related Terms

Acetate A lustrous, silky man-made fiber made from cellulose. Often used in blends with silk, cotton, rayon, and other man-made fibers. Has excellent draping qualities. Used for clothes, home furnishings, and linings.

Acrylic A man-made fiber used to make wool-like fabrics and knitted goods. Used for sweaters, blankets, carpets, fleece and fur-like fabrics, home furnishings, work clothes.

Alpaca A soft, luxurious, wool fabric made from the hair of the Peruvian alpaca. Also refers to fabric made from cotton or rayon and blended with alpaca. Used for suits and coats.

Angora Smooth, soft fibers from the Angora goat or rabbit; usually blended with wool.

Argyle A plaid design composed of large diamonds and contrasting diagonal stripes.

Basket weave A weave resembling the checkered pattern of a plaited basket.

Batik A cotton fabric dyed by a Javanese process of resist dyeing that produces rich and intricate multi-colored designs. Often simulated by machine printing.

Batiste A soft, sheer, very fine, plain-weave fabric made of cotton, wool, silk, or synthetic fibers. Used for linings, dresses, lingerie, handkerchiefs, infant's wear, and blouses.

Blend The combination of two or more types of fibers in one yarn, resulting in a new fabric or a tweed effect.

Block printing A process of printing fabric by hand using carved wood or linoleum blocks.

Bouclé A woven or knitted wool, cotton, silk, or rayon fabric with a nubby texture. Used for coats, suits, and dresses.

Broadcloth A closely woven fabric made in many weights, fibers, and blends. Cotton and silk broadcloths have a lustrous finish and are used to make shirts, pajamas, sport clothes, blouses, dresses, and children's clothes. Wool broadcloth has a brushed finish which gives it a napped effect; it is used for coats, dresses, and suits.

Brocade A heavy silk or rayon jacquard-weave fabric with a raised all-over design. Often accented with silver and gold threads. Used for evening dresses and wraps, foundation garments, housecoats, and slip covers.

Buckram A stiffening for clothing composed of two plain-weave fabrics glued together.

Burlap A coarse, plain-weave fabric made of jute, hemp, or cotton. Used for wall coverings, drapery, and sometimes for clothing.

Calico A plain-weave, lightweight cotton fabric, printed with a small figured pattern. Used for dresses, blouses, sportwear, and children's clothes.

137

Camel's hair A luxurious, soft fabric with a rich nap made from the undercoat of a camel, often combined with wool. The classic coating fabric.

Canvas A heavy, strong, firmly woven cotton, linen, or synthetic fabric. In clothes-making used for stiffening in coat and suit lapels.

Carding Cleansing and disentangling fibers preparatory to spinning.

Cashmere A soft fabric made from the fine hair of the cashmere goat. Usually combined with wool for durability. Used to make sweaters, coats, and sports jackets.

Challis A soft, lightweight fabric of wool, rayon, cotton, or blends which is usually printed with delicate floral patterns. Used for making dresses and sleepwear.

Chambray A fine-quality, plain-weave cotton or silk with a colored warp and white fill. Has a linen-like finish and comes in stripes and checks. Used for dresses, shirts, children's clothes, and sportswear.

Chenille Fabric woven with soft tufts that appear as tiny balls or ribs. Usually used for bathrobes, bedspreads, and as trimmings and fringe on draperies.

Chiffon A delicate, sheer, plain-weave fabric of silk or rayon, with a soft or stiff finish. Used for evening dresses, formal blouses, and lingerie.

China silk A plain-weave silk fabric that comes in various different weights. The lighter weights are primarily used for linings and scarves. The heavier weights are for blouses and custom shirts.

Chinchilla A soft, heavy coating material (usually wool) with a nubby surface.

Chintz A fine, plain-weave cotton fabric, usually brightly printed with floral designs and sometimes glazed. Used more in home decorating than in dressmaking. Great for draperies, slip covers, and cushions.

Colorfast fabric Fabric that won't fade or run during cleaning or laundering.

Combed cotton Cotton yarn that has been carded to remove impurities.

Corduroy A heavy, soft, plain or twill-weave fabric of cotton or rayon, with lengthwise wales of cut pile. Comes in pinwale, medium wale, heavy wale, wide wale, and no-wale. Used for sportswear, children's wear, dresses, draperies, and slip covers.

Cotton Fabric made from the seed pod of the cotton plant. Available in many weaves and grades, e.g.

batiste, broadcloth, **burlap**, calico, canvas, chambray, chintz, combed cotton, corduroy, crinoline, denim, dimity, duck, faille, **flannel**, flannelette, lawn, madras, muslin, organdy, percale, **pique**, polished cotton, sailcloth, sateen, satin, **seersucker**, sharkskin, terry, and velveteen.

Crepe A soft, plain-weave silk, cotton, wool, synthetic, or blend fabric with a crinkled surface. Available in weights that range from light and sheer to heavy and opaque. Used for dresses, blouses, soft suits, and lingerie.

Crepe-back satin A silk or rayon fabric with a satin face and a crepe back. Used for dresses, blouses, lingerie, and linings.

Crepe de chine A light-, medium-, or heavy-weight plain-weave crepe, usually made of silk.

Crinoline A stiff, open-weave fabric of cotton, silk, or synthetic fibers. Used as a stiffening agent in dressmaking.

Damask A reversible, firm, jacquard-weave fabric, similar to brocade only flatter. Available in linen, cotton, rayon, or silk. The cottons and linens are used for table linen; the light-weight silks and rayons are used for dresses, blouses, linings; and the heavier weights are used for draperies and upholstery.

Denim A sturdy, twill-weave cotton fabric.

Dimity A sheer, crisp, lightweight cotton fabric with a fine corded stripe or check effect. Used for curtains, dresses, lingerie, blouses, aprons, and infants wear.

Doeskin A wool, cotton, or spun rayon fabric with a heavy, short nap on one side. Used most often for men's suits, coats, and sportswear.

Dotted swiss A crisp, transparent, fine cotton fabric decorated with raised woven dots. Used for curtains, dresses, blouses, and bedspreads.

Double-knit fabric A wool or synthetic knit fabric made on two sets of needles. The result is a double thickness of fabric that has excellent body and stability. Used for dresses, soft suits, and sportswear.

Duck A strong, heavy, tightly woven cotton or linen fabric, plain or ribbed. Very durable and somewhat water-resistant. Used for work clothes, shirts, trousers, coats, and awnings.

Eyelet A cotton fabric covered with decorative, edge-stitched cutouts.

Faille A soft, lightweight silk, rayon, or cotton fabric with pronounced crosswise ribbing. Used for suits, dresses, sportswear, summer coats, and bags.

Fake fur A heavy, soft knit or woven fabric of wool, silk, or rayon with a pile surface that resembles fur. Used for coats and jackets.

Felt A dense nonwoven fabric of wool, cotton, or rayon produced by matting fibers together under heat and pressure. Used for hats, belts, bags, and table mats.

Fibers Natural and man-made filaments from which yarns are spun.

Flannel A cotton, wool, or rayon plain- or twill-weave fabric that is slightly napped on one or both sides. Available in different weights. The lightweights are used for shirts, blouses, and children's wear; the mediumweights for dresses and sportswear; and the heavyweights for suits and coats.

Flannelette A soft, warm, plain- or twill-weave cotton fabric with a nap on one side. Used for sleepwear and infants clothes. Also called outing flannel.

Fleece A soft, heavy coating material with a deeply napped, fleece-like surface.

Gabardine A firm, tightly woven, twilled fabric of wool, cotton, rayon, or blends. Excellent for tailoring. Used for suits, coats, sportswear, and raincoats.

Gauze A sheer, thin, woven fabric like cheesecloth.

Georgette A sheer, soft, dull-textured wool fabric, heavier than chiffon with a crinkled crepe-like surface.

Gingham A crisp, lightweight, plain-weave cotton fabric available in stripes, checks, plaids, or solids. Used for dresses, blouses, and children's wear.

Herringbone An irregular twill-weave that produces a zigzag design.

Homespun A loose, coarse, plain-weave wool, linen, cotton, or blend fabric with a tweedy appearance. Used for shirts, suits, coats, jackets, and dresses.

Hopsacking A coarse, rough-textured cotton, linen, or rayon fabric with an open weave. Used for men's slacks and shirts, women's sportswear, and draperies.

Jacquard A loom that produces the intricate woven designs of damasks and brocades.

Jersey A soft, plain-knitted fabric with a smooth surface made from cotton, wool, synthetics, or blends. Comes tubular or flat. Used for lingerie, dresses, blouses, sports shirts, gloves, and bathing suits.

Khaki A sturdy twilled cotton or wool fabric in an olive-drab color. Used in sportswear.

Knit fabrics Any fabric made by single- or double-needle knitting. Knitting is a method of constructing fabric by interlocking a series of loops of one or more yarns. These fabrics have much more flexibility than wovens (which are made of intersecting threads rather than interlocking loops). Available in wool, cotton, silk, synthetics, and blends. Widely used in all types of clothes for men, women, and children.

Lace A fine, open-worked fabric of silk, rayon, cotton, nylon, or blends consisting of a network of threads formed into a pattern or design.

Lamé A plain-weave or brocaded fabric made of metallic threads, sometimes combined with silk or rayon. Used to make evening wear and as trim.

Laminated fabric Two or more layers of fabric fused together by means of adhesives or heat. Also, a foam-backed fabric. Used for dresses, jackets, sportswear.

Lawn A sheer, fine, plain-weave cotton fabric often with a crisp finish. Used in infants wear, dresses, blouses, underwear.

Leatherette An imitation leather made of paper, cloth, or plastic that has been varnished, lacquered, grained, and finished.

Linen A strong, lustrous fabric made from natural flax fibers. Available in various weaves and weights. Used for sheets, slip covers, draperies, dresses, suits, handkerchiefs, and tablecloths.

Madras cotton A fine, hand-loomed cotton fabric from India available in natural color or dyed with bleeding vegetable dyes and woven into plaids and stripes. Used for shirts, dresses, sportswear.

Matte finish A fabric with a dull nonlustrous surface.

Matte jersey Tricot fabric with a dull, or matte, surface. Used to make dresses, blouses, and evening wear.

Mercerizing Treating cotton thread to a process that makes it stronger and more lustrous.

Mesh A knitted, knotted, or woven open-textured fabric with even spaces between the yarns. It can be made of fine or coarse threads or yarns.

Metallic cloth Shiny, crisp fabric with silk, rayon, or cotton warp threads and metallic filling threads.

Modacrylic A synthetic, modified acrylic fiber that is wrinkle-resistant, resilient, warm, soft, and wash-and-wear. Used for blankets, carpets, draperies, fur-like pile fabrics, and knit wear.

Mohair The fabric made from the long, silky, lightweight fiber from the Angora goat blended with wool and other fibers. Available in many weaves, patterns, and colors. Used for dresses, coats, jackets, and sportswear.

Monk's cloth A coarse, heavy cotton or linen basket-weave fabric. Used for draperies, upholstery, bedspreads, and pillows.

Muslin A firm, durable, bleached or unbleached, plain-weave cotton fabric. Available in various weights and grades. Used for undergarments, shirts, pillowcases, sheets, dresses, lingerie and children's wear.

Nap A soft, fuzzy fabric finish, usually produced by brushing.

Natural fibers The fibers that occur in nature: cotton, linen, silk, and wool.

Net A silk, cotton, or synthetic mesh fabric which ranges from sheer and fine (such as tulle) to coarse and open (such as fish net). Used in making curtains, evening gowns, and veiling.

Organdy A very fine, sheer, plain-weave cotton fabric with a crisp finish. Used in party dresses, curtains, bedspreads, and blouses.

Organza A silk, rayon, or nylon organdy fabric. Used for blouses, curtains, party dresses.

Oxford cloth A shiny, soft, medium-firm, plain- or basket-weave cotton fabric. Available in different weights. Used for shirts, summer suits, dresses, sportswear, children's wear, and draperies.

Peau de soie A rich, smooth, soft satin-weave dress material made of silk, rayon, or blends. Used for evening wear.

Percale A fine, firm, plain-weave lightweight cotton fabric with a smooth, dull finish. Used for dresses, children's wear, and draperies.

Permanent press A term describing fabric performance with regard to wrinkle-resistance, shape-retention, and washability.

Pile A fabric woven with an extra set of threads which stand up to form a soft, thick, deep, furry surface.

Pinstripe A fabric with fine, slender stripes approximately the width of a straight pin. Used for tailored suits.

Piqué A firm cotton, silk, or rayon fabric with a wale, waffle, or diamond woven in to create patterned effects. Used for sportswear, children's wear, dresses, collars, and cuffs.

Plaid A textile pattern of colored blocks and/or intersecting stripes.

Plain-weave The most basic type of weave; each filling yarn passes alternately over and under each warp yarn.

Polished cotton A satin-weave or waxed-cotton fabric with a glossy face. Used for dresses, sportswear, and children's clothes.

Polyester A generic term for a synthetic fiber with superior wrinkle-resistance and easy-care properties. Used successfully in blends with cotton, rayon, and wool. Used in permanent press fabric, carpets, curtains, cushions, home furnishings.

Pongee A plain-weave, lightweight silk fabric (usually a natural or ivory color). Used for curtains and linings.

Poplin A medium-firm, plain-weave silk, cotton, wool, synthetic, or blend fabric with a fine rib running from selvage to selvage. Used for coats, suits, dresses, pajamas, sportswear, and children's wear.

Pure silk Silk fabric containing no more than ten percent metallic weighting or finishing.

Qiana A soft, lustrous man-made fabric. Has excellent draping qualities and is machine washable. Used for dresses, blouses, and shirts.

Rajah A silk fabric, similar to pongee, with a rough surface.

Raw silk Silk fibers before the natural gum has been removed.

Rayon The oldest of the man-made fibers. Made of certain solutions of modified cellulose (wood pulp). Now produced in many versions; best used in blends with all other fibers. Adds comfort and lustre to fibers with which it is combined. Used for apparel, home furnishings, linings, rugs, and carpets.

Reversible fabric A fabric that is finished and usable on both sides.

Sailcloth A strong, heavy plain-weave fabric of cotton, linen, or jute. Originally used for sails; now available, plain or printed, in weights suitable for clothing.

Sateen A satin-weave mercerized cotton fabric with a

high lustre and crease-resistant finish. Used for costumes, slip covers, draperies, and linings.

Satin A silk or synthetic satin-weave fabric with a soft, shiny surface. Comes in many varieties. Used for dresses, evening wear, negligees, draperies, and bedspreads.

Seersucker A crisp, lightweight plain-weave cotton fabric with crinkled stripes woven lengthwise at alternating intervals. Comes in stripes, plaids, and checks. Used for dresses, children's wear and sportswear.

Shantung A crisp, lightweight silk, rayon, wool, or cotton plain-weave fabric made with thick and thin yarns to give a nubbed surface. Used for sportswear, women's suits, dresses, blouses, pajamas and robes.

Sharkskin A twill-weave wool fabric with white and colored yarns that create a small-dot effect. Also a smooth, lustrous, closely-woven silk, cotton, or synthetic fabric. Used for suits and sportswear.

Shetland wool A warm, soft, fine, lightweight knitted or woven fabric made from the wool of the Shetland sheep. Used for coats and suits.

Silk A filament produced by silkworms that is woven into fabrics noted for their soft lustre, strength, and luxurious feel, such as China silk, chiffon, crepe de chine, faille, Lyon's velvet, peau de soie, pongee, satin, shantung, surah, and taffeta.

Sizing A finishing process that gives stiffness and strength to textiles.

Spandex A synthetic fiber with great elasticity, or fabric made of spandex fiber. Used for foundation garments, swim wear, and hosiery.

Suede cloth A heavy cotton, wool, synthetic, or blend woven or knit fabric, finished to resemble suede. Used for dresses, coats, and sportswear.

Surah A soft, lightweight, lustrous silk, rayon, or synthetic twill-weave fabric. Used for neckties, dresses, and blouses.

Synthetic fibers Man-made fibers produced by chemical means.

Taffeta A crisp, lightweight, lustrous silk, cotton, synthetic, or blend plain-weave fabric. Available in several weights and varieties. Used to make dresses, children's wear, blouses, suits, slips, draperies, and bedspreads.

Tattersall A simple over-check pattern in two colors.

Terry cloth A soft woven or knitted cotton fabric with a loop pile on one or both sides. Very absorbent. Available in stretch form. Used for bath towels, bathrobes, wash cloths, beach robes, and play clothes.

Thread count The number of threads per inch in warp-and-weft woven fabric.

Ticking A firm, strong, durable twill-weave cotton fabric that usually has stripes. Used for play clothes, upholstery, mattress and pillow coverings.

Triacetate A synthetic fiber similar to acetate, but higher in heat-resistance and easier to care for.

Tricot A soft knit fabric with vertical wales on the face and crosswise ribs on the back. Highly run-resistant; very little lengthwise stretch.

Tulle A fine, soft silk, cotton, rayon, or synthetic net used for veils and trimmings.

Tussah Uncultivated silk with coarse, strong, uneven filaments; tan in color.

Tweed A rough, nubby wool, cotton, silk, or blend fabric. Tweeds can be plain-, twill-, or herringbone-weave, and have a homespun look. Available in various colors, patterns, and weights. Used for coats, suits, jackets, slacks, and dresses.

Twill A basic weave that produces a diagonal rib.

Ultrasuede A very expensive, nonwoven, synthetic, suede-like fabric. Washable and lightweight; tailors beautifully. Used for sportswear, dresses, coats, jackets, hats, and handbags.

Velour A soft, strong, closely-woven, plain- or satin-weave fabric made of cotton, wool, silk, or rayon. Has a nap on one side and is used to make coats, suits, upholstery, and draperies.

Velvet A luxurious, smooth, rich, soft fabric of silk or rayon with a short thick pile on one side. Used for dresses, suits, coats, evening wear, and draperies.

Velveteen A soft, thick, short-pile, all-cotton fabric resembling velvet. Can be plain-weave or twill-back. Used for dresses, coats, suits, children's dresses, draperies, upholstery, and bedspreads.

Vicuña The world's finest and costliest fabric; made from the wool of the South American vicuña. Used to make coats.

Vinyl A plastic material that usually has a fabric backing.

Voile A plain-weave, lightweight, crisp, sheer fabric of cotton, silk, wool, or synthetics. Available in plain colors and prints. Used for dresses, blouses, curtains, and lingerie.

Wale One of a series of ribs or cords in a woven fabric such as corduroy.

Warp The lengthwise threads in a woven fabric that run parallel to the selvages.

Wash-and-wear Refers to the wrinkle resistant quality of a fabric, after laundering.

Weft The threads that run across the warp in woven fabric. Also called "filler."

Wool Fabrics woven from the soft fibers in the coats of sheep, camel, alpaca, Angora rabbit and goat, and vicuña. Types of wool include angora, batiste, broadcloth, camel's hair, cashmere, challis, chinchilla, flannel, sharkskin, Shetland, tweed, vicuña, and worsted.

Worsted A fine, strong, crisp fabric woven from combed wool yarn.

Woven fabrics Fabrics made by threading yarn lengthwise on a loom and weaving a filler thread across the width.

Yarn A strand of textile fiber spun of short fibers or composed of continuous filaments.

Fabric Qualities

FABRIC DURABILITY	Strong	Not so Strong	Shrinks	Moths Love It	Weakened by Light	Mildews
Naturals:						
Cotton	X		X		X	X
Linen	X		X			X
Silk	X				X	
Wool		X	X	X	X	X
Synthetics:						
Acetate		X			X	
Acrylic	X					
Nylon	X					
Polyester	X					
Rayon		X	X		X	X

FABRIC CARE AND QUALITIES

	Machine Washable	Dry Clean Only	Wrinkles Yes	Wrinkles No	Clings Yes	Clings No	Absorbent Yes	Absorbent No	Seasonal Summer	Seasonal Winter	Elastic Yes	Elastic No	Holds Shape Yes	Holds Shape No
Naturals:														
Cotton	X		X			X	X		X			X	X	
Linen		X	X			X	X		X			X	X	
Silk		X		X	X		X		X	X	X		X	
Wool		X		X			X			X	X			X
Synthetics:														
Acetate		X	X		X			X	X	X	X		X	
Acrylic	X			X	X			X	X	X			X	
Nylon	X			X	X			X	X	X	X		X	
Polyester	X			X	X			X	X	X			X	
Rayon		X	X		X		X		X	X	X			X

Guide C

Sewing on Special Fabrics

In this section:

1. Knits and Stretchables
2. Fabrics with Nap: Velvet, Velveteen, Corduroy, and Velour
3. Leather, Suede, Vinyl, and Ultrasuede
4. Sheer Fabrics
5. Metallic Fabrics
6. Bias-Cut Fabrics

1. Knits and Stretchables

Preparation

Most knits tend to have directional shading, so use the pattern layout marked "with nap." (If a "with nap" layout isn't specified, buy an extra ⅝ yard of fabric and lay out all pattern pieces so that the grain is running in the same direction.) Use a pattern that is designed for use with knits. It's best to stick with patterns that have a minimum of seam details.

Some tubular knits have creases pressed into them so sharply that they can't be removed. Check this *before* cutting out a garment and refold if necessary to avoid the crease when you cut. Use only *very* sharp shears, and be sure that the fabric *does not* hang over the edge of the table while you are cutting.

Put the stretch of the fabric to good use! The stretch should run across the shoulders in blouses, shirts, dresses, and jackets; from waistline to ankle in pants or slacks; and from side to side in skirts and shorts.

Don't forget to preshrink knits. Launder the fabric as you would the finished garment to remove fabric finishes and prevent future shrinkage.

Sewing the Garment

Use ball point or silk pins and a fresh ball point needle for each knit garment. (The ball point separates fabric threads instead of piercing them.) Use polyester thread and a stitch length of between 10 and 15, depending on the stretch of the knit. *Always test stitch a seam on a scrap* to determine the best stitch length.

A roller presser foot helps feed fabric layers evenly while you're stitching. Hold seams taut while sewing, but *don't stretch*. If you are having difficulty sewing a stretchy seam, place a piece of tissue paper between the bottom fabric layer and the machine throat plate. Use

144

straight seam tape to stabilize areas (shoulders, neck-lines, waistline) that you don't want to stretch.

Zigzag stitches are great for sewing knits—they provide elasticity so that the stitches don't snap when stretched. If your machine won't do a zigzag stitch, sew 2 rows of straight stitches very close together. The second row will provide the necessary back up in case a stitch breaks.

Seam allowances on knits won't ravel, so there is no need for seam finishes. To keep seam allowances from curling, stitch ⅛ inch from each edge, using a straight machine stitch.

Linings are usually taboo with knits. Use interfacing *only* when necessary (use polyester featherweight inter-facing, or a piece of garment fabric itself); and never interface turtlenecks or soft collars.

Be sure to baste and fit the garment as you sew.

The Finishing Touches

Let the garment hang for twenty-four hours before hemming. Edge-stitch the hem edge to prevent it from rolling. Catch-stitch hems are best for knits (see Sew-Easy Guide 12).

Test-press a scrap of fabric before touching an iron to the garment. The fiber content of the fabric should determine the temperature setting. Use brown paper under seam allowances when pressing to avoid im-prints of the seam edges showing on the front of the garment.

2. Fabrics with Nap: Velvet, Velveteen, Corduroy, and Velour

Preparation

Important: Handle fabrics with nap as little as pos-sible; they are easily crushed and easily marred.

Choose patterns with simple style lines and use "with nap" layouts. (If your pattern doesn't show a "with nap" layout buy ⅝ of a yard more fabric than specified.)

Which way to use the nap is up to you. When the nap is running up, the color appears richer. Garments made with the nap running down are shinier and sturdier. So, take your pick. The most important thing to remember is that all pieces must be cut out with the nap running in the same direction. Find the direction of the nap by running your hand along the lengthwise grain of the fabric. If the fabric feels smooth, the nap is down; if the fabric feels rough, the nap is up.

Use tailor's chalk and/or tailor's tacks to transfer pattern markings to the fabric. A tracing wheel will mar napped fabrics. In fact, pins may mar, so pin in seam allowances and within dart areas only. And don't forget to preshrink all napped fabrics.

Sewing the Garment

Experiment with stitch lengths on scrap fabric until you find the perfect length for an unpuckered seam line. Sew in the direction of the nap to prevent stretch-ing and use a roller presser foot so that seams won't slip while you stitch. When joining a napped to an un-napped fabric, sew in the direction of the nap, with the unnapped fabric on top.

It's a good idea to baste seams with silk thread before doing the final stitching. This will allow you to double check the fit before you sew. Remember, these fabrics are easily marred; *avoid ripping* whenever pos-sible. If you do have to remove stitches, do so carefully and brush the fabric to remove stitch marks.

Use an overlock or zigzag stitch to finish raw edges. For a particularly nice finish, encase raw edges in bias seam binding (Sew Easy Guide 17).

The Finishing Touches

Always test-press on a scrap when working with pile fabrics; the pile is very easily squashed. Use a needle board (a board covered with fine pieces of wire), press cloth of the garment fabric (self-fabric), or a terry towel for pressing. Place brown paper under the seam allowances to prevent imprints.

Freshen up a slightly wrinkled napped garment by hanging it in a steamy shower; the creases disappear and you won't have to iron.

Top-stitching is a nice finish for "with nap" gar-ments, but be sure to top stitch in the direction of the nap.

3. Leather, Suede, Vinyl, and Ultrasuede

Preparation

Here is one time when you get off easy: No pre-shrinking is necessary for these fabrics.

Use simply styled patterns that require few seams, darts, and a minimum of easing.

Pin marks will show, so pin in seam allowances and within dart areas only. Transfer pattern markings with chalk to the wrong side of the fabric.

Be sure to fit the pattern to your body *before* cutting—mistakes are much too costly when working with these gems.

Use very sharp scissors for cutting.

Sewing the Garment

Use a leather needle (size 14 to 16) and heavy-duty thread for sewing on leather, suede, and vinyl. Use a very fine needle and polyester thread on Ultrasuede. Test stitch on a scrap to determine the ideal stitch length (a large stitch, but not a basting stitch).

Stitching errors will show, so be *very* careful. Don't pin seams when working with leathers; use paper clips or scotch tape instead. Use very fine pins with Ultra-suede. If skins slip or stick when sewing, place tissue paper between the bottom skin and the throat plate of the machine. Use a roller presser foot so the fabric will roll easily and evenly under the needle.

You'll probably want to line these fabrics; they are usually uncomfortable next to the skin. Use medium- to lightweight perma-press linings. Use fusable interfacings with Ultrasuedes.

If leather seams curl, roll, and won't stay put, glue the seam allowances to the back of the fabric with rubber cement. Top stitching also helps keep seam edges in their place.

The Finishing Touches

Ultrasuede hems are fused into place with a fusable web found in most notions departments. Glue hems on leather garments with rubber cement.

Never steam press on leather, vinyl, or suede. Press with a warm, dry iron over a press cloth or a sheet of brown paper.

When pressing Ultrasuede, use steam only, a synthetic temperature setting, and press on the *wrong side*. If you must press on the right side, use a scrap of Ultra-suede for a press cloth. Restore the nap by brushing if necessary.

4. Sheer Fabrics

Preparation

Most sheer fabrics are soft and drape easily. Choose soft, unfitted styles or styles with gathers. Avoid the tailored look.

Sometimes you'll want to use an underfabric with sheers, for modesty's sake. Be sure to choose an underfabric that is compatible in care requirements with the garment fabric (use a washable lining with a washable sheer.)

Sheers have a tendency to slip and slide as you cut. Prevent this by pinning the fabric to the cutting board or to a sheet that is secured to a table.

Test tailor's chalk or carbon on a scrap *before* using; if they leave permanent marks, use tailor's tacks. When using an underfabric, mark this fabric instead of the sheer.

Sewing the Garment

Always test stitch on a scrap before sewing a seam. Use a very fine, sharp needle. Ball-point needles are great because they won't cut fabric threads. Use fine thread and lightweight nylon zippers. (Snap closings are good on sheer fabrics.)

Loosen the top tension a bit when stitching seams. Support the fabric while you sew; hold the seam at the back of the presser foot and gently guide it with your hands. Use tissue paper on one or both sides of the seam while stitching and for best results, use French seams (see Sew Easy Guide 19).

Sometimes a nice effect is achieved by eliminating the facings. Bind the raw edges instead with self- or contrasting fabric (see Sew Easy Guide 17).

The Finishing Touches

Always test-press on a scrap before ironing on these delicate fabrics. Use steam with discretion; it can cause fibers to permanently pucker.

Hand- or machine-rolled hems are best on circular sheer skirts. (By hand, this hem is made by turning the raw hem edge under twice; one quarter inch each time; and sewing with invisible slip stitches. A machine attachment exists that does this job in a flash.)

5. Metallic Fabrics

Preparation

Choose simply styled patterns to work with and use "with nap" layouts (or buy ⅝ yard more fabric than called for and lay out all pattern pieces in the same direction).

Pin only in the seam allowances and transfer markings with tailor's chalk or tacks; the tracing wheel might break the metallic threads.

This is one time when you definitely *don't* want to use your best scissors; the metallic threads will dull the blades.

Sewing the Garment

Use very fine ball-point pins and needles and synthetic thread. Change needles as they become dull. Use tissue paper while stitching if the fabric sticks or slips, and avoid restitching—ripping may leave permanent marks.

Most metallics will fray, so finish the seam edges with a zigzag stitch.

Metallics are usually irritating to the skin; line these garments for comfort.

The Finishing Touches

For a smooth finish, face the hem with lining material instead of turning up a regular hem.

Always test-press! Creasing a garment too heavily may break threads, and steam may tarnish some metallics. If pressing with an iron is impossible, seams can be pressed with your finger. If your test fabric passes the press test; press on the *wrong* side using a press cloth and a warm setting. Be sure to use a towel when pressing metallics that have a raised surface, and don't press too heavily with the iron.

6. Bias-Cut Fabrics

Preparation

The bias grain is the grain that lies 45 degrees from the vertical grain of a piece of fabric. Find the bias grain by folding a lengthwise edge to meet a crosswise edge—the diagonal line thus formed is the bias grain.

Bias-cut garments have a wonderful draped quality about them. They gracefully flow and glide with you as you move; and they are usually as comfortable as they are elegant (see Figure C. 1).

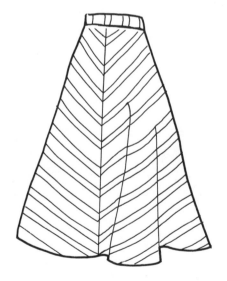

FIGURE C.1. *A striped skirt cut on the bias.*

A stripe fabric cut on the bias produces a chevron effect if you use a pattern with center seams and carefully match all pattern notches.

Virtually any garment (or garment section) can be cut on the bias—skirts, pants, dresses, ruffles. Stick to simple styles for best results and choose a fabric that "gives" or stretches equally in both directions.

The first step is to establish a bias-grain line on each pattern piece. Using a protractor, draw a straight line 45 degrees from the vertical grainline on each pattern section (see Figure C.2). Use the new grain lines to lay out the pattern. If you use patterns that are especially designed to be cut on the bias skip this step entirely. Bias-cut patterns are clearly marked in the pattern catalogues. (Beginners should use these for a while.)

Sewing the Garment

It's a good idea to baste seams and let them hang a day to "stretch out." Refit and then do the final stitching. Always test-stitch on scrap fabric first and be careful not to stretch bias-cut seams as you sew. Pin tissue paper to the back of seams for added protection. The tissue will tear away easily after the seams are sewn.

When joining a piece cut on the bias with a piece cut on the straight of the grain, sew with the bias section on top and be careful not to stretch as you stitch. Use straight seam binding to stabilize a bias-cut seam (see Sew Easy Guide 17), especially when putting in a zipper.

The Finishing Touches

Let a bias-cut garment hang for a day before turning up the hem. Rehang the garment another day after pinning and before stitching the hem. Refit the garment, make the necessary corrections, and then do the final stitching.

Don't forget to test on scrap fabric before pressing. Steam gently; never press sharp creases; and press diagonally across seam lines (with the straight grain of the fabric).

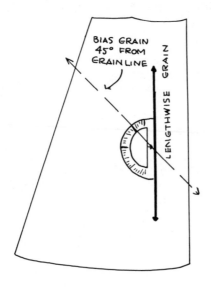

FIGURE C.2. *Establishing a bias grain line.*

Guide D

The Sewing Machine

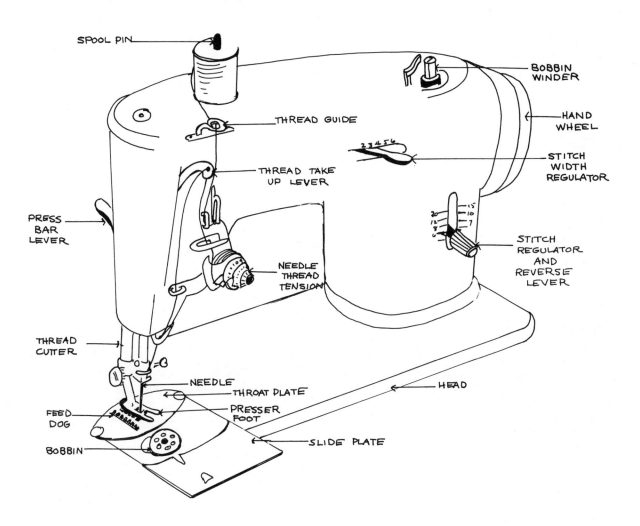

Guide E

Trouble-Shooting Guide for the Sewing Machine

Possible reasons for the needle thread breaking:

The needle is the wrong size. (Replace with correct needle.)

The needle is of inferior quality. (Replace with high-quality needle.)

The needle is blunt or bent. (Replace with new needle.)

The needle is the wrong one for the fabric. (Replace with correct needle.)

The thread is inferior in quality. (Replace with high-quality thread.)

The machine is threaded incorrectly. (Rethread.)

The upper tension is too tight. (Loosen it.)

The needle thread is knotted. (Break the thread, dispose of the knot, and rethread.)

The needle is not fully inserted in the clamp. (Re-insert the needle.)

The needle thread is too thick for the needle. (Replace with correct thread.)

The needle thread is too fine for the fabric. (Replace with correct thread.)

The machine needs cleaning. (Clean it.)

Possible reasons for the bobbin thread breaking:

The bobbin is threaded incorrectly. (Rethread.)

There is a knot in the bobbin thread. (Break the thread, cut off the knot, and rethread.)

The bobbin is wound unevenly. (Dispose of the thread and rewind.)

The bobbin tension is too tight. (Do not try to adjust the bobbin tension. Let the sewing machine service man check and correct this.)

Possible reasons for the machine skip-stitching:

The needle is in backwards. (Take it off and replace it correctly.)

The needle is inserted incorrectly in the clamp. (Re-insert the needle.)

The needle is bent. (Replace with a new needle.)

The machine is threaded incorrectly. (Rethread.)

The needle is the wrong type for the machine. (Replace with correct needle.)

The thread is too thick for the fabric. (Replace with correct thread.)

150

The thread is too thick for the needle size. (Replace with correct thread.)
The needle is the wrong size for the fabric. (Replace with correct needle.)
The thread is inferior in quality. (Replace with high-quality thread.)
The tension is set incorrectly. (Adjust the upper tension. The bobbin tension must be adjusted by a service person.)

Possible reasons for the fabric puckering:

The tension is too tight. (Adjust the upper tension; have the bobbin tension adjusted.)
The stitch is too long. (Shorten it.)
The thread is too thick. (Replace with correct thread.)

Possible reasons for the fabric feeding unevenly:

The feed dog is clogged with dirt or it's disengaged. (Clean and adjust.)
The needle plate is not inserted properly. (Adjust.)
The foot is not suitable for the type of material. (Replace with correct foot.)
The stitch length is wrong. (Change it.)
A loose thread is caught in the presser foot. (Remove it.)

Possible reasons for the needle breaking:

The needle is bent or blunt. (Replace with a new needle.)
The needle is inserted incorrectly or perhaps poorly centered. (Replace the needle.)

The fabric was pulled. (Replace the needle and allow the fabric to move at its own pace.)
You sewed over too thick a seam.
The thread has knots. (Rethread.)
The needle is of poor quality. (Replace with a high-quality needle.)
The upper tension is too tight. (Loosen it.)
The needle is the wrong size. (Replace with correct needle.)

If the machine runs too slowly:

Oil it!

If the machine is too noisy:

Oil it! (Follow the instructions in your owner's manual.)

If the machine won't run:

Plug it in!
The machine is plugged in, but the electrical supply isn't getting through.
If the motor runs, but the machine doesn't, tighten the flywheel.
If the whole machine jams and the needle and bobbin become immobile, don't try to force the machine to work. Disconnect the power source. Carefully remove the material, needle, and bobbin and check for a piece of caught material or thread. Clean the bobbin area and rethread the machine. If it still won't run, call the friendly service man.

Pattern-Size Charts

Women's Sizes

Miss

Size	6	8	10	12	14	16	18	20
Bust	30½*	31½	32½	34	36	38	40	42
Waist	23	24	25	26½	28	30	32	34
Hip	32½	33½	34½	36	38	40	42	44
Back-waist length	15½	15¾	16	16¼	16½	16¾	17	17¼

*Note: All measurements are in inches unless otherwise marked.

Miss Petite

Size	6mp	8mp	10mp	12mp	14mp	16mp
Bust	30½	31½	32½	34	36	38
Waist	23½	24½	25½	27	28½	30½
Hip	32½	33½	34½	36	38	40
Back-waist length	14½	14¾	15	15½	15½	15¾

Junior

Size	5	7	9	11	13	15
Bust	30	31	32	33½	35	37
Waist	22½	23½	24½	25½	27	29
Hip	32	33	34	35½	37	39
Back-waist length	15	15½	15½	15¾	16	16¼

Junior Petite

Size	3jp	5jp	7jp	9jp	11jp	13jp
Bust	30	31	32	33	34	35
Waist	22	23	24	25	26	27
Hip	31	32	33	34	35	36
Back-waist length	14	14¼	14½	14¾	15	15¼

Young Junior/Teen

Size	5/6	7/8	9/10	11/12	13/14	15/16
Bust	28	29	30½	32	33½	35
Waist	22	23	24	25	26	27
Hips	31	32	33½	35	36½	38
Back-waist length	13½	14	14½	15	15⅜	15¾

Women's

Size	38	40	42	44	46	48	50	
Bust	42	44	46	48	50	52	54	
Waist	35	37	39	41½	44	46½	49	
Hips	44	46	48	50	52	54	56	
Back-waist length	17¼	17⅜	17½	17⅝	17¾	17⅞	18	

Half-Sizes

Bust	33	35	37	39	41	43	45	47
Waist	27	29	31	33	35	37½	40	42½
Hips	35	37	39	41	43	45½	48	50½
Back-waist length	15	15¼	15½	15¾	15⅞	16	16⅛	16¼

Many of you will want to select a pattern size that is one inch smaller in the bust than your actual bust measurement. Pattern companies add two to three inches to the pattern bust measurement when they print the paper pattern to allow for a comfortable fit. Two to three inches is a little more room than you will want or need, so rather than buy a pattern by your exact bust measurement and have to take it in, buy a pattern with a bust measurement slightly smaller than your own and it will fit perfectly. (This applies to the bust measurement *only*).

Children's Sizes

Babies
For infants who are not yet walking.

Size	Newborn (1-3 months)	6 months
Weight	7-13 pounds	13-18 pounds
Height	17-24 inches	24-26½ inches

Toddlers

Between a baby and a child. Toddlers' pants have a diaper allowance. Dresses in Toddler sizes are shorter than the similar Child's size.

Size	½	1	2	3	4
Breast/chest	19	20	21	22	23
Waist	19	19½	20	20½	21
Finished-dress length	14	15	16	17	18
Approx. height	28	31	34	37	40

Children

Size	2	3	4	5	6	6x
Breast/chest	21	22	23	24	25	25½
Waist	20	20½	21	21½	22	22½
Hips			24	25	26	26½
Back-waist length	8½	9	9½	10	10½	10¾
Approx. height	35	38	41	44	47	48
Finished-dress length	18	19	20	22	24	25

Girls

For the girl who has not yet begun to mature.

Size	7	8	10	12	14
Breast/chest	26	27	28½	30	32
Waist	23	23½	24½	25½	26½
Hips	27	28	30	32	34
Back-waist length	11½	12	12¾	13½	14½
Approx. height	50	52	56	58½	61

Chubby

For the growing girl who is over the average weight for her age and height.

Size	8½c	10½c	12½c	14½c
Breast	30	31½	33	34½
Waist	28	29	30	31
Hips	33	34½	36	37½
Back-waist length	12½	13¼	14	14¾
Approx. height	52	56	58½	61

Boys' and Men's Sizes

Boys and Teen-boys
For growing boys and young men who have not yet reached adult stature.

	Boys					Teen-boys		
Size	7	8	10	12	14	16	18	20
Chest	26	27	28	30	32	33½	35	36½
Waist	23	24	25	26	27	28	29	30
Hips	27	28	29½	31	32½	34	35½	37
Neck	11¼	11½	12	12½	13	13½	14	14½
Neckband**	11¾	12	12½	13	13½	14	14½	15
Height	48	50	54	58	61	64	66	68
Shirt sleeve	22⅜	23¼	25	26¾	29	30	31	32

Men's
For men of average build about 5′10″ without shoes.*

Size	34	36	38	40	42	44	46	48
Chest	34	36	38	40	42	44	46	48
Waist	28	30	32	34	36	39	42	44
Hips	35	37	39	41	43	45	47	49
Neck	13½	14	14½	15	15½	16	16½	17
Neckband**	14	14½	15	15½	16	16½	17	17½
Shirt sleeve	32	32	33	33	34	34	35	35

*Men over 5′10″ tall, buy the pattern closest to actual size and lengthen it to fit. (see Chapter 7 on altering patterns.)
**This is a ready-to-wear figure, not a body measurement, and is given here for reference.

Glossary of Sewing Terms

Adjustable space guide An adjustable attachment for the sewing machine that aids in quilting and in sewing perfectly even seams.

Adjustment line A double line printed on a pattern piece that indicates where the piece can be lengthened or shortened.

Alterations Adjustments for fit made on the pattern *before* cutting. Also, adjustments made in fitting the basted garment.

Appliqué A separate design motif sewn to a fabric or garment.

Armhole, or Armscye The opening in a garment for the arm or sleeve.

Assembling Joining the major pieces of a garment together.

Back-stitching Hand or machine stitching used to reinforce the stitching at the beginning or end of a seam.

Ball-point needle A needle with a rounded tip which separates fabric threads instead of piercing them.

Basting Long stitches made by hand or by machine to hold two pieces of fabric together temporarily. Used to join garment sections together for fitting and to keep fabric from slipping during final stitching.

Belting Stiffening used at the waistline of garments and to back belts.

Bias The diagonal grain of the fabric—45 degrees from the straight of the grain. The true bias is found by folding the crosswise edge to the lengthwise edge. The diagonal line thus formed is the bias.

Bias tape A thin, folded strip of cotton, nylon, or rayon cut diagonally—on the bias—so that it will stretch smoothly over curved and straight edges.

Blind-stitch A hand stitch used for hems and finishing work that is invisible from the right side of the garment. Most modern zigzag machines have a blind-stitch pattern.

Bonding A foundation of lining attached to a weakened fabric to give it strength.

Bobbin The spool holding the lower of the two threads of a sewing machine.

Bodice The portion of a garment above the waist not including the sleeves or collar.

Bodkin A blunt needle-type gadget used to pull material through narrow, enclosed spaces. Excellent for making belt loops and for drawing elastic, ribbon, and cord through casings.

Bolt The unit in which fabric is packaged and sold by

the manufacturer. There are usually twelve to twenty yards to a bolt.

Bound buttonholes Buttonholes finished with a fabric binding.

Box pleat Two pleats that turn away from one another to form a box shape on the right side.

Buttonhole twist A strong silk thread used to attach buttons and fasteners to garments. Also used for making eyelets, worked buttonholes, and belt loops.

Carriers Thread or fabric loops attached to a garment to support a belt or sash.

Casing A hem through which ribbon, tape, cord, elastic, or a curtain rod can be run.

Catch-stitch A cross-stitch made by hand, used to hold a raw edge in place. An excellent hem-stitch for knits.

Center line The vertical center of the bodice, skirt, or yoke section of a garment.

Chain-stitch An interlocking stitch used in hand-embroidery.

Clip A snip into the seam allowance or selvage with the point of the scissors. Used on curved seams, square corners, and buttonholes so seams will lie flat when pressed.

Closure The area on to which zippers, buttons, and fasteners are placed to open and close a garment.

Convertible A notched collar that can be worn either buttoned at the neck or open with lapels.

Crease A line made by folding the fabric and pressing the fold. Also refers to the line that may result when the manufacturer folds the fabric and rolls it onto the bolt.

Crosswise grain The threads that run across the width of the fabric, from selvage to selvage.

Cutting line A long, unbroken line printed on the pattern that indicates where to cut (sometimes accompanied by a drawing of scissors).

Dart A stitched fold of fabric that tapers to a point at one or both ends. Used to shape the garment to the body.

Decorative stitching Zigzag machine-stitching done for decorative effects; and hand-embroidery.

Directional stitching Stitching seams *with* the grain of the fabric to prevent stretching.

Dolman sleeve A sleeve cut all in one piece with the bodice. The armhole usually extends to the waist, or just above.

Drape The result of a fabric falling gracefully into folds.

Dressmaker's carbon A marking carbon, available in several colors, used with a tracing wheel to transfer pattern construction symbols to the fabric.

Ease Process of fitting two unequal-sized pieces of fabric together (without forming gathers or tucks) by evenly distributing the fullness along the seam. Used most commonly to set in sleeves.

Ease allowance The extra width added to body measurements in a pattern to leave room for movement.

Edge-stitch Machine-stitching on the right side of a garment, close to a finished edge or seam.

Embroidery Decorative needlework done on fabric with either silk, cotton, or metal threads. Can be done by machine or by hand.

Emery bag Small bag filled with emery powder used to sharpen and remove rust from pins and needles.

Eyelet A small hole in a garment, finished by hand or with a metal ring, to hold the prong of a buckle or lacings.

Facing A second layer of fabric (usually the same as the garment) sewn to necklines, front and back openings, armholes, and sleeves to finish raw edges.

Fastenings Any device used to open and close a garment—zippers, hooks and eyes, snaps, buttons, frogs, etc.

Feed dogs The ridged pieces of metal or plastic on the bed of the sewing machine that move back and forth and push the fabric along beneath the needle.

Finish (see Seam finish).

Flat-fell A sturdy, double-stitched seam used on men's clothes, tailored blouses, and sportswear.

Fly front A finished closing used in pants and top coats that conceals the zipper or buttons.

Foot A sewing machine attachment used to hold fabric in place while stitching. Comes in a wide variety of designs.

French seam A small, neat, double-stitched seam used in children's wear and on sheer fabrics.

Gathering Fabric pulled up on rows of stitching to create fullness.

Gore A section of a skirt that's fuller at the bottom than at the top.

Grading Trimming seam allowances to different widths to reduce bulk and make the seam lie flat.

Grain The direction of fabric threads. In woven fabrics there are lengthwise and crosswise yarns which produce lengthwise and crosswise grains. When the two threads are at right angles, the fabric is "on the true grain."

Grain-line arrow The double-ended arrow on the pattern piece which indicates how it should be placed on the fabric for cutting—on the lengthwise, crosswise, or bias grain of the fabric.

Gusset A small triangular piece of fabric set into a slash to give added ease; usually placed at the underarm.

Hand The feel of a fabric.

Haute couture High fashion.

Heading The top edge of curtains—above the casing.

Hem An edge finish where the edge is folded under and stitched into place. Usually used at the bottom of a garment.

Hemline The line on which a hem is marked and turned under.

Hoop A two-part circular wood, metal, or plastic frame used to hold fabric taut when embroidering. Available in various sizes.

Inset A piece of fabric or trim inserted into a garment for fit or decoration.

Instruction sheet A guide enclosed with each pattern showing how to identify and assemble the pattern pieces.

Interfacing A special fabric sewn between the garment and facing fabrics at necklines, collars, cuffs, pockets, plackets, armholes, and waistbands to strengthen, shape, support, stiffen, and prevent stretching.

Intersecting seams Seams that cross one another when the major garment sections are sewn together.

Inverted pleat Pleats pressed toward each other.

Iron-ons Interfacing fabrics, patches, seam bindings, and fusing agents that are pressed rather than sewn into place.

Joinings The points at which one section of a garment is joined to another—skirt and bodice, sleeve and bodice, etc.

Kick pleat A short pleat at the bottom of a skirt to give walking room.

Kimono sleeve A sleeve cut all in one with the bodice.

Knife pleats A series of pleats that all turn in the same direction.

Lap To extend or fold one piece of fabric over another.

Lapel The section of a garment, between the top button and collar, which is turned back along a fold line.

Lapped seam A seam in which one seam allowance is laid over another and top-stitched.

Layout The way pattern pieces are laid on the fabric for cutting (indicated by diagrams on the pattern instruction sheet).

Lengthwise grain The threads of a fabric running parallel to the selvages, and perpendicular to the crosswise grain.

Line The style or effect given by the cut and construction of a garment.

Lining A suitable fabric constructed in the shape of the garment to cover and finish the inside of the garment. Adds body and helps hold the shape of the garment.

Markings The pattern construction symbols that are transferred from the pattern to the fabric by means of tailor's tacks, chalk, bastings, or tracing wheel.

Matching The joining together of construction markings—notches, for example.

Miter The diagonal line formed when fabric, a band, or lace is joined at a square corner. After seaming, the excess fabric is usually cut away on the underside.

Motif Unit of design in a decoration or pattern.

Muslin A garment made of muslin or inexpensive fabric that serves as an alteration and cutting guide for making the same garment in a more expensive fabric.

Needle board A board, covered with fine pieces of wire, used for pressing napped fabrics.

Notches V-shaped markings on pattern edge that indicate which edges are to be seamed together and where. Matching notches are to be joined.

Notions Sewing supplies, usually small items, such as thread, needles, pins, buttons, etc.

Off-grain Fabric that is *not* cut or printed on the true grain; or fabric that was pulled out of shape when it was rolled on the bolt.

Overcasting A zigzag or slanting stitch used over the raw edge of a fabric to keep it from raveling.

Overlap The part of a garment that extends over

another part, as at the opening of a blouse, jacket, coat, or waistband.

Patching A mending technique using an extra piece of fabric to cover a hole.

Patchwork Fabric formed by joining different patches of fabric together. Formerly used for quilts; now popular in dressmaking.

Pattern layout guide Instructions and diagrams included in a pattern that show how to place the pattern pieces on the fabric for cutting.

Piecing Sewing pieces of fabric together to form a single larger piece of fabric.

Pin-basting A form of basting for machine-stitching where pins are placed perpendicular to the seam line.

Pivot To turn the fabric on the machine needle while the needle is still in the fabric—used when stitching square and pointed corners.

Placement line A line printed on a pattern that indicates where buttonholes, pockets, pleats, and trims are to be placed.

Placket An opening in a garment that is finished with a visible strip of fabric running the length of the opening. Usually closed by a zipper, snaps, or hooks and eyes.

Pleats Folds of fabric used to add fullness to a garment. Many varieties exist.

Preshrinking Shrinking of fabric before cutting so that the dimensions of the finished garment won't alter during washing or dry cleaning.

Presser foot The part of a sewing machine that holds fabric steady during sewing.

Press cloth A cloth used between the iron and the garment fabric to protect the fabric during pressing.

Press mitt A padded mitt used in pressing and shaping a garment section.

Pressure The force exerted by the pressure foot on the fabric during stitching. Pressure can be regulated to suit the fabric.

Quilting A design of hand- or machine-stitches running through two thicknesses of fabric with a layer of padding in between.

Raglan sleeve A sleeve joined to the bodice along a diagonal line extending from the armhole to the neckline.

Ravel To unweave or fray, as when threads pull out from the edge of the fabric.

Raw edge The unfinished edge of a piece of fabric.

Reinforcing Strengthening an area that will be subjected to strain—either with an underlay of fabric, or with extra rows of stitching.

Remnant An unsold end from a bolt of fabric; or a leftover piece of fabric.

Return The distance from the curtain rod to the wall. Curtains and draperies are made to extend around the curved return.

Right side The finished side of a piece of fabric; or the outside of a garment.

Ripping Removing machine-stitching with a seam ripper.

Ruffle A band of fabric that is gathered and added to a garment as trim or decoration.

Running-stitch The simplest hand-stitch. The thread appears on both sides of the fabric, with stitches of approximately equal length.

Sag The degree to which a garment stretches after handling or wearing.

Satin-stitch An embroidery stitch, done by hand or machine, consisting of rows of closely spaced zigzag stitches.

Seam The line of stitching formed by sewing two pieces of fabric together.

Seam allowance The amount of fabric extending beyond the stitching line, usually ⅝ inch.

Seam binding Rayon, silk, or nylon ribbon, one-half to one inch wide, used to reinforce certain seams or to finish raw edges.

Seam finish The finish used on the raw edge of a seam allowance to keep it from raveling or fraying.

Seamline (also called **Stitching line**) The long broken line printed on the pattern designating where a seam is to be sewn; usually ⅝ inch from the cutting line.

Seam ripper The tool used for removing machine stitches.

Secure To fasten permanently with a knot or backstitch.

Self Of the same material as the rest of the garment.

Selvage The finished narrow border on the lengthwise edges of all woven fabric.

Shank The stem between the button and the garment, made with thread or part of the button, that allows the buttonhole to fit smoothly over the button.

Shirring Two or more rows of hand- or machine-gathering, usually used decoratively.

Slash A long, straight cut in a fabric; longer than a clip.

Sleeve board A small padded board (sometimes two joined together) used for pressing small areas, sleeves, and pant legs.

Smocking A decorative way of gathering fabric. Can be done by hand or machine.

Stay-stitch A line of machine stitching, just outside of the seam line, made before assembling the garment to prevent curved or bias cut edges from stretching.

Straightening Working with fabric to correct the grainline.

Straight of the goods The lengthwise grain of the fabric.

Tack Small hand-stitches used to hold two pieces of fabric together. Used to attach a facing to a seam allowance.

Tailor's ham A large cushion (in the shape of a ham) used for ironing the shaped sections of a garment such as darts and sleeve caps.

Tailor's tacks Temporary hand-stitches used to transfer pattern markings to the fabric.

Take-up lever The lever on the sewing machine used to raise and lower the presser foot.

Taper Cutting or stitching at a slight angle. Usually used to make a garment gradually smaller.

Tension The degree of looseness or tightness of the bobbin and needle threads of the sewing machine. When the needle and bobbin threads are drawn into the fabric to the same degree, the tension is balanced.

Thread tracing Basting over pattern markings on the wrong side of the fabric so that the markings will show on the front side of the fabric.

Throat plate A flat metal piece in the bed of the sewing machine with a hole in it through which the needle passes as it stitches.

Top-stitching A line of machine-stitching done on the outside of a garment, parallel to a seam or finished edge. Used for decoration and to accent style lines.

Tracing wheel A small wheel with serrated edges used with dressmaker's carbon to transfer pattern markings to the fabric.

Trapunto A quilting technique in which the design is outlined with stitches; and then each part of the design is filled separately, giving a high relief effect.

Trimming Cutting away excess fabric in the seam allowance after a seam has been sewn. Also, a decorative lace, ribbon, or braid.

Tucks Evenly stitched, straight folds of fabric.

Underlap A part of a garment that extends under another part; as in the opening of a jacket, coat, or waistband.

Under-stitching A row of stitches through the facing and seam allowance and close to the seamline that holds the facing in place and prevents it from rolling to the outside.

Vent A lapped opening used in the hems of tailored jackets, and elsewhere.

Weights Metal discs sewn into hemlines for proper hang.

With nap Pattern designation indicating that napped fabric is to be used and therefore all pattern pieces must be laid out in the same direction on the fabric.

Wrong side The unfinished side of the fabric, or the inside of a garment.

Yardage The amount of fabric needed to make a garment.

Yoke The fitted portion of a garment, usually at the shoulders or hips, from which the rest of the garment hangs.

Zigzag stitch A machine-stitch made by a back-and-forth sideways needle movement. Great for finishing raw edges and for sewing knits; also used for decorative purposes. (The satin-stitch is no more than a closely spaced zigzag stitch.)

Zipper foot A sewing machine foot designed especially for stitching zippers.

Guide H

Sew-Easy Guide to Basic Procedures

In this section:

Altering Patterns. See Chapter 7

Altering Second-Hand Clothes. See Chapter 10

Appliqué. See Chapter 11

1. Basting

Basting is a temporary stitch used to hold pieces of fabric together until after the final machine-stitching, at which time the basting stitches are removed. Basting makes seaming and fitting easier and guarantees a look of quality craftsmanship to the finished product.

Hand-basting

Always baste on a flat surface. Wear a thimble, and use thread that contrasts with the fabric so that the basting stands out.

Use silk thread on fine fabrics or when basting on the top side of a garment to hold the layers of fabric in place during the final pressing. Silk thread doesn't leave marks that show after pressing and it won't mar fine fabrics.

To prepare for basting, pin seams together at the ends, the notches, and at the center. Then, starting from the center and working toward the seam ends, place pins at equal intervals. Pin at right angles to the seam line (Figure H.1).

Thread a long, slender needle with a single strand of thread no longer than thirty inches in length. Knot the longer end of the thread and baste a fraction of an inch outside of the seam line with an even *running-stitch*. When you reach the end of a line of basting, fasten with a *back-stitch* (see Sew-Easy Guide 11).

Remove bastings by clipping stitches every three to five inches. Pull out the threads. Clip the back stitch separately; don't try to pull it out.

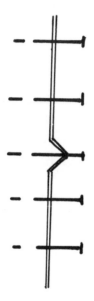

FIGURE H.1. *Pinning seams together.*

Machine-basting

Machine-basting is particularly handy when you want to double-check a questionable fit. Be sure the needle marks won't show on the fabric before using this technique.

Pin seams together. Set the stitch length at 6 (or to the longest stitch on your machine) and stitch a fraction of an inch outside of the seamline.

To remove, clip the top thread every five stitches or so and pull the bottom thread out.

Pin-basting

I use this technique whenever possible. It's a time-saver, but can only be used successfully on straight seams and on easy-to-handle fabrics. If the fabric is expensive, slips and slides easily, or is marred by ripping, you'd better forget this trick and hand-baste instead.

Pin the seams as with other kinds of basting, only pin more often.

Pin at right angles to the seam line, on the top side of the fabric, barely nipping the fabric at the seam line with each pin. If you're using a seam guide, be sure that the pins point toward the seam edge.

Machine stitch very carefully and for best results, use a hinged presser foot. If the machine has difficulty sewing over pins, remove each pin just before it passes under the needle. After a few needle breaks, take the hint and slow down.

2. Belts and Belt Loops

Belts

The basic belt consists of a stiffening called belting, a buckle, eyelets, and a piece of the garment fabric.

Cut the belting four inches longer than your waist and shape one end to a point (Figure H.2). Cut a strip of fabric three inches longer than the belting and twice the width plus 1¼ inches for seam allowances. Fasten a safety pin to the right side and close to one end of the fabric piece. (The pin will be helpful in turning the belt.) Fold the fabric around the belting, wrong side out. Be sure the safety pin is at the pointed end of the belting.

Stitch close to the belting using a zipper foot. Don't catch the belting in the stitches. Slide the fabric around so that the seam is in the center of the belt. Trim the seam allowance to one-quarter inch and press open. Stitch the shaped end close to the belting, back-stitching at each end. Trim the seam allowance to one-quarter inch and remove the belting (Figure H.3).

FIGURE H.2. *Shaping the belt.*

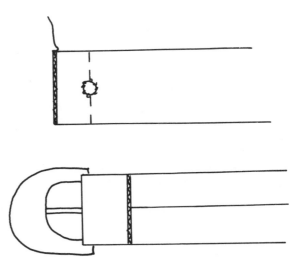

FIGURE H.4. *Adding the belt buckle.*

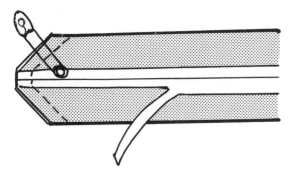

FIGURE H.3. *Trimming the seam allowance on the belt.*

Turn the belt right side out, working the safety pin toward the open end. Push the pointed end out with an orange stick, center the lengthwise seam, and press.

Insert the belting. *Top-stitch* around the right side of the belt close to the edge, if desired for effect (see Sew-Easy Guide 21).

Try on the finished belt. Mark the center front line on each belt end. Trim the unfinished end to 2 inches from the center line. Machine-stitch one-quarter inch from the unfinished end and overcast the edges.

Pierce a hole for the buckle on the center line marking at the unfinished end of the belt. Overcast the edges of the hole by hand using a buttonhole stitch (see Sew-Easy Guide 11). Slip the buckle prong through the hole. Turn back the unfinished end and fasten it to the belt with *slip-stitches* (Figure H.4; Sew-Easy Guide 11).

Insert one eyelet on the center line marking at the pointed end of the belt and one on either side of this mark. Use commercial eyelets and install according to the package directions.

As an alternative to assembling the belt components yourself, buy a belt kit complete with belting, a self-cover buckle, and eyelets. Construct the belt according to the kit instructions. Belt kits are found in the notions section of most fabric stores.

Or why not splurge and go all out for quality craftsmanship? Find a belt manufacturer in the Yellow Pages. Sometimes professional buttonholers make belts as well. Do a little comparative phone shopping for the best deal. Take the belter as much fabric as you can spare (one-fourth yard is more than enough); any unused fabric will be returned

Belt Loops

Thread Loops

Thread loops hold a belt in place at the waist of a dress—one at each side seam does the trick.

Mark the position for the loops with pins on the right side of the garment at the side seams.

Use buttonhole twist or a double strand of thread and knot one end. Take a few back-stitches on the underside of the garment at the top marking. Bring the needle through to the front side of the garment at this spot. Make a stitch at the bottom mark, leaving enough slack between the top and bottom marks for the belt to fit through.

Sew back and forth between the two marks a few times. Using the *buttonhole stitch*, work over the strands of thread, drawing the stitches firmly up against one another along the length of the thread loops (Figure H.5; Sew-Easy Guide 11). Fasten the threads to the underside of the garment with back-stitches.

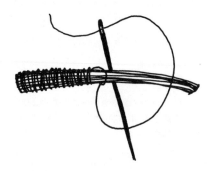

FIGURE H.5. *Finishing a thread loop.*

Fabric Loops

Fabric belt loops are placed on the waistband of skirts, pants, and shorts. Usually five or seven loops fit on a garment (one at each side seam; one at the center back; two more in back, spaced equally from the center back loop; and two more in the front.)

Cut a fabric strip, on the lengthwise grain, for each loop. Each belt loop should be long enough to accommodate the belt, plus three-fourths inch. The width of each strip should be two times the finished width of the loops (usually one-quarter to one-half inch wide), plus one-half inch for seam allowances.

Fold each strip lengthwise (right sides together) around a piece of string cut two inches longer than the fabric strip. Stitch one-quarter inch from the length-

wise edge and stitch the loop closed very close to one end (Figure H.6). (Be sure to catch the string in the closing stitches.) Trim the lengthwise seam to one-eighth inch and press the seam open with your fingers.

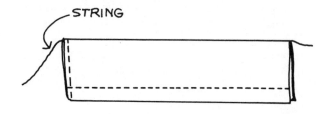

FIGURE H.6. *Stitching a fabric loop.*

Pull the string from the unstitched end; the loop will easily turn right side out. Clip off the stitched end and string; center the lengthwise seam; and press.

Finish the ends of each belt loop with a machine overcast or zigzag stitch. Mark the top and bottom position of each loop on the waistband with pins. Fold the finished ends of each loop under one-eighth to one-quarter inch and press.

Position each loop on the waistband and top-stitch into place. Carefully stitch back and forth over the first line of stitching to secure the loop (Figure H.7). Pull the thread ends to the underside and tie (see Sew-Easy Guide 19).

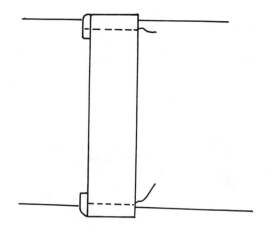

FIGURE H.7. *Securing the fabric loop.*

3. Buttonholes

Several types of buttonholes exist to choose from: Bound buttonholes add a touch of class to any creation; the machine-worked kind are suitable for sportswear.

Here are a few basic rules that apply to *all* buttonholes:

Buy the buttons *before* constructing the garment.

The pattern indicates the size of the buttons to be used and the exact positioning of the buttonholes on the garment.

Transfer all buttonhole markings to the *wrong side* of the fabric and baste (thread trace) over these markings so they'll show up on the *right* side of the garment (Figure H.8).

Use a ruler to make sure that the buttonholes are perfectly aligned with one another. The vertical placement lines should lie on the vertical grain of the fabric and be exactly parallel to one another. Make sure that the horizontal buttonhole markings are at right angles to the vertical markings.

Respace buttonholes after lengthening or shortening the pattern section where the buttons occur. The buttons should be evenly spaced; the last button no closer than four inches from the bottom of the hem. If you change the size of the buttons, be sure to make the necessary changes in the size of the buttonholes. The buttonhole width is equal to the diameter of the button plus one-eighth inch to allow for the shank. For a thick button, add one-quarter inch to the button diameter and add one-quarter inch to the distance around a ball button. Test the buttonhole length on a scrap of fabric.

Interface all areas containing buttonholes using a lightweight interfacing. Baste the interfacing into position before beginning the buttonholes so it won't slip or slide while you work.

Always make a trial buttonhole on scraps using the same fabrics and the same number of layers you'll be working with on the garment.

One more rule to remember: Women's buttonholes belong on the right side of a garment and men's on the left. Pay attention to this little bit of convention—you'd be surprised how difficult it is to get in and out of a shirt that buttons backwards.

Bound Buttonholes

Bound buttonholes are made in the garment *before* the facings are attached.

This simple procedure requires that an extra strip of garment fabric be cut on the crosswise grain for each buttonhole. Each fabric strip should be 1 inch wide and 1 inch longer than the width of the buttonhole.

Baste down the center of each fabric strip. With the wrong side of the fabric facing up, fold the edges of the strip to meet at the center marking (Figure H.9).

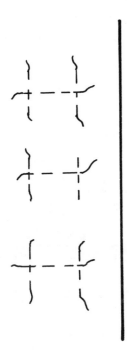

FIGURE H.8. *Transferring the buttonhole markings to the right side of the fabric.*

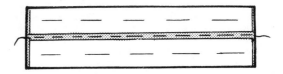

FIGURE H.9. *Making bound buttonholes; basting the fabric strip.*

Baste the center of the strip over the buttonhole marking, with the cut edges facing up. The ends of the strip should extend one-half inch beyond the ends of the markings.

Starting along one side, machine-stitch one-eighth inch from the center marking using small stitches. Cross each end at the vertical marking, being sure to take the same number of stitches on each side of the center line (Figure H.10). Overlap the stitches where you began and tie off the thread ends (see Sew-Easy Guide 19).

Sew the hook to the underside of the left-hand closing, ⅛″ from the edge. Sew the round eye to the underside of the right-hand closing so that the eye protrudes just beyond the edge of the garment. Fasten the hook and eye; the garment edges should meet exactly (Figure H.17).

Turn the garment so that the right side faces up. Fold the garment back at each end of the buttonhole. Pull the triangular sections away from the hole to square the corners. Secure the ends by stitching back and forth across the triangular sections and the ends of the fabric strip (Figure H.12). Trim to one-quarter inch.

Add the facings to the garment after the buttonholes are finished. Slit the facing behind each buttonhole, turn under the raw edges, and slip-stitch the facing to the back of the buttonhole (see Sew-Easy Guide 11).

The easiest way to make a series of bound button-

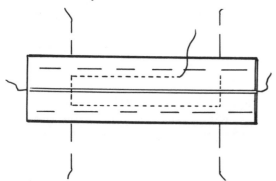

FIGURE H.10. *Machine-stitching bound buttonholes.*

FIGURE H.11. *Cutting the buttonhole.*

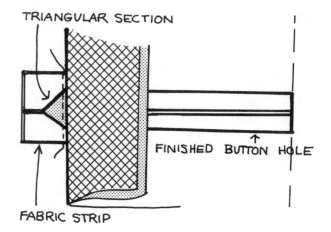

FIGURE H.12. *Finishing the bound buttonhole.*

holes is to complete the same step on each buttonhole before moving on to the next step. This kind of organization saves time.

Machine-worked Buttonholes

Machine-worked buttonholes are best suited for casual clothes, especially if they will be machine-washed frequently.

Always make a sample buttonhole on scrap fabric first.

Attach the facings *before* making machine-worked buttonholes.

Use the buttonhole attachment or a special built-in zigzag mechanism, and follow the directions for making buttonholes in your sewing machine instruction manual. For extra strong buttonholes, restitch the buttonhole a second time.

4. Buttons and Other Fastenings

Buttons

Always use the correct thread to attach buttons to a garment: buttonhole twist, heavy duty thread, or a double strand of cotton pulled through beeswax. Beeswax prevents annoying knots from forming while sewing. The thread should be no longer than eighteen inches in length.

The placement of the buttons on a garment is important. Poorly spaced buttons can destroy a good fit.

Finish the buttonholes first, then pin the garment closed matching the centers vertically. Insert a pin through each buttonhole to mark the button position on the underlapped section (Figure H.13). Buttons should be placed exactly on the center line and directly underneath the horizontal buttonholes and one-eighth inch below the top of vertical buttonholes.

Buttons that don't have metal shanks should be sewn on to the garment with a thread shank. Take several small stitches on the right side of the garment where the button is to be placed to secure the thread. Bring the thread up through the button. Place a matchstick, heavy pin, or toothpick on top of the button and sew back and forth through the button and the fabric until the button is secure.

Bring the thread to the right side of the fabric underneath the button. Pull out the pin, matchstick, or toothpick. Holding the button up to the top of the stitches, wind the thread around the stitches between the button and the fabric to form a shank. Take a few small back-stitches into the shank to secure the thread (Figure H.14).

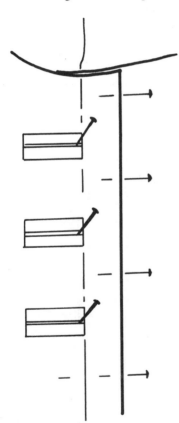

FIGURE H.13. *Marking for button placement with pins.*   FIGURE H.14. *Making a thread shank.*

SEW-EASY GUIDES TO BASIC PROCEDURES   **167**

Don't sew buttons on too tightly. They will work loose and fall off, the thread will break; or the fabric underneath the buttons will tear.

Snaps

Snaps are seldom used by themselves, but are usually used with hooks and eyes, or buttons to hold an edge flat.

Place the ball part of the snap on the wrong side of the garment one-eighth inch from the finished edge of the overlapping section. Sew it into place taking about five stitches in each hole. Stitch underneath the snap between each hole (Figure H.15). Stitch only through the facing and interfacing so that the stitches won't be visible from the top of the garment. Fasten with two small back stitches underneath the snap.

Chalk the ball part of the snap and press it against the underlapping section as you would in closing the garment. Position the socket over this mark and sew into place, using the same technique as for attaching the ball section.

Hooks and eyes

Hooks and eyes are most commonly used at neck edges and waistbands. Overlapping edges take a hook on the overlap and a straight eye on the underlap.

Sew the hook to the underside of the overlap about one-eighth inch from the edge. Stitch around each metal ring, sewing through the facing and interfacing *only* so that the stitches won't show from the top of the garment. Slide the needle under the hook and sew the hook end to the garment to hold it in place. Secure with a back-stitch.

Close the overlap and mark the underlap with a pin where the bend of the hook falls. Place the straight eye over the marking and sew through each metal ring catching all layers of fabric. Secure the thread with a back-stitch (Figure H.16).

Edges that meet rather than overlap take a hook on the one side of the closing and a round eye on the other. Sew the hook to the underside of the left-hand closing, ⅛" from the edge. Sew the round eye to the under-

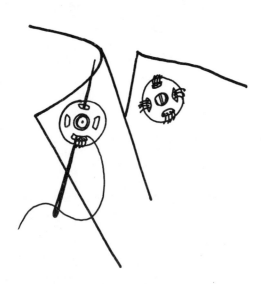

FIGURE H.15. *Sewing on snaps.*

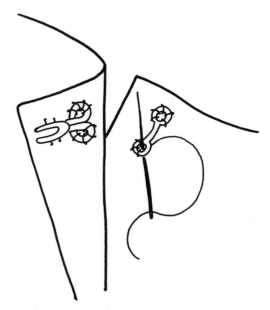

FIGURE H.16. *Sewing a hook and eye on an overlapping opening.*

side of the right-hand closing so that the eye protrudes just beyond the edge of the garment. Fasten the hook and eye; the garment edges should meet exactly (Figure H. 17).

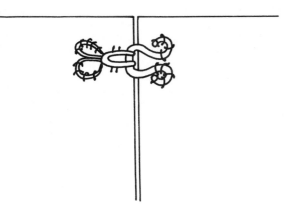

FIGURE H.17. *A hook and eye on edges that meet.*

5. Collars

There are about as many different types of collars as there are dress styles. Instructions on the two most commonly used collars follow.

The Classic Collar (or, the Convertible Collar)

This collar is made up of a top collar, an under collar, and an interfacing. The *interfacing* gives the collar its shape.

Cut the interfacing from the top collar pattern piece. Draw the stitching line and pivot points lightly on the interfacing with colored chalk or pencil. Pin the interfacing to the wrong side of the collar. Clip the corners of the interfacing diagonally inside the pivot point. Baste the interfacing into place, and trim it close to the bastings at the neckline edge only.

Pin the undercollar to the top collar, right sides together, matching the pattern markings. Baste the two collar sections together around the three outside edges —leave the neck edge open.

Machine-stitch the two collar sections together with

FIGURE H.18. *The classic collar.*

the interfacing side up so you can follow the stitching guide-line (Figure H.19).

Trim the interfacing to one-eighth inch and the collar seam allowance to one-quarter inch along the sides and the bottom edge. If the bottom edge of the collar is curved, clip the seam allowance every one-half inch or so. Clip the points diagonally.

Turn the collar to the right side and *carefully* push out the points of the collar with an orange stick—*never push out the points with a scissors.*

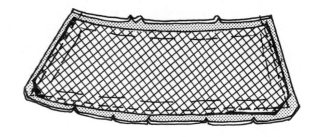

FIGURE H.19. *Machine-stitching the classic collar.*

SEW-EASY GUIDES TO BASIC PROCEDURES **169**

Gently roll the collar seams slightly to the underside so that the seams are not visible from the top of the collar. Baste with silk thread to hold the seams in place and press *using a press cloth*.

Stay-stitch the neckline of the garment, (see Sew-Easy Guide 20) and clip the neck edge every one-half inch, being careful not to clip across the stay-stitching. Pin and baste the collar to the garment neckline with the interfaced side up (Figure H.20).

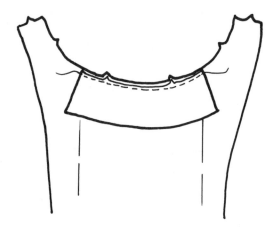

FIGURE H.20. *Basting the classic collar to the garment.*

Pin, baste, and stitch the extended facing to the back facing, right sides together. Press seams open, and finish the facing edges (see Sew-Easy Guide 9).

Fold the extended facings back along the fold lines, right sides together. Pin, baste, and stitch the facings to the collar and the garment neckline. Trim the seam allowances to one-quarter inch. *Under-stitch* (see Sew-Easy Guide 9) to prevent the facings from rolling out (Figure H.21).

Turn the facings to the inside and press. Tack the facings to the garment at the shoulder seams with small hand-stitches (Figure H.22).

Shirt Collars

Shirt collars are sewn first to a neckband which is attached to the garment.

Construct the collar section the same as for the classic collar. Stay-stitch the garment neckline and clip

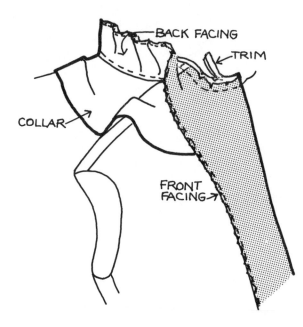

FIGURE H.21. *Attaching the facing to the classic collar.*

at one-half inch intervals. Then, instead of attaching the collar directly to the garment, follow this procedure.

Cut an interfacing for the neckband using the neck-band pattern piece. Pin and baste the interfacing to the wrong side of the outer neck band. Trim the interfacing close to the bastings.

Pin and baste the curved edge of the interfaced neckband to the underside of the collar (right sides together), matching pattern markings.

Pin the other neckband piece to the top side of the collar, right sides together. Baste the two neckband pieces together along the curved edge. Machine-stitch along the stitching line to within ⅝ inch of the neck edge.

Trim the interfacing to one-eighth inch and the seam allowances to one-quarter inch. Clip the trimmed seam allowances at one-half inch intervals.

Turn the neckband to the right side and press.

Pin, baste, and stitch the interfaced neckband to the neckline of the garment, right sides together. Trim the seam allowances to one-quarter inch and clip where necessary. Press the neckline seam allowance toward the band.

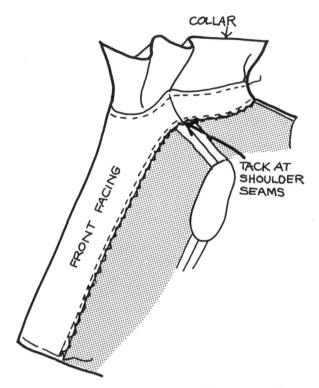

FIGURE H.22. *Tacking the facing of the classic collar to the garment.*

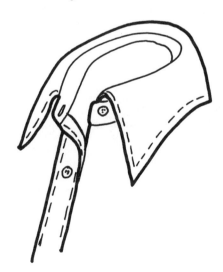

FIGURE H.23. *The shirt collar.*

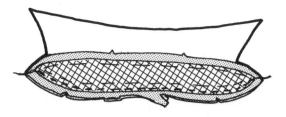

FIGURE H.24. *Sewing the neckband to the collar.*

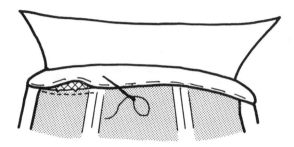

FIGURE H.25. *Slip-stitching the shirt-collar neckband on-to the garment.*

Turn the free neckband edge under ⅝ inch, trim to one-quarter inch, and pin it over the neckline seam. Slip-stitch the neckband into place on the garment (Figure H.25, and Sew-Easy Guide 11).

6. Cuffs

Cuffs are another one of those items in sewing that *must* be interfaced—sad-looking cuffs are as disappointing as limp, lifeless collars.

Blouse Cuffs

The blouse cuff is made all in one piece and softly folds under to finish the sleeve edge.

Cut the cuff interfacing using the cuff pattern piece. Fold the interfacing in half lengthwise and cut along the fold. Use the half with the notched edge to interface the cuff.

Pin and baste the interfacing to the cuff. Trim the interfacing close to the bastings along the outer three edges (Figure H.27).

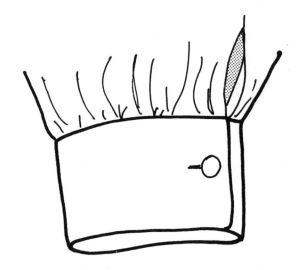

FIGURE H.26.   *The blouse cuff.*

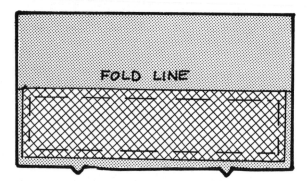

FIGURE H.27.   *Basting the interfacing to the blouse cuff piece.*

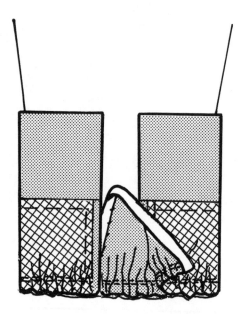

FIGURE H.28.   *Basting the cuff to the sleeve edge.*

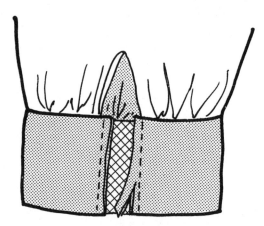

FIGURE H.29.   *Sewing and trimming the cuff ends.*

Pin, baste, and stitch the notched edge of the cuff to the sleeve edge (right sides together), matching all pattern markings. If the bottom sleeve edge is gathered, distribute the fullness evenly around the cuff before stitching (Figure H.28). Trim the cuff seam allowance to one-quarter inch, fold the cuff down, and press the seam allowances toward the cuff.

Turn the sleeve right side out. Fold the cuff along the foldline, right sides together, so that the wrong side of the cuff faces out. Pin, baste, and stitch the cuff ends. Trim the seam allowances to one-quarter inch (Figure H.29).

Turn the cuff right side out. Fold under the free cuff edge along the seam line and trim the seam allowance to one-quarter inch. Slip-stitch the folded edge into place over the cuff seam (Figure H.30).

FIGURE H.30. *Stitching the sleeve edge over the cuff seam.*

Finish the cuff with buttonholes following the pattern markings. (Bound buttonholes must be made before the cuff is attached to the sleeve and faced.)

Shirt Cuffs

Cut a cuff interfacing using the cuff pattern piece. Pin and baste the interfacing to the wrong side of the cuff piece. Trim the interfacing close to the bastings.

Pin and baste the cuff to the cuff facing, right sides together, leaving the notched edge open. Machine-stitch to within ⅝ inch of the notched edge. Trim the seam allowance to one-quarter inch and clip all curves (Figure H.32). Turn the cuff right side out and press, making sure that the seam is not visible from the top side of the cuff.

Turn the sleeve right side out and pin the top of the cuff to the sleeve edge (right sides together), matching all notches. If the sleeve edge is gathered, distribute the fullness evenly around the cuff. Baste and machine-stitch the cuff to the sleeve (Figure H.33). Trim the seam allowance to one-quarter inch. Turn the cuff right side out and press the seam allowance toward the cuff.

Turn the free cuff edge under along the stitching line, trim the seam allowance to one-quarter inch and slip-stitch the folded edge in place over the cuff seam (see Sew-Easy Guide 11).

Top-stitch the cuff for a tailored finish and make *buttonholes* following the pattern markings (see Sew-

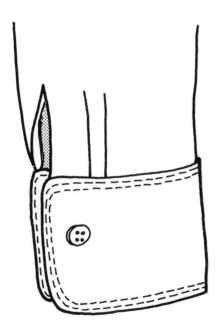

FIGURE H.31. *The shirt cuff.*

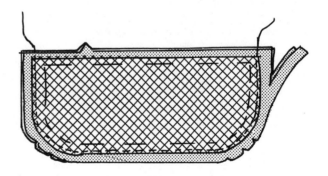

FIGURE H.32. *Trimming the seam allowances on the shirt cuff.*

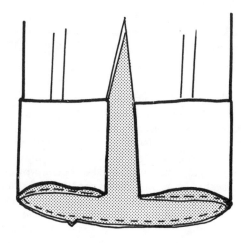

FIGURE H.33. *Attaching the shirt cuff to the sleeve.*

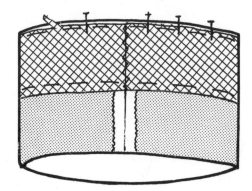

FIGURE H.34. *Pinning, basting, and trimming interfacing on the band cuff.*

Easy Guides 3 and 21). Be sure the buttonholes are placed correctly or the cuffs will button backwards. (Bound buttonholes must be made before the cuff is faced and attached to the sleeve.) Decorative snap fasteners also make a nice finish to a tailored cuff.

Band Cuffs

Bands of fabric added to sleeves and pant legs turn back to become cuffs. These cuffs *do not* have buttoned openings like the others, so be sure to leave enough room for slipping the garments on and off.

Cut two strips of fabric as wide as you like (twice the width of the intended cuff, plus 2¼ inches for seam allowances and turning). Cut the strips either on the lengthwise grain or on the bias. Each band should be as long as the sleeve or pant leg edge, plus 1¾ inches for seam allowances and ease. Since the band is cut double, there will be no need for a separate facing.

Cut an interfacing for each band as long as the band and half the width. Make each interfacing into a circular band by stitching the ends together using a *lapped seam* (see Sew-Easy Guide 9). Make the cuffs into circular bands by stitching the ends of the cuffs, right sides together, and press the seams open.

Pin and baste the interfacing to the wrong side of the cuff, matching seams. Trim the interfacing close to the basting along the raw edge (Figure H.34).

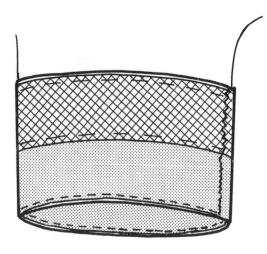

FIGURE H.35. *Attaching the band cuff to the sleeve.*

Pin, baste, and stitch the noninterfaced edge of the cuff to the sleeve, right sides together (Figure H.35). Trim the seam, press the cuff down, and press the seam allowances toward the cuff.

Fold the cuff to the inside along the foldline. Turn under the unfinished cuff edge ⅝ inch, trim to ¼ inch, and slip-stitch into place over the cuff seam (Figure H.36).

Fold the finished band up on the outside of the garment to form the cuff (Figure H.37).

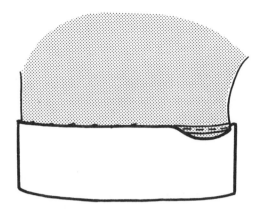

FIGURE H.36 *Slip-stitch the band cuff over the cuff seam.*

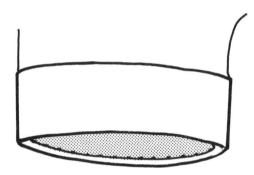

FIGURE H.37. *Folding the band up to form the cuff.*

7. Darts

A dart is one of those construction details that gives three-dimensional shape to a garment. It is responsible for fitting a flat piece of fabric to the shape of our bodies. In order to guarantee a smooth and flattering fit, the dart must be constructed carefully and tapered gradually.

Fold the dart along the center line, carefully matching the markings. Start pinning at the seam edge or at the widest part of the dart. Then pin at the point; at the midpoint; and at one-inch intervals in between.

Place pins at right angles to the seamline. Baste the dart to hold it securely in place, if necessary.

Start machine-stitching at the wide end of the dart (at the edge of the garment), reinforcing with *back-stitching* (see Sew-Easy Guide 19). Taper the stitching gradually to the point (Figure H.38). Sew a few stitches off the fabric edge at the end of the dart to guard against a puckered point.

Tie off the threads to secure the end of the dart (Figure H.39 and Sew-Easy Guide 19). Never reinforce the *end* of a dart by back-stitching; it may cause the dart point to bulge.

Most darts are pressed as they are sewn and then toward the center of the garment; bust and elbow darts are pressed *down*. With wide darts and darts in heavy fabrics, slash darts to within one inch of the point of the dart. Press the dart open and press the point toward the center (see Chapter 9, Figures 9.4 through 9.7).

Use the same procedures for sewing contour darts (darts that taper to a point at both ends).

Guarantee a perfectly smooth contour dart by sewing the dart in two steps: Start at the center of the dart and sew to one point at a time. Overlap the stitching approximately three-fourths inch at the center (Figure

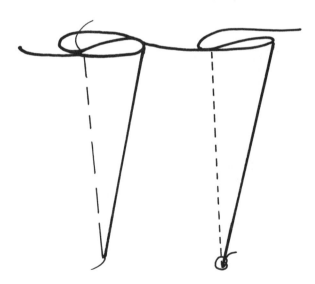

FIGURE H.38. *Basting and stitching a dart.*

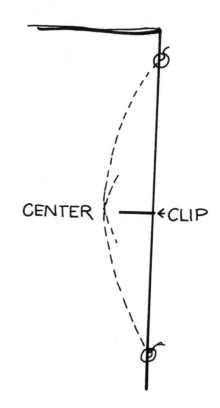

FIGURE H.39. *Tying off darts.*

FIGURE H.40. *Sewing contour darts from the center to each point.*

H.40). (Be sure the stitches overlap *inside* the seam line.)

Tie off the threads at each end of the dart and clip the dart at the center to within one-quarter inch of the stitching line. (Clip more if necessary for a smooth fit.)

8. Easing

A long piece of fabric is often joined to a shorter one along the seam at shoulders and elbows to allow for comfort in motion. The longer piece of fabric is said to be "eased" into the seam line of the smaller piece of fabric.

On the longer piece, stitch one-eighth inch outside the stitching line between the markings that indicate the area to be eased, using long machine stitches or hand basting. Leave a few inches of thread at each end of the ease-stitching.

Pin the two pieces of fabric (right sides together) between the ends of the seam and the ease markings. Leave the area to be eased open (Figure H.41).

Pull up the ease thread, gathering the longer piece, until the two pieces of fabric are equal in length.

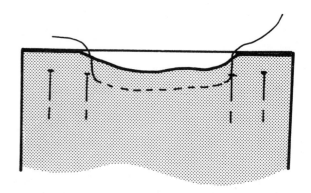

FIGURE H.41. *Ease-stitching a longer piece of fabric.*

176   GUIDES TO SEWING

Distribute the gathers evenly and pin. Baste if there is too much ease fabric to be controlled with pins. Stitch the seam (Figure H.42).

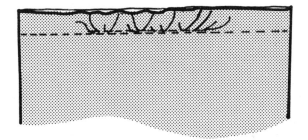

FIGURE H.42. *Stitching the seam and easing the longer fabric into the smaller.*

Embroidering. See Chapter 11

9. Facings

Facings put the finishing touch on necklines and armholes by neatly concealing the raw edges.

Here are a few facing rules to remember:

Always interface facings. Cut interfacings from the facing pattern pieces, unless the pattern includes special interfacing pattern pieces. Be sure to trim the interfacing close to the stitching so the seams won't be bulky.

Don't forget about the facings when altering a pattern to fit. Make the necessary adjustments in the pattern pieces *before* cutting out the facings.

Tack the facings to the inside of the garment loosely at the inner seams. Tight stitches give a puckered appearance to the finished garment.

Neckline Facings

Stitch the front and back bodice pieces together at the shoulder seams, finish the seam edges, and press the seams open. Stay-stitch the neckline edge just outside the seam line to prevent it from stretching while you work.

Trim ⅜ inch from the unnotched edge of the interfacings. Sew the interfacing pieces together using a *lapped seam* to eliminate bulk. Lap one edge over the other so that the seam lines meet in the center. Stitch through the center using a straight or zigzag stitch and trim close to the stitching (Figure H.43).

Pin and baste the interfacing to the wrong side of the garment, matching notches and shoulder seams (Figure H.44). Trim the interfacing close to the basting around the neckline.

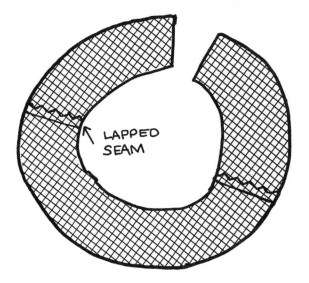

FIGURE H.43. *Sewing interfacings for neckline facing with a lapped hem.*

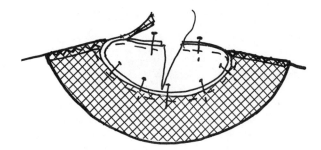

FIGURE H.44. *Pinning and basting interfacing for neckline facing.*

Install the zipper at this point if there is one (see Sew-Easy Guide 24).

Pin, baste, and stitch the front and back neckline facings at the shoulder seams, with right sides of the fabric together. Finish the seam edges and press the seams open.

Finish the unnotched edge of the facing by stitching one-quarter inch from the edge using a straight stitch. Trim to one-eighth inch and overcast or zigzag the trimmed edge. Another finish suitable for facings is to encase the free facing edge in bias seam binding. Or, if the fabric is lightweight, turn the free edge under one-quarter inch and edge-stitch (see Sew-Easy Guide 17).

Pin, baste, and stitch the facing to the garment neckline with right sides together. Trim the facing seam allowance to one-eighth inch and the garment seam allowance to one-quarter inch. Clip the neckline seam allowance every half-inch or so around the curve, being careful not to cut across the line of stitching (Figure H.45).

Turn the garment wrong side out and press the neckline seam allowance toward the facings. *Understitch* the facing by machine-stitching the neckline seam allowance to the facings, sewing very close to the neckline seam. This will prevent facings from rolling to the outside of the garment (Figure H.46).

Turn the facings to the inside of the garment and press. Roll the garment edge a little to the inside along

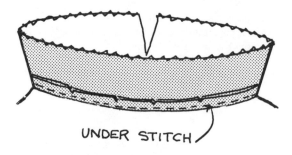

FIGURE H.46. *Understitching the neckline facing to prevent rolling.*

the neckline seam, so that the facings can't be seen from the outside.

Pin the facings to the shoulder seam allowances and slip-stitch in place using loose stitches so that the garment doesn't pucker. Turn under the facing ends so that they clear the zipper teeth and slip-stitch the facings to the zipper tape (see Sew-Easy Guide 11).

Armhole Facings

Prepare and attach the armhole facings and interfacings according to the same procedure used for facing the neckline. When machine-stitching the facing to the garment, begin and end the stitching at the underarm seam. Don't forget to understitch to prevent the facings from rolling to the outside of the armhole.

Extended Facings

An extended facing is a facing that is cut all in one with the garment section. The facing is folded back along a foldline to finish the edge. This kind of facing is most commonly found at buttoned openings at the center of a garment.

Turn the facing to the inside and press along the fold line, then turn the facing away from the garment.

Join the front and back interfacing sections using lapped seams to eliminate bulk. Trim ⅜ inch from the free edge of the interfacing. (If the pattern doesn't include a pattern piece for the front interfacing section, cut the interfacing from the extended facing portion of the garment piece using the foldline as a cutting line.)

Pin the interfacing to the wrong side of the garment, aligning the front edge of the interfacing with the

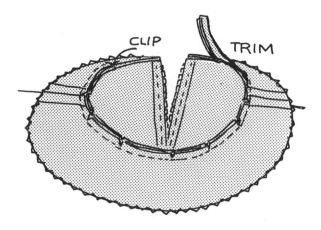

FIGURE H.45. *Clipping and trimming neckline facing.*

facing foldline. Baste the interfacing into place along the neckline, front opening, and waistline. Trim close to the bastings at the neckline and waistline; don't trim the front edge (Figure H.47).

Join the back and front facing sections at the shoulder seams. Finish the seam edges and press the seams open. Finish the free edge of the facing (Figure H.48).

Pin, baste, and stitch the facings to the garment at the neckline, with right sides together. Trim the facing seam allowances to one-eighth inch and the garment seam allowances to one-quarter inch. Clip diagonally across the corners close to the stitching for a smooth turning. Clip the neckline seam allowances at half-inch intervals around the curve (Figure H.49).

Turn facings away from the garment and press the neckline seam allowances toward the facings. Understitch the seam allowances to the facings, stitching as far around the neckline seam as possible. Turn the facings to the inside of the garment and secure the facings to the shoulder seam allowances using a slipstitch.

Don't remove the bastings holding the interfacing to the garment fabric at the center opening until *after* the buttonholes are made. This will keep the interfacing from slipping while you're working on the garment.

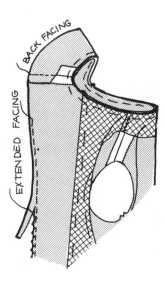

FIGURE H.48. *Joining the back and extended facings and finishing the free edge of the facing.*

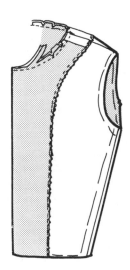

FIGURE H.47. *Basting the interfacing for an extended facing.*

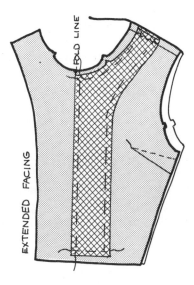

FIGURE H.49. *Attaching the extended facing to the garment.*

SEW-EASY GUIDES TO BASIC PROCEDURES **179**

10. Gathering

Gathers are small, soft folds made by pulling fabric up on a few lines of machine- or hand-stitching. Skirts are often gathered, and a ruffle is no more than a gathered piece of fabric attached to a sleeve edge, neckline, or hem.

Gather machine-stitching by setting the stitch length at about 8 stitches to the inch. Use silk thread; other thread may break mid-way through gathering. Loosen the upper tension a bit.

Stitch along the seam to be gathered a fraction of an inch outside the stitching line; stitch another line one-quarter inch outside the first line of stitching.

Do not gather over seams. Break the line of stitches one-eighth inch on either side of a seam, leaving long thread ends to use for gathering.

Pin the edge to be gathered (a skirt or ruffle) to the corresponding ungathered edge (waistband, sleeve, neckline, or hem edge) at notches, markings, and seams.

Working in sections (between seams), pull the bobbin thread and push the gathers toward the center. When the gathered edge fits the straight edge, fasten the gathers by winding the bobbin threads around a pin in a figure eight fashion (Figure H.50).

Distribute the gathers evenly between the pins and stitch the gathered edge to the ungathered edge along the seam line. Sew with the *gathered* side up.

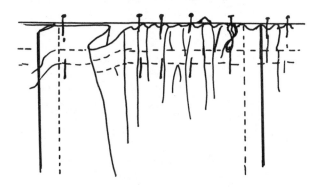

FIGURE H.50. *Fitting the gathered edge to the straight edge.*

Gathering by hand is done in the same fashion. Use a small even running-stitch instead of machine-stitching (see Sew-Easy Guide 11).

Grain. See Chapters 6 and 8

11. Hand-Stitching

Running-stitch

The running-stitch is most often used for basting and gathering (Figure H.51). Make stitches one-half inch long and space them one-half inch apart, beginning with a knot and ending with a back-stitch. Pull the thread firmly with each stitch, but loosely enough so as not to pucker the fabric.

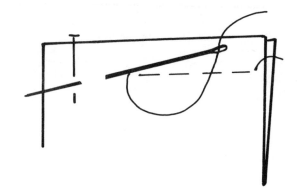

FIGURE H.51. *The running-stitch.*

Back-stitch

This stitch is usually used to secure the end of a line of stitching. Bring the needle through to the upper side of the fabric. Take a stitch back one-quarter inch and bring the needle out again one-quarter inch forward of the thread on the basting line (Figure H.52). Back stitch again directly over the first stitch for an extra secure finish.

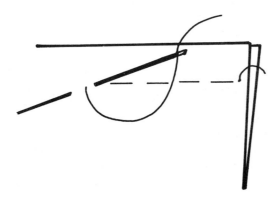

FIGURE H.52. *The back-stitch.*

Slip-stitch

The slip-stitch is used to join one piece of fabric to another so that the stitches are invisible. It is used most often in hemming and in joining linings to the garment fabric. Pick up one or two threads of the garment fabric and slide the needle horizontally through the folded edge of the lining or hem allowance one-eighth inch away from the previous stitch (Figure H.53). Pull the thread firmly, but not too tightly. Back-stitch to finish.

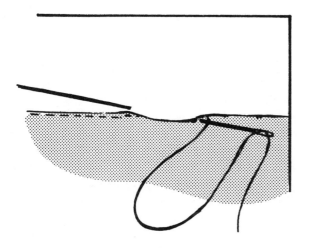

FIGURE H.53. *The slip-stitch.*

Catch-stitch

The catch-stitch is also used in hemming; it is particularly good for hemming knits (Figure H.54). Work from left to right. Secure the thread to the hem edge with several back stitches. Point the needle to the left and pick up one or two threads of the garment fabric, just above the hem edge. Point the needle to the left again and take a small stitch in the hem allowance one-quarter inch below the edge and one-quarter inch to the right of the previous stitch. Continue sewing in this zigzag fashion along the entire length of the hem, working from left to right.

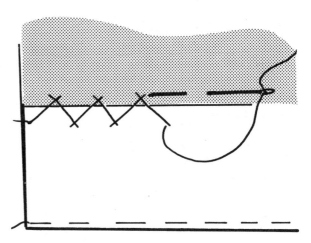

FIGURE H.54. *The catch-stitch.*

Buttonhole- or Blanket-stitch

This stitch is used to make hand worked buttonholes, thread belt loops, and to decoratively finish a raw edge.

Working from left to right, hold the thread to the left with your thumb and circle the thread around to the right, forming a loop. Insert the needle vertically into the fabric (or underneath the foundation threads, when making belt loops). As the needle emerges, be sure that it passes *over* the thread loop. This forms a small knot, called a purl, at the end of each stitch (see Sew-Easy Guide 2, Figure H.5).

SEW-EASY GUIDES TO BASIC PROCEDURES **181**

Satin-stitch

The satin-stitch is an embroidery stitch used to fill in the area between two lines of a design. Make parallel stitches close together over the area to be filled in (Figure H.55). For a raised effect, pad the design area first with small running-stitches.

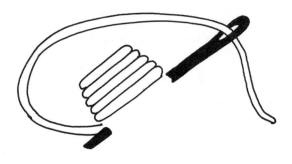

FIGURE H.55. *The satin-stitch.*

Stem- or Outline-stitch

This is an embroidery-stitch used for exactly what you'd expect—stems and outlining. Work from left to right along a guideline (Figure H.56). Pull the needle through to the right side of the fabric. Let the thread drop below the guideline. Point the needle to the left and take a small stitch on the guideline one-quarter inch to the right of where the needle emerged. Continue stitching to the right in this fashion.

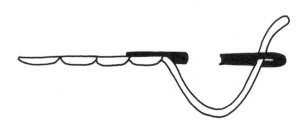

FIGURE H.56. *The outline-stitch.*

Chain-stitch

I use this stitch both for outlining and for filling in large areas of a design (Figure H.57). With the needle pulled to the right side of the fabric, circle the thread from left to right. Hold the loop down with your thumb and insert the needle back into the fabric at the point where it emerged. Bring the needle to the top side of the fabric again one-quarter inch below the previous stitch, being sure to keep the thread loop under the needle point.

FIGURE H.57. *The chain-stitch.*

12. Hems

Hemlines fluctuate year by year, but the mark of a finely crafted hem remains the same—invisible handicraft is what we're aiming for. Settle into a comfortable chair, and take your time.

No matter what the garment, the hemming procedure is basically always the same: mark, pin, trim if necessary, finish the edge, and stitch into place.

Here are some general hints that apply to all hems:

Let the finished garment hang at least overnight before hemming.

Don't be fooled into thinking you can hem adequately by measuring an equal distance from the waist to the hem edge around the skirt. The *only* way to ensure an even hem is to measure from the floor to the hem edge with a yardstick or hem marker. Try to get someone else to turn up the hem.

Wear the undergarments and shoes you plan to wear with the new garment. Determine the skirt length by turning the hem up in front and in back and checking the length in the mirror.

Stand very still, with arms at your side, while your helper circles around you with a yardstick or hem marker. The hem should be marked at three-inch intervals with pins.

Take the garment off and pin the hem up along the markings, matching all seams. Baste the hem next to the fold (Figure H.58).

Trim the raw hem edge so that the hem is even all the way around the skirt. Most hems are two to three inches deep; check the pattern for the exact measurement and use the sewing gauge for fast and easy measuring.

Ease-stitch the raw hem edge of full skirts and distribute the gathers evenly around the hem (see Sew-Easy Guide 10). If the garment is wool, shrink out the excess fullness with a steam iron.

Pin, baste, and stitch seam tape or binding to the hem one-quarter inch from the raw hem edge. Turn each tape end under one-quarter inch and overlap one-half inch at the starting point. Substitute a sexy lace seam binding for the plain utility kind to pretty up the hem edge.

Hem without a seam binding if you're so inclined. Overcast the raw edges or, if the fabric is lightweight, turn the hem edge under a quarter-inch and stitch close to the fold.

Pin and baste the hem edge to the skirt, being sure to match all seams. Stitch the hem in place using an invisible, evenly spaced slip-stitch (Figure H.59, Sew-Easy Guide 11). Don't pull the thread too tightly or the hem will pucker.

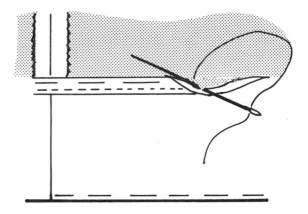

FIGURE H.59. *Stitching the hem edge to the garment with a slip-stitch.*

Hemming Knits

Hem a knit skirt using a catch-stitch instead of a slip-stitch (sew-Easy Guide 11, Figure H.59). The catch-stitch "gives" more than a slip-stitch and is less likely to snap when the stretchables expand and contract.

Skirts with Front Openings

A skirt that opens down the front calls for slightly different treatment. Turn up the hem and finish the hem edge as for any skirt, but don't attach the seam

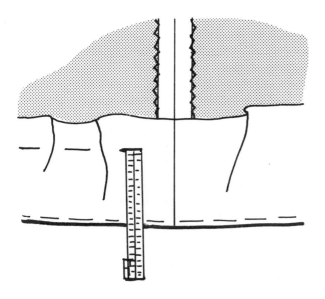

FIGURE H.58. *Basting the hem next to the fold.*

tape to the facing hem edge—stop the tape at the front foldline to reduce bulk.

Hem the skirt using a slip-stitch, being sure to sew all the way to the edge of the facing (Figure H.60).

Fold the facing to the inside of the garment along the front foldline. Pin the facing to the hem and slip-stitch into place (Figure H.61).

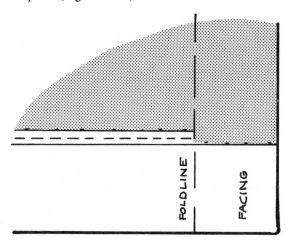

FIGURE H.60.   *Hemming a front-opening skirt.*

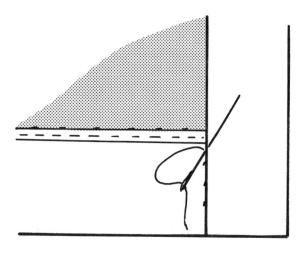

FIGURE H.61.   *Slip-stitching the facing into place on a front-opening skirt.*

Hemming Pleats

Measure up each pleat seam from the hem edge to the depth of the hem and clip the seam allowance. Press the seam open within the hem area and hem the skirt as usual. Edge-stitch the fold of the pleat so that the pleated hem stays creased (Figure H.62). Repeat for each pleat.

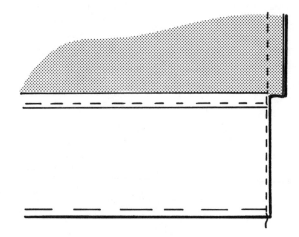

FIGURE H.62.   *Hemming pleats.*

Machine-stitched Hems

A word to the hurried. A hand-sewn hem is a sign of quality, but there are times when sacrifices are justified. If you are sewing a lot of school clothes and casual wear at once you might want to hem by machine.

Follow the instructions in your sewing machine manual for using the blind-stitch (or ask for a demonstration at your sewing machine shop). Practice a bit until you master the technique.

Adding a Bias-band Hem

Adding a bias-band hem—a band of new fabric to replace the old hem—is a great way to refurbish tired old clothes.

Find the bias grain of the band fabric. Use a protractor to establish the bias grain—45 degrees from the vertical grain. Or, fold a lengthwise edge of the fabric to meet a crosswise edge. The diagonal thus formed is the bias grain.

Cut a piece on the bias that is double the width of the finished band, plus 1¼ inches for seam allowances. The length of the band should be equal to the circumference of the skirt edge, plus 1¼ inches for seam allowances. Sew the band-ends, right sides together, to form a circular strip.

Save fabric by cutting two bias strips, each one-half the circumference, plus 1¼ inches for seam allowances. Sew the two bias-cut pieces together at the sides and press the seams open.

Fold the strip lengthwise, wrong sides facing in, and baste the raw edges together. Remove the old hem from the skirt or dress and trim the bottom edge so that the skirt will be the desired length with the bias-band addition. Make sure the skirt edge is perfectly even. Pin, baste, and stitch the band to the skirt, making sure that the raw edges of the skirt are even with the raw edges of the band and that the seams match (Figure H.64).

Finish the raw edges, press the bias band down, and press the seam allowances toward the garment.

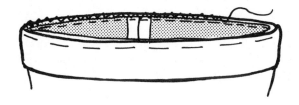

FIGURE H.64. *Joining the bias-band hem to the skirt and finishing the edges.*

13. Linings

Whether or not to line a garment is a matter of personal preference these days, though heavyweight garments, such as coats and suits *must* be lined. There are obvious advantages to lining other garments as well. Lining prolongs the life of the garment; it improves the "hang" and adds body to limp fabrics. It gives a garment a custom-made look and a smooth luxurious feel. Lining reduces wrinkling and clinging, prevents the fabric from changing shape, and conceals construction details, making seam finishes unnecessary unless the fabric frays easily. An added bonus: A lined skirt doesn't require a separate slip.

A lining is cut from the pattern pieces or from separate lining pieces if the pattern has them. It is constructed independently of the garment, and is attached to the garment fabric at the neckline, armhole, or waistline seam. Be sure to make the same fitting adjustments on the lining as you do on the garment.

Follow this procedure for lining a garment: Construct the garment and lining separately. (Do not line collars, cuffs, facings, and waistbands.)

Turn the lining inside out and slip it inside the garment so that the wrong sides of the fabrics are together (Figure H.65). Match the lining and garment at seams and darts and baste the lining to the garment at the unfinished edges. Let the hems hang free. Join the lining to the garment at the zipper opening using a slip-stitch (see Sew-Easy Guide 11).

Finish the garment according to the pattern instructions.

Hem the lining separately from the fabric. The lining should be an inch shorter than the garment at the skirt bottom and one-half inch shorter at the sleeve edges.

Lining a Jacket

Most jackets are left unlined these days for easy care. A lined jacket takes longer to construct and is more expensive than an unlined jacket. But lined jackets have a professional finish and fit better. And slippery fabrics are easier to slide on and off over sweaters and shirts than the rough jacket fabric would

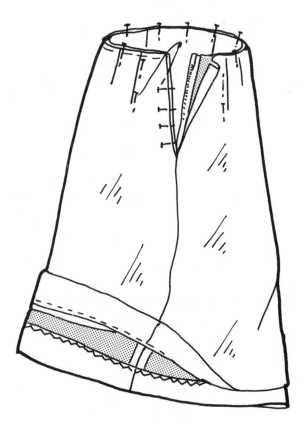

FIGURE H.65. *Matching the lining to the garment.*

be. Ask the salesperson at the fabric store to direct you to linings appropriate for jackets.

Jacket patterns that require lining contain lining pattern pieces and instructions on how to line. If you care to add a lining to an unlined jacket pattern, here's how to go about it.

Cut sleeves and the back sections of the jacket out of lining fabric. Add two inches at the center back of the lining for an ease pleat that will allow for comfort in action and a good fit. (If the back pattern section is placed on the fold, move the pattern out one inch from the fold when you cut. Since the pattern is cut double, this adds two inches. If the jacket is seamed up the back, add an inch to each center back seam allowance.)

Cut the front jacket sections out of the lining fabric

—cutting only to the fold line (or interfacing line) of the jacket front.

Stitch all the darts and seams within the front and back jacket sections. Join the front and back sections together at shoulder and side seams.

Turn the raw neckline and center front edges under about one inch and press, clipping where necessary so that the lining lies flat. Position the lining over the jacket, wrong sides together.

Baste the lining to the garment at the armholes (see Figure H.66).

Pin and baste the turned-under edges of the lining to the center front of the jacket, and around the neckline, stopping at the shoulder seams.

Lay a pleat at the center back of the lining; press to one side; and baste across the upper and lower edge. Tack the pleat in place at the neck, waistline, and lower edge, using small hand stitches. Pin and baste

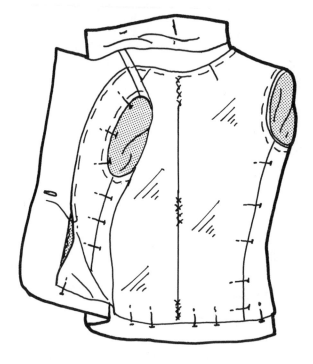

FIGURE H.66. *Pleating the lining and basting it to the garment.*

the turned-under edge of the lining along the back neckline.

Try on the jacket and check for a smooth fit and hang.

Slip-stitch the lining to the jacket along the neck and down the front of the garment (see Sew-Easy Guide 11).

Stitch the underarm seam of the sleeve lining; press the seam open; and run a line of ease-stitching along the sleeve cap, between the notches (see Sew-Easy Guide 8).

Turn the sleeve right side out and position it over the wrong side of the garment sleeve. Pull up the ease stitches so that the sleeve lining fits over the armhole seam allowance. Pin the sleeve lining into place and finish with invisible slip-stitches (Figure H.67).

Turn the sleeve and bottom edges of the lining under so that they overlap the jacket hems but don't show from the outside. Hem both using a slip stitch. Fold the lining hem edge back one-fourth to one-half inch, and stitch the lining hem allowance *only* to the jacket.

Bonding

Bonding is a foundation of lining attached to a weakened fabric to give it strength. Select a lining that supports the fabric without making it too stiff, and match the color of the bonding fabric to the garment fabric.

Work on a flat surface; cut lining to match each pattern piece. Bond the lining to the fabric with wrong sides together. Use diagonal hand-basting stitches to hold the fabrics together and machine-baste around the outer edge of each bonded section (Figure H.68). Now, treat the two layers as one in remaking the garment.

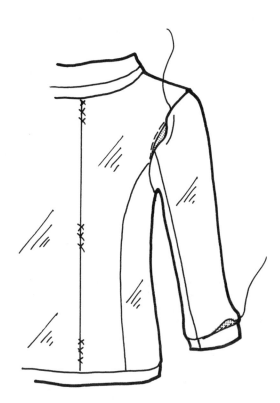

FIGURE H.67. *Attaching the sleeve lining.*

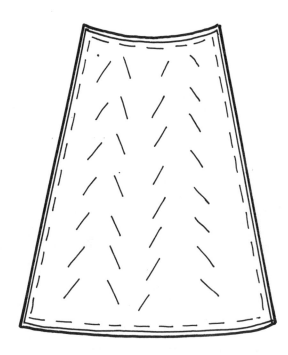

FIGURE H.68. *Bonding lining to weakened fabric.*

Measurements. See Chapters 3 and 7

Mitering. See Chapter 11

Needles. See Chapter 5

Patchwork. See Chapter 11

14. Pleats

There is an array of pleats to choose from: box pleats, inverted pleats, pleats that turn to one side (Figure H.69), pressed pleats, unpressed pleats, and pleats top-stitched to the finish.

To make perfect pleats be sure you transfer pleat markings accurately; fold, pin, and baste pleats care-

fully; and press pleats correctly. Time, patience, and care are the key ingredients.

With the chalk or carbon transfer to the wrong side of the fabric the pattern markings for fold lines, placement lines (the lines against which the folded pleat is placed), and symbols to indicate where the top-stitching is to end. If you are making pleats from the top side of the fabric, run a line of basting (called *thread-tracing*) through all marked lines to transfer them to the right side (Figure H.70). Use a different color thread for fold and placement lines for easy pleating.

Fold each pleat on the fold line. Pin the foldline against its placement line, pinning from the bottom to the top to guarantee an even hemline.

Baste the folded pleats one-quarter inch from the fold, working from the bottom to top and being sure to

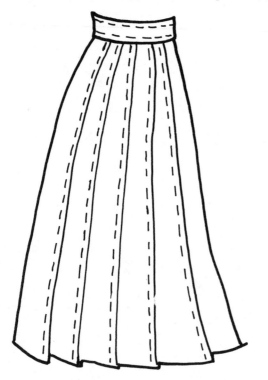

FIGURE H.69. *One-way pleats.*

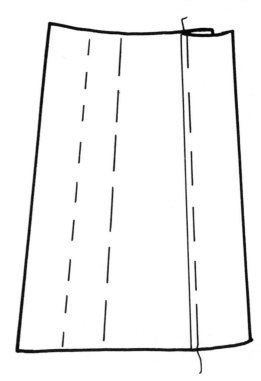

FIGURE H.70. *Thread-tracing fold and placement lines for pleats and basting a pleat into place.*

sew through all the layers of fabric. Machine-baste around the top of the skirt, a fraction of an inch outside the waistline seam, to hold the pleats into place. Do not remove the basting until after the garment is completed. The result will be unpressed pleats that hang in soft, graceful folds from the waist.

For crisp, sharp pleats, press the pleats before any bastings are removed. Press the pleats on both sides of the fabric. Use a press cloth when pressing the right side of the fabric to prevent a shine. If pressing on the wrong side creates imprints on the right side of the fabric, insert strips of brown paper under the fold of the pleat before pressing.

Treat the top-stitched pleat a little differently. After pressing the pleats but *before* removing any bastings, stitch on the right side of the fabric one-eighth to one-fourth inch from the edge of each pleat. The pattern tells you how far down each pleat to topstitch.

Take out just enough of the bastings so that the skirt can be hemmed. Repress the pleats after hemming and remove the remaining bastings.

Putting a sharp-edged pleat into perma-press fabrics and fabrics that have been treated with a crease-resistant finish takes an additional step. After the pleats are pressed and hemmed evenly, edge-stitch the front and back edges of each pleat. Use the presser foot as a gauge and place a line of straight machine-stitches one-eighth inch from each edge (Figure H.71).

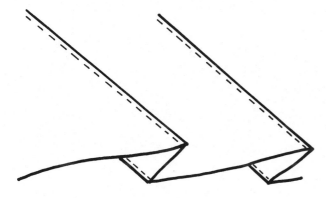

FIGURE H.71. *Edge-stitching front and back edges of each pleat in crease-resistant fabric.*

15. Pockets

Patch Pockets

Interface patch pockets made of lightweight or loosely woven fabric. Cut interfacings using the pocket pattern piece and baste the interfacing to the wrong side of the pocket.

Turn under the top edge of the pocket one-quarter inch and edge stitch. Fold the upper edge of the pocket to the outside along the foldline so that right sides of the hem are together. Stitch the hem ends and trim to one-quarter inch. Trim the corners of the hem edges diagonally. If the pocket is rounded on the bottom,

FIGURE H.72. *Patch pockets.*

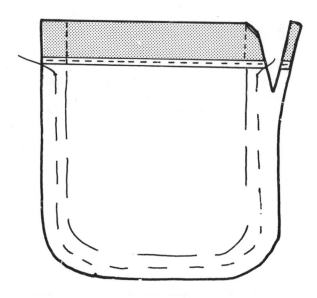

FIGURE H.73. *Trimming the patch pocket seam allowance.*

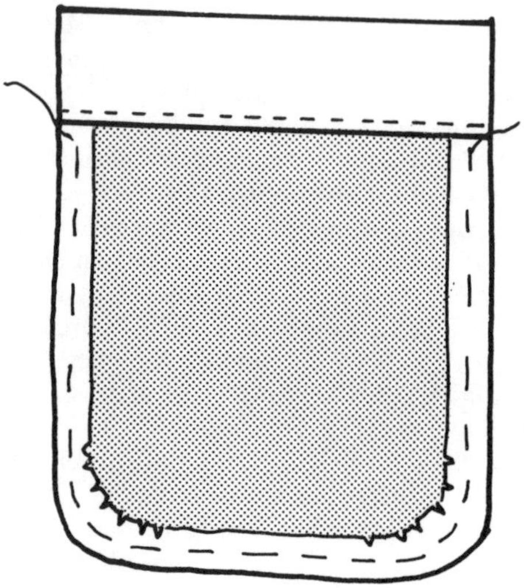

FIGURE H.74. *Notching a rounded patch pocket to reduce fullness.*

ease-stitch the rounded area one-eighth inch from the stitching line. Trim the pocket seam allowance just outside of the ease stitches (Figure H.73).

Turn the pocket hem and the seam allowances to the inside. Pull in the ease stitches on the rounded pockets. Baste around the pocket edges to hold the seam allowances in place. Notch the curves on the rounded pocket every one-half inch or so to remove excess fullness (Figure H.74).

Transfer pocket placement markings to the wrong side of the garment fabric. Baste through all markings to transfer them to the front of the garment.

Place the pocket wrong side down on the front side of the garment, aligning the pocket edges with the basted placement lines. Pin the pocket to the garment using one pin every inch or so (Figure H.75).

Try on the garment to check the positioning of the pockets. Pockets located below the waist should be positioned so that you can slip your hands into them naturally and comfortably. If you altered the pattern, the pockets may have to be relocated to retain symmetry and balance.

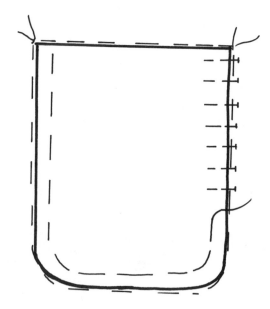

FIGURE H.75. *Pinning the patch pocket to the garment.*

Baste the pocket to the garment one-quarter inch from the pocket edge.

Sew the pocket to the garment by hand, using an invisible slip-stitch (Sew-Easy Guide 11), or machine-stitch very close to the pocket edge. Add a row of *top-stitching* for a classy finish (see Sew-Easy Guide 21).

In-seam Pocket

The in-seam pocket is cut from the lining fabric and sewn to the garment at special openings in the side seams (Figure H.76).

Before sewing the pocket pieces together, sew each pocket piece to the appropriate garment section, matching notches (Figure H.77). Press the seam toward the pocket.

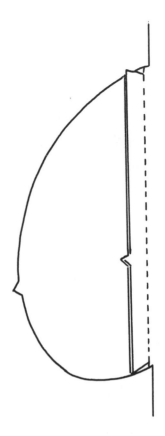

FIGURE H.77. *Attaching the in-seam pocket pieces to the garment piece.*

FIGURE H.76. *In-seam pocket.*

Baste the garment sections together at the side seams, basting across the pocket openings (Figure H.78). Baste the pocket pieces together around the outside edges.

Machine-stitch the side seams, starting at the lower edge of the seam, pivoting at the pocket corners, and sewing around the pocket openings.

Remove the bastings and turn the pocket toward the front along the foldline. Press the side seam allowances open, clipping the facing extension above and below the pocket as necessary.

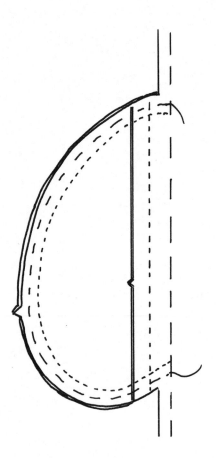

FIGURE H.78. *Basting and stitching the in-seam pocket.*

Preshrinking. See Chapter 6

Quilting. See Chapter 11

Restyling. See Chapter 10

16. Ruffles

Make a ruffle by cutting a strip of fabric 1½ to 2 times as long as the edge to which the ruffle is to be attached; and twice the width, plus 1¼ inch for seam allowances.

If the ruffle is to go on a sleeve end or hem, make the ruffle into a circular band by sewing the ends of the strip, right sides together. Press the seam open. Fold the ruffle in half with wrong sides facing, and baste the raw edges together.

Skip this step if the ruffle is to attach to a straight edge rather than a circular one. Fold the ruffle right sides together instead, and stitch each end taking a normal seam allowance. Trim the seams and turn the ruffle to the right side. Baste the raw edges together.

Gather the ruffle along the raw edges (Figure H.79, Sew-Easy Guide 10). Pin the ruffle to the edge of the garment, lining up the raw edges, and distribute the gathers evenly. Baste and machine-stitch the ruffle into place. Press the seam towards the garment and finish the seam allowances so they won't fray (Figure H.80).

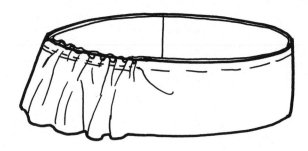

FIGURE H.79. *Gathering a ruffle along the raw edges.*

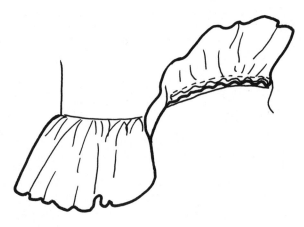

FIGURE H.80. *Attaching the ruffle and finishing the seam allowances.*

17. Seam Finishes

What's happening inside that dress is as important as how it looks on the outside. You're in for a big disappointment if, after a few washings, the fabric ravels through at the seams. (See Sew-Easy Guide 19 for sewing seams.)

Several seam finishes are listed below. Select the technique best suited to your fabric. Always pretest the method on a scrap. Will the seam finish keep the fabric from raveling? Will the seam finish show from the outside? If it does, use a less bulky technique.

Use a *straight machine-stitch* to finish fabric that ravels only moderately. Simply stitch a line one-half inch from the seam line (Figure H.81).

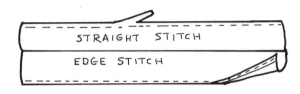

FIGURE H.81. *Two types of seam finishes.*

If the fabric is light to medium weight, and ravels, turn under the raw edges of the seam allowances ⅛ inch and machine-stitch close to the edge. This technique is called *edge-stitching*. Do not edge-stitch on bulky fabrics.

Finish the edges of tweeds; heavy, coarse, and bulky weaves; and easily frayed fabrics with *double-fold bias tape* (available in the notions department). This is the perfect finish for an unlined coat or jacket.

Encase each raw seam edge in the bias tape, placing the narrow edge of the tape on the top. Stitch close to the edge of the tape. Since the wider edge of the tape is on the bottom, both edges of the tape will be sewn to the seam allowance at once (Figure H.82).

A simple finish for ravely fabrics is a line of *zigzag stitching* one-half inch from the seam line. Trim close to the zigzag stitching to remove the excess seam allowance. Use this finish on fabrics that "give"; the stitch is as flexible as the fabric.

If your machine makes *overcast-stitches*, use them to finish seams on tweeds, raw silks, and heavy wool-

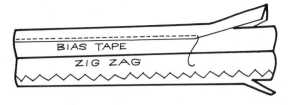

FIGURE H.82. *Two types of seam finishes.*

ens (Figure H.83). Stitch along the seam edge so that the stitches overcast the raw edges. If the seam allowance draws up during overcasting, clip it at intervals so that the seam will press flat.

FIGURE H.83. *Two types of seam finishes.*

If you don't have a new machine, but have a zigzag model, use the *blind-stitch* zigzag as you would an overcast stitch, making sure to form the stitches over the edge of the seam.

Some fabrics just don't ravel. Finish them anyway for a professional look. Finishing strengthens seams so the shape of an otherwise limp-looking gown will improve if you finish the seams.

Knits are among the fabrics that won't ravel, but the seam allowances will sometimes roll. To prevent this, sew a line of straight-stitching one-quarter inch from the edge of each seam allowance.

18. Set-in Sleeves

The sleeves of a garment must be cut *very* carefully; pay particular attention to those nearly inconspicuous notches. Without notches you can easily set the right sleeve into the left armhole or vice versa.

The sleeve cap of a set-in sleeve must be larger than the armhole into which it fits so that the arm can move freely. The trick is to put in the sleeve without causing puckers to appear.

Ease-stitch (see Sew-Easy Guide 8) between the notches of each sleeve cap, just outside the stitching line. Ease-stitch again one-quarter inch outside the first row of stitching. Leave the thread ends one to two inches long.

Finish the sleeve opening—before stitching the underarm seam—following this procedure:

Stay-stitch around the sleeve opening and slash the opening in between the lines of stitching (Figure H.84).

Cut a strip of fabric on the lengthwise grain, 1½ inches wide and twice the length of the opening. Pin and baste the strip of fabric to the sleeve opening, right sides together. Machine-stitch around the opening just outside the stay stitching (Figure H.85).

Turn the fabric strip right side out and press the seam allowance toward the strip. Turn the free edge of the fabric strip under one-quarter inch and press. Pin the folded edge over the seam allowance on the inside of

the sleeve so it just covers the machine-stitching and slip-stitch into place (Figure H.86; see Sew-Easy Guide 11).

Fold both fabric strips under; stitch to the sleeve at the bottom edge; then stitch diagonally across the top of the folded fabric strip.

Stitch the sleeve underarm seams and press the seams open.

Stitch the side seams, darts, and shoulder seams of the garment bodice. Press the seams open and turn the garment inside out.

Pin each sleeve to the garment, right sides together, matching armhole notches and underarm seamlines. Pin the shoulder marking of the sleeve to the garment

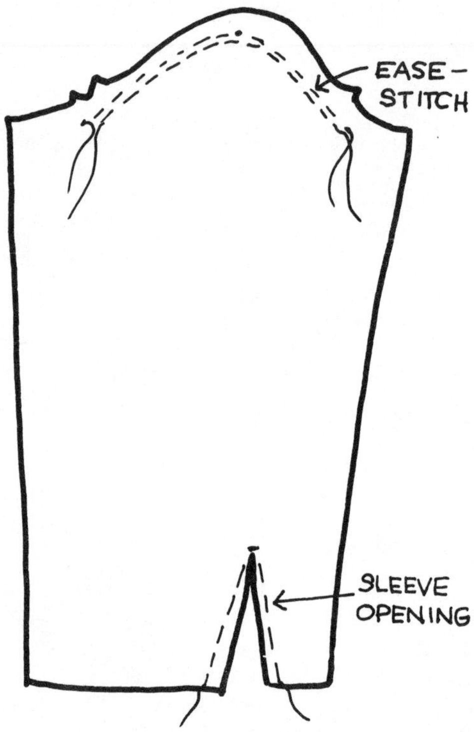

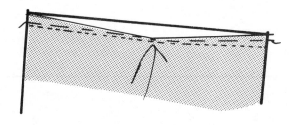

FIGURE H.85. *Attaching a strip of fabric to the sleeve opening.*

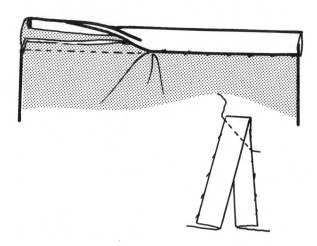

FIGURE H.86. *Slip-stitching the fabric strip to the sleeve opening.*

FIGURE H.84. *Ease-stitching the sleeve cap; and slashing and stitching at the bottom.*

shoulder seam and be sure the shoulder seam allowances are pinned open.

Pull the ease-stitching up until the sleeve fits the armhole of the garment. Wrap the thread ends around a pin in a figure-eight fashion to secure the gathers (see Sew-Easy Guide 10; Figures H.50 & H.87). Distribute the gathers evenly around the sleeve cap, pinning every quarter-inch or so. Leave a one-inch flat area at the shoulder seam.

Woolens require a little steam heat to shrink out excess fullness. Unpin the sleeve from the armhole, keeping the ease threads securely wrapped around the pins. Using a press cloth and sleeve board, press around the sleeve cap with a steam iron to remove the fullness. Don't skip this important step or the fabric will pucker.

Repin the sleeve and baste into place. Machine-stitch around the armhole edge on the sleeve side (the garment side facing down to the throat plate) so that you can press out any fullness in the sleeve cap with

your fingers as you sew (see Figure H.88). Make a second line of stitches in the seam allowance, one-quarter inch outside the first line of stitching to give additional strength to the armhole seam. Trim the seam allowance close to the second line of stitching and finish the edges with a zigzag or overcast stitch to keep the seam edge from raveling. Finish the seam edge with bias seam binding, if you prefer. Press the armhole seam toward the sleeve.

There is another procedure for attaching sleeves to a garment. After stitching the garment shoulder seams, but *before* stitching the garment side seams, or the sleeve underarm seams, machine-stitch the sleeve to the garment at the armhole openings. (Be sure to match all notches and carefully distribute the ease in the sleeve.) After the sleeve is attached pin, baste, and stitch the garment side seams and sleeve underarm seams. (Make a continuous line of stitches on each side of the garment starting at the bottom edge of the garment, sewing up the side seam, and down the sleeve underarm seam, ending at the wrist.)

This procedure is easier than the regular way, but there is one drawback to consider. There is no way to double check the fit of the sleeve at the shoulder before doing the final stitching. If you use this technique, be sure to alter the paper pattern for the perfect fit *before* you cut and sew.

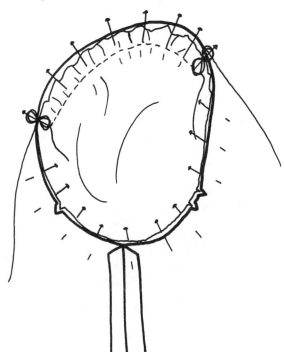

FIGURE H.87. *Setting in the sleeve.*

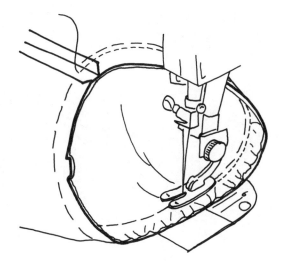

FIGURE H.88. *Machine-stitching the sleeve to the garment.*

SEW-EASY GUIDES TO BASIC PROCEDURES   **195**

19. Sewing Seams

A seam is a line of stitching used to join two pieces of fabric together. Seams are sewn with the right sides of the fabric facing in.

Straight Seams

Always make a trial run of machine-stitching on a swatch of fabric and make the necessary adjustments (stitch length, and tension) before sewing seams (see Chapter 9).

Lower the presser foot at the beginning of a seam ⅝-inch from the seam edge. Sew forward a few stitches. Then sew back and forth over the first few stitches to fasten the seam end.

Using a seam guide or a guideline on the throat plate, sew ⅝ inch from the seam edge, letting the machine feed the fabric under the needle by itself. Guide the fabric along the stitching line with your hands: Never tug or pull.

Be sure to stitch seams *with* the grain of the fabric. If arrows are printed on the pattern to indicate the direction of stitching, follow them.

When you reach the end of the seam, sew back and forth over the last few stitches to reinforce the seam

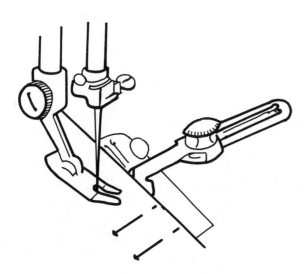

FIGURE H.89.   *Sewing a straight seam.*

end (called *back-stitching*). If your machine doesn't sew in reverse, secure the seam ends by *tying off the threads*. (See Sew-Easy Guide 17 for seam finishes.)

Tying off Thread Ends

Turn the garment over after stitching a seam. Pull the bobbin thread up until the top thread is partially pulled to this side of the garment. Slip the tip of the seam ripper underneath the thread loop and pull up until the top thread end is pulled to the bobbin (under) side of the fabric (Figure H.90). Tie the threads together in a knot. Don't pull too tightly.

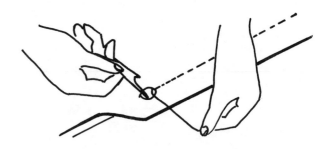

FIGURE H.90.   *Pulling the thread through for tying off.*

What to Do at Corners

To sew a seam that turns a sharp corner sew to the point of the corner. Leave the needle in the fabric, raise the presser foot, and pivot the fabric the necessary amount. Drop the pressure foot and continue sewing along the other line. If the corner is very sharp (at the point of a collar, for instance), take two or three stitches diagonally across the point (Figure H.91). Trim the seam allowances diagonally and close to the stitching for a smooth corner, without the lumps (Figure H.92).

Sewing Around Curves

Practice sewing curved seams a few times on scrap material before stitching on the garment. Guide fabric around a curved seam with your hands. If you are using a seam guide, angle it a bit for a perfectly even seam

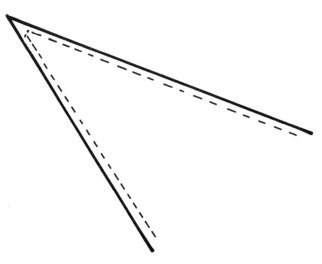

FIGURE H.91. *Sewing seams on a sharp corner.*

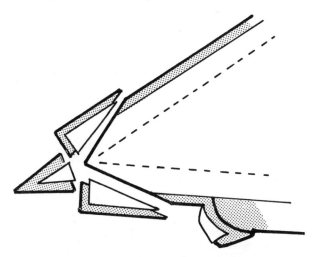

FIGURE H.92. *Trimming seam allowances at a sharp corner.*

allowance. Use a slower machine speed and smaller stitches than those used for sewing straight seams.

Pressing Seams

Seams should be pressed as sewn first; then pressed open. Curved seams should be pressed over a tailor's

ham or mitt. Press a seam open before stitching another seam across it, and press several seams at once to save time (see Chapter 9, Figures 9.3 through 9.8).

Flat-fell Seam

Flat-fell seams are commonly used in boy's and men's wear. They give a tailored appearance to women's sportswear, and they are sturdy as well as decorative. This seam is *not* suitable for bulky fabrics.

With *wrong* sides together, make a regular seam. Press the seam allowances to one side. Trim the bottom seam allowance to one-eighth inch. Turn the top seam allowance under one-quarter inch and press it over the trimmed seam allowance. Top-stitch very close to the folded edge (Figure H.93).

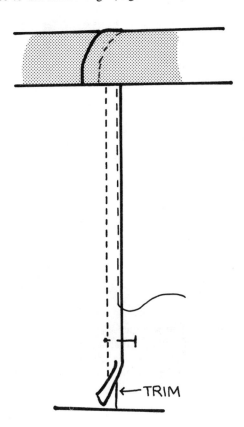

FIGURE H.93. *Flat-fell seam.*

French Seam

Use the French seam on sheer fabrics, children's clothes, men's shirts, and lingerie. This is *not* a good finish for curved seams.

Place the *wrong* sides of the fabric together and stitch a ⅜ inch seam (Figure H.94). Trim the seam to within ⅛ inch of the stitching and press the seam to the right.

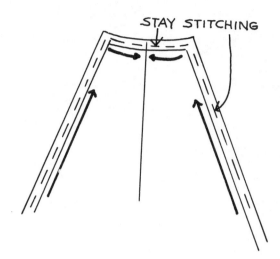

FIGURE H.95. *Stay-stitching hip- and waistlines.*

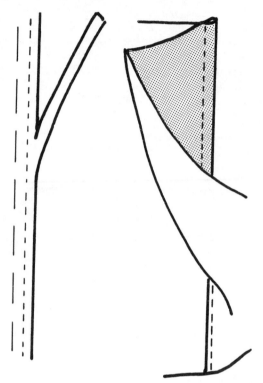

FIGURE H.94. *French seam.*

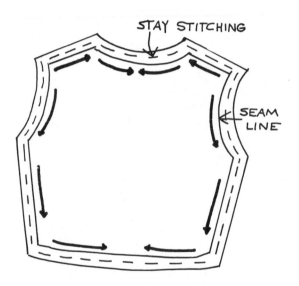

FIGURE H.96. *Stay-stitching neck, shoulder, and bodice lines.*

Turn the *right* sides of the fabric together and stitch a ¼ inch seam, being sure that the trimmed edges are covered. This produces a seam within a seam which is sturdy and there's no chance of seam edges raveling.

20. Stay-stitching

Stay-stitching is a line of machine-stitching in the seam allowance of a single thickness of fabric. It is used to prevent the fabric from stretching while you work. Necklines, shoulder lines, waistlines, and hip lines are stay-stitched.

Pay attention to the direction in which you stay-stitch; sew in the direction indicated on the diagrams (Figures H.95 and H.96).

Use the same thread and stitch length that you will use for sewing seams.

Thread. See Chapter 5

21. Top-stitching

Top-stitching on seams, style lines, and finished edges gives a garment the look of distinction. Even the simplest easy-sew design takes on a high fashion flare with a few rows of top-stitching selectively used to emphasize seams.

Top-stitching can be done as a finishing touch after the garment is complete or in sections as the garment is being constructed.

Use regular or buttonhole-twist thread (the latter is best for thick fabrics); a size 18 needle; and a stitch length of 6-8 stitches per inch. Increase the top tension a bit when using buttonhole-twist thread.

Attach, grade (Sew-Easy Guide 22), and turn facings and interfacings before top stitching. Baste the layers to be top-stitched together with silk thread to prevent them from slipping while you sew.

Top-stitch on a scrap first. Fold the scrap to simulate a seam edge and include the same type of linings and interfacings that are used in constructing the garment.

The key to professional-looking top-stitching is straight, even stitching. Stitch slowly, very carefully on curves, and pivot precisely at corners.

Use one of the following guides to guarantee a smooth, even line: a guideline marked on the throatplate of the machine; a seam guide attached to the bed of the machine; or a strip of tape carefully attached to the throatplate of the machine (Figure H.97). If the top-stitching line is over three-fourths inch from the finished edge, use a line of edge-stitching or a nearby seam as a guideline. When there is no such seam or guideline to use as a reference, baste a fraction of an inch from the top-stitching line with silk thread. (Stitch very close to this basting, being careful not to sew on top of it.)

When top-stitching, be sure to leave thread ends long enough so that the top threads can be pulled to the wrong side of the fabric and tied off (see Sew-Easy Guide 19).

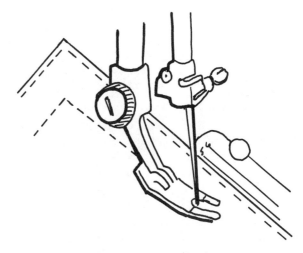

FIGURE H.97. *Top-stitching*.

Use contrasting thread to add interest, or let several rows of top-stitching, one next to the other, enhance the importance of collars, cuffs, pockets, and hems. Use the presser foot to gauge the additional rows for perfectly parallel lines of stitching.

22. Trimming, Grading, Clipping, and Notching

Trim seam allowances to reduce bulk. Enclosed seams should be trimmed to one-quarter inch from the stitching line (Figure H.98).

Grade enclosed seams when the seam allowance is to be turned in one direction, as with facings. To grade, trim the facing seam allowance to one-eighth inch and the garment seam allowance to one-quarter inch. If an interfacing is sewn into the seam, trim the interfacing seam allowance to one-sixteenth inch.

Curved seams must be *clipped* or *notched* so they'll lie flat when pressed open (Figure H.99). Cut small notches in the seam allowances of outside curves and clip the seam allowances of inside curves. Space clips and notches evenly on the curve at one-half inch to one-inch intervals, depending on the angle of the curve and the flexibility of the fabric. Don't clip or notch across the stitching line.

Seams must be trimmed or graded before being clipped and notched.

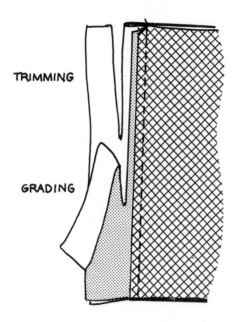

FIGURE H.98. *Trimming and grading.*

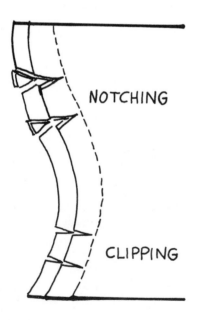

FIGURE H.99. *Clipping and notching.*

Always trim, grade, clip, and notch where called for in your pattern instructions.

Trims. See Chapter 11

23. Tucks

Tucks are extra folds of fabric that are top-stitched, edge-stitched, or blind-stitched, depending on the effect you have in mind (Figure H.100). Tucks can be used on the outside of a garment for a decorative effect; or they can be used on the inside of children's clothes —in which case they provide built-in room to grow.

Tucks can be made on the lengthwise or crosswise grain. To estimate how much extra yardage you'll need to add tucks to a garment, decide on the width of each tuck and multiply by two (each tuck is a double fold of fabric). Then multiply this number by the number of tucks. Cut the garment section out wide or long enough to accommodate this additional yardage.

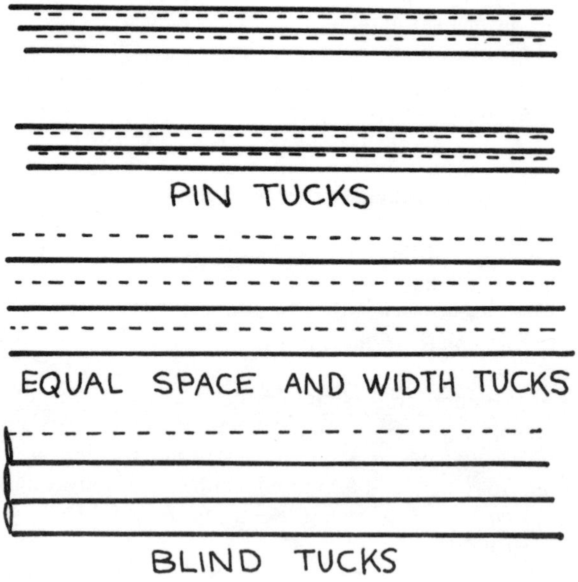

PIN TUCKS

EQUAL SPACE AND WIDTH TUCKS

BLIND TUCKS

FIGURE H.100. *Kinds of tucks.*

Mark the tucking lines on the wrong side of the fabric with chalk and transfer to the front of the fabric with thread tracing. Fold and press along each line. Machine-stitch along each fold to form the tuck.

Top-stitch each tuck using a decorative machine-stitch, or space tucks in a unique way to add individuality to your hand-made creations.

24. Waistbands

There is no reason to put up with a waistband that bulges, binds, creases, slips, slides, wrinkles, folds over, or stretches. Avoid waistband disasters by incorporating these tricks into the sewing routine: Cut the band on the *lengthwise grain*; *always interface*; and attach a waistband to the garment *before* finishing off the ends of the band, *not* after.

Cut the waistband interfacing from the waistband pattern piece, using the foldline as the cutting line.

Place the interfacing on the wrong side of the waistband, matching all notches. Pin the two pieces together and machine-baste along the notched edge and both ends. (Don't stitch along the center fold line.) Trim the interfacing close to the machine-basting. Carefully hand-stitch the interfacing to the waistband along the center foldline, using matching thread, and invisible slip-stitches (Figure H.101, Sew-Easy Guide 11).

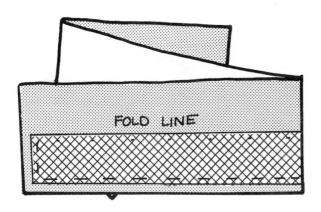

FIGURE H.101. *Slip-stitching the interfacing to the waistband.*

Pin the waistband to the skirt with right sides together, matching notches, center-front, center-back, and side markings (Figure H.102). The waistband will extend ⅝ inch at one side of the zipper opening and several inches on the other side to form an overlap.

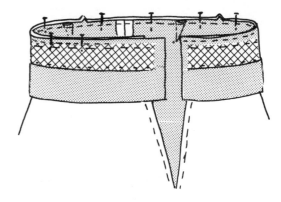

FIGURE H.102. *Pinning the waistband to the garment.*

Distribute any ease in the skirt evenly around the waistband (Sew-Easy Guide 8). Baste the waistband into place and remove the pins. Machine-stitch around the waist, back-stitching to reinforce each end.

Trim the waistline seam to one-quarter inch. Turn the waistband away from the skirt, and press the seam allowances toward the waistband.

Fold each end of the waistband in half, right sides together. Pin, baste, and stitch across the short end (Figure H.103). Trim this seam to one-quarter inch and press. Pin, baste, and stitch across the end of the overlap section and along the lower edge as far as the zipper opening. Trim and press.

Turn the waistband to the inside, and baste along the fold (Figure H.104). Turn the free edge of the waistband under ⅝ inch. Trim to ¼ inch and pin the edge over the waistline seam, enclosing the raw seam allowances. Finish the waistband by hand, using a slip-stitch (see Sew-Easy Guide 11).

Attach the appropriate closing devices to the waistband (hooks and eyes, buttons and buttonholes, or decorative snap fasteners) (see Sew-Easy Guides 3 and 4).

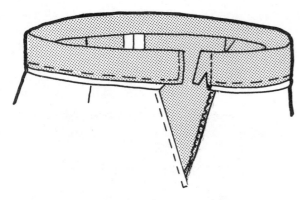

FIGURE H.103. *Folding the waistband over; stitching and trimming.*

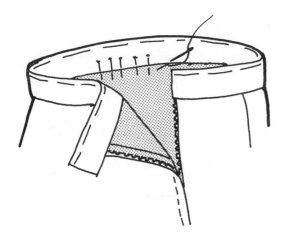

FIGURE H.104. *Joining the waistband and the inside of the garment.*

Elasticized Waistbands

Knowing how to put in an elasticized waistband is one of the handiest sewing techniques you can know. If you are a novice at sewing, nothing is easier to make than a skirt or pants with elastic at the waist—no zippers, no buttonholes, and they can't be beat when it comes to comfort. The elasticized waistband is also the perfect answer to a child's growing waistline.

There are two ways to put elastic into a waistband. (Use these same techniques to put elastic anywhere—at sleeve edges, or at the bottom of sweat-suit pantlegs.) One way is to make a casing through which the elastic is threaded. The other way is to sew the elastic directly onto the fabric.

Casings are usually one-half to one inch wide (one inch is best for waistlines). Turn the top edge of the waistline under one-quarter inch; then turn under a one-inch hem. Top-stitch very close to the hem edge, leaving a one-inch opening for the elastic.

Cut the elastic one inch longer than the waist (or arm or leg) measurement. Attach a safety pin to one end of the elastic and thread it through the casing. Overlap the ends one-half inch and sew them together securely by hand. Close the opening with top stitches, being sure to overlap the stitches on both sides of the opening.

The second type of elastic waistband (the elastic is sewn directly to the garment fabric), is perfect for children's wear and for replacing the elastic in men's boxer shorts. Cut a piece of elastic one inch longer than the waistline. Lap one end of the elastic over the other one-half inch and join the ends together with two rows of zigzag stitching. Divide the waistline of the garment and the circle of elastic into quarters and mark with pins.

Finish the raw edges of the waistline hem. Press the waistline hem under along the foldline. Fold the hem away from the garment.

Pin each edge of the elastic to the waistline hem at the quartered intervals. Keep an edge of the elastic aligned with the crease for the hem.

Stitch the elastic to the waistline along the edge closest to the crease (Figure H.105). Use a medium-width zigzag stitch and stretch the elastic between the pins as you sew.

Turn the elastic and the hem to the underside, along the foldline, and pin at the quartered intervals. Stitch the waistband hem into place close to each edge of the elastic using a zigzag stitch. Pull the threads to the underside and tie off the ends (see Sew-Easy Guide 19).

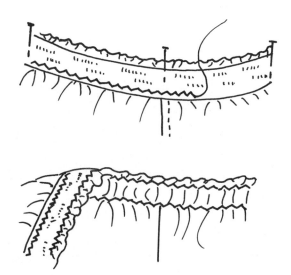

FIGURE H.105. *Sewing the elastic directly to the waist-band.*

25. Zippers

Use a zipper that is the same color as the fabric, and buy the kind and the length of zipper that is specified on the pattern.

Press the zipper flat before installing it. Always use a press cloth when pressing an installed zipper from the right side of the garment.

Don't even consider putting in that zipper without a zipper foot on your machine (unless you are sewing by hand).

There is no trick to stitching past the pull tab of a zipper: Leave the needle in the fabric; raise the presser foot; move the pull tab one way or the other; lower the presser foot; and continue to sew. Don't stitch too close to the teeth or the tab won't pull at all. Install the zipper at the first opportunity during the construction procedure—before that garment takes shape.

If you alter the pattern you may have to change the zipper length. If a zipper is too long, allow the excess zipper tape to extend beyond the top edge of the garment during the installation. To shorten the zipper, machine baste across the zipper tape one-half inch from the garment edge (be sure the pull tab is *below* the basting) and then trim the zipper tape even with the edge. If the zipper is too short, you're out of luck; exchange it for the correct size.

Centered Zippers

The centered zipper is the most common zipper installation. It's used for center front and center back openings, at necklines, waistlines, and on sleeves.

Machine-stitch the seam into which the zipper is to be installed, leaving an opening one inch longer than the zipper.

Pin the zipper opening together along the seam line and machine-baste. Press the seam open.

Working from the wrong side of the fabric, position the zipper face down over the machine-basted seam. The zipper teeth should be lined up with the basted seam and the pull tab should by ⅞ inch below the top of the garment.

Pin the zipper into place; place pins at right angles to the seam, through all thicknesses, and underneath the teeth portion of the zipper (Figure H.106). Baste one-quarter inch from either side of the center seam. Baste carefully; this will be your stitching guide.

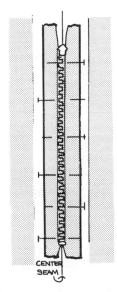

FIGURE H.106. *Positioning a centered zipper.*

Using a zipper foot, machine-stitch around the zipper, on the front side of the fabric, stitching just outside the bastings. Leave the needle down and pivot the fabric on the needle at the corners. Take the same number of stitches on either side of the center seam as you stitch across the bottom of the zipper tape (Figure H.107).

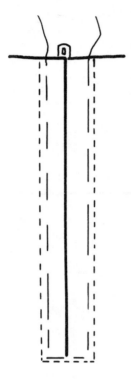

FIGURE H.107. *Stitching a centered zipper using basting as guidelines.*

Finish off the zipper installation with a hand-stitch instead of a machine-stitch. Use a fine needle and a single strand of matching thread. Sew around the zipper using a very neat back-stitch; picking up only one or two threads of the garment with each stitch (see Sew-Easy Guide 11). Hand-finishing makes for an inconspicuous zipper application particularly suited to soft wools, silks, sheers, and knits.

Lapped Zipper

Less common than the centered zipper is the lapped zipper which is most often found at side openings of skirts and dresses. The overlapped section hides the zipper completely; only one row of stitching is on display.

Turn in the edge of the opening that is to be underlapped ⅜ inch and baste. Turn in and baste the full seam allowance of the other opening edge.

Working from the front of the garment, position the underlapped edge over the zipper tape, aligning the bottom zipper stop with the bottom of the opening. Carefully baste the zipper to the underlapped edge. Using the basting as a guide, machine- or hand-stitch the zipper into place.

Pin the overlapping edge to the zipper, making sure to overlap just enough to cover the first row of stitching and baste. Machine- or hand-stitch this side of the zipper, starting at the center of the seam just below the bottom of the zipper (Figure H.108). Pivot the fabric on the needle at the corner and stitch to the top of the zipper, staying very close to the bastings. Remove all bastings and press.

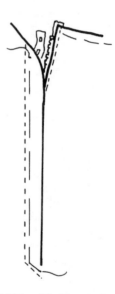

FIGURE H.108. *Stitching the lapped zipper.*

Invisible Zippers

Don't follow the directions above or the directions on the pattern if you're using an invisible zipper. Follow the directions on the zipper package and use a special zipper foot designed for use with invisible zippers only.

Fly-front zippers

Take a look at what goes into the man's fly-front zipper: a left fly-front extension, a right fly-front extension (the extension is usually cut in one piece with the front pant-leg section), and a right fly shield (which is a separate, lined insert).

Use this type of zipper installation only when the pattern calls for it, and count on having to shorten the zipper a bit. It's hard to find a standard zipper size to fit most fly-front openings.

Stitch the crotch fronts together. Put in the zipper before attaching the waistband using the following procedure.

Turn both fly-front extensions under along the fold line and baste each extension very close to the fold (Figure H.109).

Working from the front side of the garment, pin the right side of the zipper opening to the unopened zipper, keeping the basted fold close to the teeth. Align the zipper stop with the bottom of the zipper opening and pin from bottom to top. If the zipper is too long for the opening, let the excess extend beyond the waist of the pants. Baste the zipper in place and remove the pins.

Lap the left front extension over the zipper so that the extension just covers the last line of basting. Baste into place (Figure H.110).

Working from the wrong side of the garment, open out the left front extension and pin the left zipper tape to it. Pin from bottom to top, being careful not to catch the front of the garment in the pins. Baste the zipper to

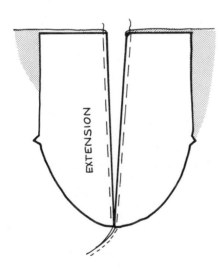

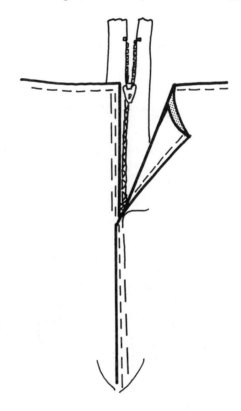

FIGURE H.109. *Basting the fly-front extensions in place for a fly-front zipper.*

FIGURE H.110. *Lapping the left extension over the zipper and basting into place.*

the extension and remove the pins. Using a zipper foot, machine-stitch very close to the bastings and then stitch another row, one-quarter inch away from the first row of stitches (Figure H.111).

Turn the left front extension back into place and baste it to the garment at the waistline. On the left front of the garment, stitch along the stitching line (a line 1½ inches from the center-front fold that curves in to meet the center-front seam at the bottom of the zipper) (Figure H.112). Be sure to stitch through all thicknesses. Pull the top thread through to the wrong side and tie off the ends (Sew-Easy Guide 19).

Make the right fly shield by sewing together the fly insert and lining along the stitching line. Trim the seam, turn, and press.

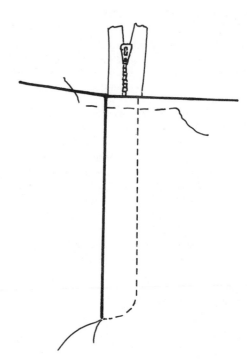

FIGURE H.112. *The stitching line of the fly-front zipper.*

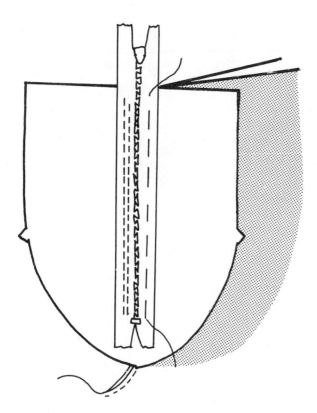

FIGURE H.111. *Machine-stitching two rows, joining the left extension and the zipper.*

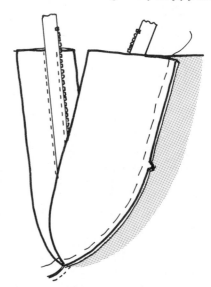

FIGURE H.113. *Basting the fly-shield onto the right front extension.*

Working from the wrong side, pin and baste the fly shield over the right front extension and the zipper, making sure to line up the raw edges of the extension with the raw edges of the fly shield (Figure H.113).

Turn the garment over. Remove the bastings holding the left fly front in place and open up the zipper. Keeping the left side out of the way, stitch the right side of the zipper in place from the front side of the garment. Stitch very close to the line of basting and stitch through all thicknesses.

If the zipper is too long machine-baste across both sides of the zipper tape at the waistline seam. The line of basting will prevent the zipper tab from sliding off the end of the tape. Trim the ends of the zipper flush with the upper edge of the garment (Figure H.114).

Finish the zipper installation by sewing the raw edges of the right fly extension and the right fly shield together using one of the new overlock stitches or a wide zigzag.

Reverse this procedure when putting a fly-front zipper into women's slacks—the right side should overlap (the left side overlaps in Levis and in all men's wear). You may eliminate the fly-shield in women's slacks entirely to reduce bulk, but remember that the fly shield serves a purpose—it protects tucked in sweaters and blouses from the zipper.

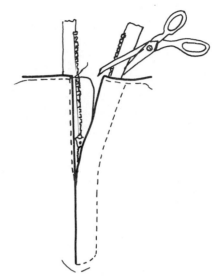

FIGURE H.114. *Trimming the zipper flush with the upper edge of the garment.*

Index

Note: Definitions found in Glossaries are not included in this Index. Consult proper Glossary (Fabric terms: pages 137-142; Sewing terms: pages 156-160), where terms are listed in alphabetical order.

S

Satin-stitch   182
Scissors   21, 68
Seam ripper   21, 73-74
Seams   196-198;
   finishing   193;
   flat-fell   197;
   French   198;
   on knits   145;
   pressing   74-75;
   ripping   73-74
Selling home-sewn items   130-133
Sewing aids   22-23
Sewing machines, attachments   17-18;
   adjusting   18;
   adjusting for knits   144;
   decorative stitching with   92-94;
   diagram of   149;
   how to buy   15-16;
   maintenance   18, 48;
   needle sizes   46;
   stitch sizes   73;
   tension   18, 73;
   trouble-shooting guide   149-151
Sewing center, setting up   18-21
Sheers   146-147
Shirt, collars   170-171;
   cuffs   173-174
Sizes   27-28
Ski clothes   108-109
Skirts, hemming   183-184;
   patchwork   96-97
Sleeve board   23
Sleeves, set-in   193-195
Slipstitch   181
Snaps   168
Spot removal   76-77
Stay-stitching   198-199

Stem-stitch   182
Stitches   180-182;
   embroidery   97, 181-182
Straightening the grain   50-51
Stretch fabrics   42, 144-145
Stripes (see Patterned fabrics)
Styles   28-31
Suede   146
Swimwear   111

T

Tablecloths   122-123
Tailor's ham   23
Tailor's tacks   70-71
Tennis wear   110
Tension (see Sewing machines, tension)
Tents, camping   110
Thread   22, 46
Top-stitching   91, 92, 145, 199
Tote bags   110-111
Tracing wheel   22, 68-69
Transferring pattern markings   68-71
Trimmings   89-103
Tucks   102, 105, 200-201

U

Ultrasuede   146

V

Vinyl   146

W

Y

Z

Dian Davis has been sewing for twenty years. She began sewing at the age of ten under the direction of her mother, an expert seamstress, former fashion artist, and illustrator. Dian enjoys sewing as a hobby, as a creative outlet and as an inexpensive way to stay well-dressed. She makes everything she wears and admits that she feels more comfortable in her own clothes.

Five years ago, Dian decided to pursue a career in sewing and designing. Since then she has been studying the technical aspects of sewing and designing, as well as continuing to make special order clothes for her private customers and designing clothes for sale to boutiques in Los Angeles, San Francisco, Sausalito and Berkeley. Her line of appliquéd decorator pillows was very successful and her ethnic-inspired caftans were given a special showing at "The Egg and I", an arts and crafts gallery in Los Angeles.

Dian lives in the Oakland Hills in a two-story log cabin, built around 1900. Part of her house has been converted into a studio where she enjoys many hours sewing and designing.

215